ICONOCLASM AS CHILD'S PLAY

ICONOCLASM AS CHILD'S PLAY

Joe Moshenska

STANFORD UNIVERSITY PRESS

Stanford, California

STANFORD UNIVERSITY PRESS
Stanford, California

Printed in the United States of America on acid-free, archival-quality paper

Library of Congress Cataloging-in-Publication Data
Names: Moshenska, Joe, author.
Title: Iconoclasm as child's play / Joe Moshenska.
Description: Stanford, California : Stanford University Press, 2019. |
    Includes bibliographical references and index.
Identifiers: LCCN 2018033510 (print) | LCCN 2018038306 (ebook) |
    ISBN 9780804798501 (cloth: alk. paper) | ISBN 9781503608740 (ebook)
Subjects: LCSH: Play—Religious aspects. | Iconoclasm.
Classification: LCC BL65.P6 (ebook) | LCC BL65.P6 M67 2019 (print) | DDC 306.4/81—dc23
LC record available at https://lccn.loc.gov/2018033510

Typeset by Kevin Barrett Kane in 10/15 Minion Pro

Cover art: Shelley and Pamela Jackson, *Josh McBig*

Cover design: Rob Ehle

For Alejandro and Beatriz

CONTENTS

PREFACE

LET US BEGIN IN A PARTICULAR TIME AND PLACE. The place can be specified with some precision—Redcliffe Cross in Bristol, in the west of England. The exact time is less certain, but it is sometime in the 1530s. A preacher named Roger Edgeworth stands and delivers one of a series of sermons that he gave on this spot during this period. For some years he has been fighting a fierce battle for the souls of the local people with Hugh Latimer, the evangelical preacher who has risen to great prominence in this region thanks to the patronage of Thomas Cromwell and Archbishop Cranmer.[1] Edgeworth remained a constant irritant to the reformed cause with his insistence that the new and emerging forms of religion had produced not heightened piety but a widespread irreverence and ribaldry among the Christian laity.[2] Although the theme of Edgeworth's sermon on this particular day sounded somewhat abstruse—"treatying of the fift gift of the holy gost, called the spirite of Science"—his denunciation of what he saw as the recent upsurge in impiety took a striking form. He crystallized the behavior that shocked him into a particular and peculiar domestic scene. "Now at the dissolution of Monasteries and of Freers houses," Edgeworth claimed,

many Images haue bene caryed abrod, and gyuen to children to playe wyth all. And when the children haue theym in theyr handes, dauncynge them after their childyshe maner, commeth the father or the mother and saythe: What nasse, what haste thou there? the childe aunsweareth (as she is taught) I haue here myne ydoll, the father laugheth and maketh a gaye game at it. So saithe the mother to an other, Iugge, or Thommye, where haddest thou that pretye Idoll? Iohn our parishe clarke gaue it me, saythe the childe, and for that the clarke muste haue thankes, and you shall lacke no good chere.[3]

Edgeworth's account of the dangerous irreverence that he saw around him is startling. He is describing the removal of holy objects from churches for the purpose of their humiliation and destruction—a process that should be easily identifiable as iconoclasm. This is not, however, iconoclasm in its usual guise. Surely iconoclasts were grim-faced men bearing hammers and flaming torches, fanatics or stern killjoys who destroyed the beautiful and integrated fabric of late medieval religion in an orgy of burning, smashing, and rending.[4] Here, however, the hand that is placed on the sacred item does not exert a furious grip: it is a child's clutching fingers, dancing the object, laughing with it, making it into a game. What Edgeworth describes is not iconoclasm as sternly pious violence; it is iconoclasm as child's play.

In its most modest formulation my aim in this book is to make sense of the scene that Edgeworth describes, and I will return throughout the chapters that follow to its several dimensions. This was, however, by no means a unique or isolated incident: as I will show, there is scattered but definitive evidence, distributed across a range of geographical locations, that holy things were made into playthings with sufficient frequency for it to be considered an established and recognized part of iconoclastic practice in the early modern period. This, then, is my first and more limited aim: to present this evidence and to try to understand why this activity, in some ways so surprising to modern eyes, became possible. I will place this activity in its context, asking what it tells us about early modern iconoclasm that it could periodically become play, and what about early modern play made it potentially iconoclastic. What were the precise discourses in the culture of the period with which iconoclastic child's play chimed, which it illuminates and by which it is illuminated?

In developing interpretations of this sort, I might seem to be historicizing iconoclasm as child's play or to be using Edgeworth at his West Country pulpit, a moment seemingly from the margins of early modern culture, as a somewhat belated form of the arresting new historicist anecdote. I wish both to invoke these possible models and to hold them at bay. For as I have ruminated on the scene from Edgeworth's sermon, in which the playing children dance the idols that have been wrenched from religious houses and thrust into their hands, I have become less certain that I know what it would mean to put the sermon into context and to determine its meaning solely as an "early modern" event.

I have, to be frank, been seduced by this passage from Edgeworth's sermon— caught up in its folds, brought back to it time and again, finding myself compelled to wonder at it and to speculate about what is really going on in this scene and what it means. Who were these children? Were they aware of the iconoclastic significance of their actions or blithely indifferent to them? Did they enjoy such play more or less than their other forms of playing? What went through the minds of the parents who gave the children these objects? Were they gleeful at their own daring? Did they do so nervously or with brazen triumphalism? Or perhaps with deep ambivalence? Did they do so because they hated these objects and were sure of their worthlessness? Or because they feared them and found the children's play reassuring of each object's inert triviality? Or, if they could not decide, was this a way of keeping the object around—literally keeping it in play—and absorbing it into the household, not so much taming its power as hiding it in plain sight? I have not been able to stop asking these questions of Edgeworth's scene, even though I began by trying to remain focused on the way in which the scene is mediated by his words and their polemical intent, defined by the framing of a sermon that is in turn framed by its immediate context. To speculate about the feelings, intentions, and complex inner lives of historical actors from several centuries ago is a perilous and disreputable enterprise at the best of times; to do so with figures who may never have existed in anything like this form, conjured up in the service of a controversial sermon, is to risk floundering "in the bog of hermeneutic narcissism," to use Thomas M. Greene's chastening phrase.[5]

Nonetheless, I have become convinced that the value and significance of Edgeworth's scene—and its wider implications, the elucidation of which constitutes the larger ambition of this book—are inseparable from the way it has come to life for me, the way it has seemed to solicit or at least to enable a certain kind of wild imagining on my part. This has in turn affected the way that I have chosen to write about it. Like a significant number of recent scholars, I have grown impatient with the sense, rarely formulated explicitly but constantly implied by the institutional norms and structures governing academic discourse, that the ways in which we become enchanted by and affectively attached to our objects of study are at best an embarrassment and at worst a distortion rigorously to be overcome.[6] While these are arguably questions raised by any historical inquiry, I would argue that they have a specificity, a richness and a tenacity in relation to Edgeworth's scene of iconoclastic play. This is in part because I have in this instance become curiously and affectively attached to a scene that itself seems to brim with curious affective attachments of varying and conflicting sorts. The children are attached to the objects with which they play—already, before their parents arrive and intervene. The adults, too, are attached to these objects—powerfully invested in the significance that they once had and the new significance that they are supposed to accrue now that they have been placed in the children's hands; and they are also attached to the children themselves, determined to ensure that their playing takes the right form and confers the right meaning on its objects. Then there is Edgeworth himself, who wants to inspire a radically different form of attachment in his auditors— who wants them to be appalled by this irreverence, to feel horror at the account of holy objects treated in this way, and to reaffirm, by contrast, the proper way that such objects are supposed to matter.

This scene, read from a distance of nearly five centuries, does not offer a straightforward snapshot of facts from the past so much as a crystallized sense of what a particular group of people in the past wanted from one another and from some of the objects that they encountered, as well as a crystallized sense of how we might imagine this past and what we might want it to be. The once-holy object in transit, moving from the monastery or religious house to the playing child's hand, encapsulates much wider questions about what we want from objects, both historical and contemporary, and suggests the divergent and potentially conflicting forms of investment to which they are subject; the way in which playing occurs, and comes to be carefully guided and shaped by the parents, raises the question of what we want play to be, what meanings we want it to have, and what possibilities it might open up; and, finally, the prominence of children in the scene and their involvement in the iconoclastic process raises the question of what we want children to do, what we want them to be, and what the roles are that they are sometimes asked or compelled to play.

It is this final point on which I want initially to dwell, for the question of interpretative investment in children is perhaps less frequently posed than the question of our attachment to the past or to certain objects, but no less crucial, and it will become increasingly central to my argument as it develops across the ensuing chapters. In his account of the Tambaran, the religious cult of the Arapesh people in New Guinea, Donald Tuzin attends carefully to the role played by children in sustaining a sense that the local spirit named Nggwal is dangerous and malevolent, their response of "undiluted terror" producing "the purest image of the giant ogre, the towering monster whose bloody, toothy maw waits hungrily for naughty or unwary children." Tuzin observes that "the role of children as 'culture bearers' has been largely unattended in anthropological analysis."[7] If we approach Edgeworth's scene as historical anthropologists, would it not seem explicable in just such terms, with the children asked to become bearers of the emerging culture of iconoclastic reform? Michael Taussig, however, perceptively observes that Tuzin "implies that the credulity of the child sustains the adults' secret," creating a false binary of total (childish) gullibility and knowing (adult) awareness about the nature of religious ritual and belief. Instead, Taussig insists, we should attend to "the back and forth between child culture and adult culture," and recognize that "it is not the child but *the adult's imagination of the child's imagination* that is the 'culture bearer.'"[8] This superb and curious phrase—"the adult's imagination of the child's imagination"—echoes through Taussig's book, and it will resonate through mine as well. It will be one of my central contentions that adults cannot stop imagining children—as pure and impure, innocent and guilty, gentle and violent, saintly and savage, idolaters and iconoclasts. Children, write Adam Phillips and Barbara Taylor, "tend to be seen as either wholly innocent and good, and therefore corrupted by adults, or wholly bad (vicious and sexual and rivalrous) and therefore simply small members of the unpleasant human race. This polarized view of childhood has had damaging consequences."[9] Phillips and Taylor are summarizing a widespread modern Western view, but it is possible to trace historical forms in which this binarism appears and from which it emerges; these include, for example, the repeated claim that there are two kinds of play, good and bad, and that how a child plays encapsulates his or her moral condition (though I would add that seeing children as "wholly bad" has, historically speaking, not necessarily involved seeing them as "simply small members of the unpleasant human race"; their badness can, as we will see, be construed as entirely demonic, alien, in a category all its own). It is partly the light it sheds on these ways of imagining children, their play, their imaginations and their cultural role that makes iconoclastic child's play so significant.

We might revise Tuzin's account, then, by saying that it is not merely the playing of the children in Edgeworth's scene that dramatically transforms the status of the formerly holy object but the adults' imagination of the children's imaginative play that effects this change. Because my focus is not on the child as a historical entity but on the adult's imagining of the child as a cultural process, I will have relatively little to say about the concerns that have been central to historians of childhood and of children's literature—particularly whether children were in fact recognized as a distinct group in the early modern period and when they became one.[10] Instead, I will suggest that iconoclasm as child's play illuminates with unique clarity the curious ways in which the child has been construed as "other" to reason and to culture in the West. Consider the following, from Ernst Kris and Otto Kurz's influential cross-cultural study of the image of the artist, in which they discuss the nature of "magical thinking," arising in circumstances in which "men are inclined to equate . . . the picture and the original it depicts. Such conditions," they write, "are more easily found among primitive people than among [those] who have reached our level of civilization, though in our culture they do occur in the wake of mental illness. . . . They evolve more readily in crowds than in an individual; they occur more frequently in children than in adults."[11] By aligning children with primitives and the mentally ill, Kris and Kurtz participate in a much longer history of exclusions that have been deeply formative of Western norms. As Anthony Pagden shows, Aristotle's account of the slave, the woman, and the child as innately defective in reason was frequently used during the early modern period to justify the innately slavish imperfections of non-Western peoples: "The suggestion that the Indian was a natural child . . . echoed the unreflective opinions of countless colonists and missionaries."[12] While the crucial and ongoing work of scholarship in the past decades has illuminated and indicted the habits of thought by which women, non-Western people, and the mentally ill have served as the scapegoats of Western reason—the quarantined Others that allow its smooth functioning—there has been markedly less attention to the peculiarity of the child in these narratives. The child—specifically, of course, in Aristotle's account the free male child—is a different and strange kind of Other: both external to the realm of reason and destined to join it, a rational adult *in potentia*. Children are inferior, but their inferiority is a state not of being but becoming. This is a reassuring narrative for adult reason: the child is destined to overcome its otherness and join the fold. But it also makes the child a potentially unsettling presence during its protracted meantime: the child is the Other within the household, the Other whom we once were, whose otherness has a time-limit, and who must be both clearly distinguished from the community of reason and brought progressively ever closer.

Even as I make this point, however, there seems no way to avoid at some point speaking *for* children, whether in the past or in the present—of speaking both of the child and on the child's behalf. This is the unavoidable risk identified by Jacqueline Rose when she writes of "a form of investment by the adult in the child, and . . . the demand made by the adult on the child as the effect of that investment, a demand which fixes the child and then holds it in place."[13] We might understand the scene of iconoclastic child's play, preliminarily, as a scene within which adults invest both in children and in certain objects in order to fix and hold them in place; but it is also, as I will argue, a scene in which these acts of fixing and holding are stretched to the limits, their stakes and workings thereby revealed. By owning up at the outset to my own affective investment in this scene, my own lack of cool objectivity or pure historical rigor, I also want to make clear that I by no means exempt myself from these risks, as if it is only *other*, less self-aware adults who imagine children in a certain way or try to fix them in a certain time and place. I too, inescapably, am imagining the child imagining. I aim, unapologetically, to interweave my historical and critical interpretations with further imaginings of this sort, distinguished not by their unique validity but by my attempt to make the varied historical processes by which adults have imagined children part of what I seek to understand.

My opening wager, then, is that iconoclastic child's play is worthy of sustained attention because it has the potential to illuminate in new ways our multiple and affective attachments: to particular historical details, narratives, and events; to objects holy, unholy, and otherwise; to play; and to children. The play that Edgeworth describes has this potential not because its meanings are so apparent but precisely because it is doubly inscrutable and therefore presents a particularly rich interpretative and imaginative challenge. It is inscrutable, first, because the evidence that iconoclastic child's play occurred, while indisputable, is also meager and fragmented, polemically framed and distorted, suggestive rather than decisive in its meanings. But play is inscrutable in a much deeper sense, I would argue, because the playing of children is often a particularly powerful encapsulation of the way in which human activity can be at once opaque and compelling—compelling *because* opaque. This is in no small part why it is both so tempting and so difficult to interpret and to imagine. These features are brought out in Michael Fried's influential account of the powerful hold that certain paintings seem to have on us through their depiction of figures who "exemplify . . . the state or condition of rapt attention, of being completely occupied or engrossed or (as I prefer to say) absorbed in what he or she is doing, hearing, feeling, thinking."[14] Fried pays particular attention to Pierre Chardin's "depictions of children and young people playing games or engaged in apparently trivial amusements," and he identifies Chardin's refusal to distinguish "between the pictures of games and amusements on the one hand and ostensibly more serious or morally exemplary scenes on the other." He remarks that, while a painting might seem by definition to capture an instant, "Chardin's paintings of games and amusements . . . are also remarkable for their uncanny power to suggest the actual duration of the absorptive states and activities they represent. . . . A single moment has been isolated in all its plenitude and density from an absorptive continuum. . . . Images such as these are not of time wasted but of time filled."[15]

Fried's analysis allows me to introduce what will develop into two persistent concerns of this book: first, the instability of any distinction among the playful, the trivial, and the serious; second, the crucial connections among iconoclasm, child's play, and the experience or understanding of temporality, of lived time. For now, I wish to amplify the simple but powerful argument that Fried makes in relation to Chardin's work: there is something captivating, compelling, about the sight of the child at play, not because we immediately feel able to understand the operations of such activity, or feel that it occurs for our benefit, or feel able to join in, but precisely because we are so radically excluded from it. This play does not need us to function: its meaning feels self-contained and self-sufficient, and we are made to feel utterly superfluous in its presence. We experience, before these depictions of the child at play, our separateness, our irrelevance. Whereas for Fried this is just the nature of the aesthetic response that he values, the reactions that the exclusionary self-containedness of the child at play can provoke vary, as we will see, from delight to fear and rage. But I wish to suggest that the mood of the viewer before these paintings of "games and amusements" is the mood in which we should approach the historical phenomenon of iconoclastic child's play: frank wonderment at an activity that seems to bristle with a meaning that is not, and cannot fully be, ours.

————————————

To develop an adequate response to such experiences of paradoxically rich exclusion, this book begins in a particular historical moment in which iconoclasm became child's play but spirals outward from this starting point to consider a considerably wider set of narratives, discourses, and commitments that illuminate and are illuminated by this specific historical phenomenon. My conviction that iconoclasm as child's play is acutely relevant to various ways in which we understand and imagine children, objects, and the past has informed both my structure and my approach in the chapters that follow. I make more consistent use of texts and artifacts from the sixteenth century (and, to a lesser extent, the seventeenth) than any other era, since this is the principal period in which icono-clastic child's play seems to have taken place. Each of the chapters that follows begins with a particular instance of iconoclastic child's play—or, in the case of the final two chapters, with surviving objects that were used for such play—as its point of departure; then, in order to make sense of the longer-running and sometimes tangled threads within which, I argue, this specific phenomenon is enmeshed, I go on to incorporate materials from a wide range of disciplines and historical periods. This reflects in part my own dissatisfaction with the ways in which historical materials and epochs are still carved up with excessive clarity in the modern academy and in part my desire to embrace eclecticism in the face of this sometimes dreary division of labor, to pronounce, with Ian Hacking, that "I help myself to whatever I can, from everywhere."[16] This is not to say my ap-proach is rampantly eclectic: I draw consistently on a particular set of not entirely complementary conceptual sources, especially the broadly Marxist but itself eclectic thought of Walter Benjamin and T. W. Adorno; psychoanalytic theory in the tradition of object relations (especially D. W. Winnicott and Christopher Bollas); and anthropological accounts of objecthood and play from Lévi-Strauss to the present, as well as more critical engagements with deconstruction, thing theory, and the work of Giorgio Agamben.

This approach is not so much a theory or method as the outcome of my growing conviction that eclecticism of this sort is a necessary response to the phenomenon of iconoclastic child's play itself. To treat it exclusively as an "early modern" phenomenon—to "put it in context," when this means assuming that it must be explained *solely* in terms of discourses and modes of understanding from the period in which it occurred—would be to limit and define its meaning in advance. As postcolonial, feminist, and queer theorists among others have in recent decades repeatedly and valuably shown, such seemingly innocuous acts of scholarly situating can themselves be ways of reinforcing ideologically freighted modes of understanding history and temporality as if they were the only way of doing things.[17] Elizabeth Freeman has written powerfully of these modes of "chrononormativity," by which "manipulations of time convert his-torically specific regimes of asymmetrical power into seemingly ordinary bodily tempos and routines, which in turn organize the value and meaning of time."[18] These modes affect the organization of time on every level, from the specific experiential rhythms of a single hour or day to the larger schemes within which history is organized and divided. Literary scholars such as Wai Chi Dimock and Rita Felski have begun to call for modes of writing that break out from the model of the historical "period" as enclosed and self-identical and to allow texts and ideas to act on and resonate with one another across time.[19] My aim is not just to interpret iconoclasm as child's play in context but to experiment with a mode of writing about it that moves rhythmically in and out of *its* time frame, in two senses—both the historical period in which it occurred and the multiple and shifting temporal dynamics opened up by the scene that Edgeworth describes. For this reason each of my chapters takes as its title a single word, which, I argue, reverberates in a new way when placed in relation to iconoclastic child's play and radiates out from this starting point. I aim not only to historicize the scene but, to use Dimock's term, to express, expand upon, and exfoliate the *resonance* of Edgeworth's account as a way of understanding both the scene itself and the ways in which we might relate and fail to relate to the scraps and fragments of the past.[20]

Working in this way raises one pair of questions irresistibly: do I mean this approach to be a kind of iconoclasm? And do I intend it as a form of play? Here a glance at Felski's recent work is instructive: building on Bruno Latour, she has argued that a whole array of scholarly writing, insofar as it presents and understands itself as a mode of suspicious critique, revels in its self-proclaimed iconoclastic status. "After decades of heady iconoclasm," she writes, "we are left nursing a Sunday morning hangover and wondering what fragments, if any, can be retrieved from the ruins." She subsequently offers an alternative diagnosis of what this critical activity, which presents itself as iconoclasm, truly is: "While often wary of pleasure, suspicious reading generates its own pleasures. . . . The delight it engenders is in part a ludic delight, a pleasure in creating complex designs out of textual fragments, conjuring inventive insights out of overlooked details. . . . Critique, in other words, is a form of addictive and gratifying play."[21] For Felski, then, critique is a mode of writing that takes itself to be iconoclasm when it is in fact play, and she presents this as a truth that critics cannot admit to themselves. The question emerging from these claims that drives and informs my own account is, How might it change the way we view our modes of historical and critical interpretation, if they are indeed torn in this way between the iconoclastic and the ludic, once we recognize that iconoclasm and child's play might be one and the same? Stephen K. White begins his account of "weak ontologies" in contemporary political writing with a thought experiment that speaks to the same combination of activities that Felski finds lurking in contemporary theorizing: "Imagine yourself standing by a vacant lot watching children play. Debris lies about, for a building once stood here, until its foundation gave way. Chunks of the building remain here and there, as does the gaping hole left from the foundation. As the children clamber over the remains and jump in and out of the hole, you begin to think that they are playing a game, but it is one with which you are unfamiliar. In fact, the rules still seem to be emerging, and the children themselves are sometimes uncertain how to proceed."[22] White's imagined children play *in* the ruins rather than *with* the ruins: they recall the children in certain seventeenth-century Dutch paintings, who play in ruined churches with the fragments left in the aftermath of iconoclastic fervor.[23] He develops the scene into an analogy for what it is like to observe certain theoretical schools in action. What appeals to me in his account is White's genuine fascination and bemusement before the play that he observes; in fact, it is not even clear that it *is* play, whether it has stable rules, and whether its nature is any clearer to those participating than to those observing. It unfurls open-endedly, uncertainly, and amid broken fragments, yet it remains play—or so it seems to the simultaneously absorbed and excluded observer, like the one before Chardin's paintings. The influential play-theorist Gregory Bateson, whose work I will consider in a later chapter, writes that "*play*, as a label, does not limit or define the acts that make up play," and this makes the limits of any concrete play-situation supple, provisional, prone to open up and swallow one who merely looks on in the manner that White describes: "Indeed, anybody who has tried to stop some children playing knows how it feels when his efforts simply get included in the shape of the game."[24]

It is with such an understanding—of play as unstable, polymorphous, unbounded—that I approach not just child's play as a historical phenomenon but attempts to theorize play. Two notable and influential instances merit attention here for the way in which they overlap with but ultimately differ significantly from my own. First, particularly influential in early modern studies is Stephen Greenblatt's account, in his reading of Christopher Marlowe, of a "will to play" that "flaunts society's cherished orthodoxies" and "courts self-destruction in the interest of the anarchic discharge of its energy. This is play on the brink of the abyss, *absolute* play." This Marlovian play is self-consuming and ultimately self-defeating, somewhere between a howl of despair and a gleeful cackle, and finally impotent: "the attempts to challenge this system" are "exposed as unwitting tributes to that social construction of identity against which they struggle."[25]

Greenblatt's idiom—a "will to play"—hints at the Nietzschean foundation of his argument, which is shared by Jacques Derrida's widely influential account of play as the undoing of structure, first articulated in response to the work of Claude Lévi-Strauss. "Play," Derrida writes, "is the disruption of presence. . . . Being must be conceived as presence or absence on the basis of the possibility of play and not the other way around." He then distinguishes between two types of play: "*sure* play, that which is limited to the *substitution* of *given* and *existing, present* pieces," and another conception, severed from all accounts of absolute origin and of the human as its ground, which is "Nietzschean affirmation, that is the joyous affirmation of the play of the world and of the innocence of becoming."[26] To read these exciting passages by Derrida and Greenblatt is, however, also to be reminded how easily these idioms—"absolute play," "the play of the world"—became devalued by overuse. If these various genitives involve play beyond the human, play that is always *of* some larger, transindividual entity—play of the world, play of the signifier, play of meaning—then, I want to ask, what makes it play at all? What does it share with scenes of children at play, like that described by Edgeworth, that makes them worthy of the same name? It is worth noting that Nietzsche himself was interested in the concrete nature of children playing, not just in play as affirmation and escape: "A man's maturity: having rediscovered the seriousness that he had as a child, at play."[27] I am not interested in attacking deconstruction and its derivatives as itself a form of mere playing with words, a reduction of truth and value to a game, as some have done—like Teresa Ebert, who decries what she calls "the hegemony of ludic logic" that has depoliticized and hence neutralized cultural theory.[28] Such criticisms are predicated on a conception of *mere* play, trivial and shorn of significance, whose long history I discuss in my first chapter. I prefer, instead, to take the prevalence of theoretical *lusus* in these late twentieth-century accounts as symptoms of the way in which play is both everywhere and nowhere in current critical discourse. While my opening chapters will continue to focus on the narratives and arguments in which play and iconoclasm have assumed important roles, my recursive engagement with Edgeworth's scene of iconoclastic child's play has led me not to a definition of play in general but to an understanding of its recurrent characteristics that differ markedly from these accounts of play as absolute undoing or affirmation.

Since I will emphasize these characteristics throughout, it may be helpful to enumerate them here. First, the forms of play that concern me do not involve establishing a stable relationship with an object; instead, the relationship between player and plaything is one that unfolds and changes, unpredictably, through time. As D. W. Winnicott succinctly observes, *"Doing things takes time. Playing is doing."*[29] Second, this affective, temporally uneven mode of interaction leads the plaything not only to become invested with increased significance but to verge on animation and agency. Third—and in part owing to its combination of animating intensity and unpredictability—play tends (as I have already suggested) to be opaque, its precise meaning ungraspable by those not involved in it (and perhaps by those who are). As the following chapters will suggest, these three intertwining characteristics, and the ways that we imagine them and the children engaged in them, are crystallized in iconoclasm as child's play.

My introduction, rather than considering the specific details of iconoclasm as child's play, begins with large-scale historical, cultural, and aesthetic narratives in which iconoclasm and play have been prominent but argues that these activities have tended to be opposed: insofar as iconoclasm helps to inaugurate disenchanted modernity, it is held to have driven play from the world. I argue that their convergence in the sixteenth century, therefore, has the potential to alter these larger narratives in showing that play cannot be equated with freedom nor iconoclasm with disenchantment. My first chapter begins with iconoclastic child's play in Elizabethan Lincolnshire; I relate but ultimately distinguish this practice from rhetorical strategies of trivialization and argue that we must rethink the assumption that to compare an activity to play is to trivialize it. Exploring the widespread iconoclastic term *trifle*, I argue that a strain of thought runs from scripture through the church fathers all the way to Thomas More that offers a more laudatory account of play as a way of responding to the divine and leaves play in a fluctuating position between the highest and the lowest significance. My second chapter begins with a desecrated crucifix given to children in Cologne as a plaything and argues that we should consider it as a form of what Edgeworth calls an "idoll," which I read as a hybrid of *idol* and *doll*. I present the doll as a figure perennially poised on the boundary between play and piety, and between reverence and violence, ending with our encounter with such works in the modern museum and in modern art. In Chapter 3 I continue this analysis in relation to movable puppets of doves, representing the Holy Spirit, that were given to children as playthings in Germany, and consider the marionette as a figure whose foregrounding of its constitutive brokenness paradoxically enables it to incarnate shattered Christian divinity, a foolish and material version of holiness whose implications were explored most fully by Erasmus.

My fourth chapter introduces the fetish as a theoretical term whose history has always been bound up with both iconoclasm and childhood; I approach it via iconoclastic child's play in non-European contexts, specifically Southeast Asia and New England, but also consider discussions relating to fetishism and play by modern thinkers including Lévi-Strauss and Adorno. In Chapter 5 I begin with a set of objects in Audley End House that survived partly because they spent a period as dolls. These objects guide my discussion of possible temporal models for play—especially smoothly developmental models that are held to inculcate piety and virtue—and I show how these emerge in ancient and early modern writers, but remain an issue for modern accounts of child development, building on the analyses by Ian Hacking and Christopher Bollas. I suggest that adults place children and their play into reassuringly linear temporal models in order to limit the meanings that such play can assume. In my sixth chapter I juxtapose the Audley End figures with the equally expressionless visage of an early modern wooden doll in order to explore the manner in which play does not seamlessly fill time but acts as a form of challenging blankness or vacancy within it, embodied in the figure of the masked child. I consider this alternative model of play as a neutral interlude via the writings of John Harington and others and end with an extended reading of Pieter Bruegel's painting *Children's Games* (and Hans Sedlmayr's unsettling reading of this painting) as an encapsulation of the interpretive challenges of iconoclasm as child's play and of the tendency for children to appear as demonically other in their playing. Finally, in my conclusion I discuss the category of the toy as an item that has been used to organize history into contrasting periods of playfulness and seriousness. I argue that the object of iconoclastic child's play, suspended between competing time frames and ways of meaning, encourages us to think of objects and texts as polychronic and replete with potential for surprising new meanings. I read an episode from book 1 of Edmund Spenser's *Faerie Queene* as emblematic of the kinds of reading that such a conception, inspired by iconoclasm as child's play, makes possible.

ICONOCLASM AS
CHILD'S PLAY

INTRODUCTION

IN HIS ESSAY "Le Morale de joujou" Charles Baudelaire writes: "There are some parents who try never to give toys. These are solemn, excessively solemn individuals, who have made no study of nature, and who generally make everyone around them miserable. I do not know why I think of them as reeking of Protestantism."[1] In this moment of pungent wit the poet associates a fiery commitment to reformed Christianity with an extreme solemnity that finds its natural expression in an antipathy to the playing of children. While few historians would endorse his quip as a straightforward truth, Baudelaire captures a diffuse assumption that underpins much writing about the Reformation and its implications: bluntly, that Protestantism, especially in its austerely iconoclastic form, simply reviles playfulness, especially the playing and the playthings of children.

I begin with Baudelaire's claim because it encapsulates the way in which the languages of iconoclastic religion and play can overlap with and permeate one another and the role that this overlap can assume in wider characterizations of an epoch or an attitude. While each of the following chapters begins with a historically precise instance of iconoclasm and child's play, my strategy in this introduction is rather different: since I go on to argue that this specific early modern phenomenon has a wider role to play in how we organize our narratives of the past, I start here with some of the salient features of these larger narratives. The scene of iconoclasm as child's play described by Roger Edgeworth in his sermon that I discussed in my preface assumes a wider resonance in part because there have been numerous influential narratives—of the emergence of modernity in general and of aesthetic experience in particular—in which iconoclasm and child's play have been invoked as a pair, either in parallel or in opposition to one another.

A set of claims similar in effect to Baudelaire's, though less wittily formulated, can be found at the culmination of Max Weber's influential account of the Reformation and its impact on modern mentalities. Weber claims that the reformed commitment to a worldly asceticism, defined by the productive pursuit of a particular calling, led to the widespread denigration of play as the impious abandonment of one's duties: "Waste of time is thus the first and in principle the deadliest of sins." The asceticism of this attitude, he writes, "descended like a frost on the life of 'merrie old England.' . . . The Puritan's ferocious hatred of everything which smacked of superstition . . . applied to the Christmas festivities and the May Pole."[2] For Weber the joyless, compulsively productive mindset of the puritan survives in secularized form as a prison within which modern people remain trapped: "the idea of duty in one's calling prowls about in our lives like the ghost of dead religious beliefs."[3] Weber's implicit claim that Protestant modernity is defined by the expulsion of play has since been repeated and expanded upon by influential modern play theorists, notably Johan Huizinga, who wrote in *Homo Ludens* that "mediaeval life was brimful of play: the joyous and unbuttoned play of the people . . . or the solemn and pompous play of chivalry." The hero of his story is the Roman Catholic Desiderius Erasmus, whose "whole being seems to radiate the play-spirit," but "Calvin and Luther could not abide the tone in which the Humanist Erasmus spoke of holy things."[4] Likewise Victor Turner, in his influential account of play as a liminal experience, adopts Weber's narrative entirely, arguing that English Puritanism inaugurated the total separation of work and leisure, and that "the social 'work of the Gods,' the calendrical, liturgical round . . . became 'internalized' as the systematic, non-ludic work of the individual's conscience."[5] If there is play in Protestant culture, then, according to these models, it must be, at best, furtive and repressed.

Weber's account of the Reformation as the expulsion of play correlates with his narrative of modernity as the result of a historical process of *Entzauberung*— the elimination of magic, typically translated "disenchantment"—a word now often used in various and broader senses to describe the diminished possibility of rich and immanent human meaningfulness.[6] If there is any action that would seem, on the surface, to confirm and exemplify such narratives and the prominence of the Reformation within them, it is surely iconoclasm, which aggressively seeks to banish the meanings and the forces that others would locate within certain objects, to reveal them as mute and their magic as spurious: "Protestant iconoclasm," as Joseph Leo Koerner writes, "sought disenchantment—mere wood and nothing else."[7] On this account iconoclasm as violent disenchantment is a crucial step in driving not only immanent significance from the world but play as well. Insofar as we are agents of modernity, perpetuating its disenchanting ideals in our modes of thought and action, we are akin to Baudelairean parents, solemnly and miserably restricting playfulness; insofar as we are victims of disenchantment, trapped in a world that has been iconoclastically stripped of intrinsic meaning, we are like Baudelairean children, denied toys and cruelly rendered incapable of play.

The frequent claims that the poverty of modernity makes true play impossible should be read against the backdrop of something like these assumptions, as with Huizinga's openly nostalgic lament that "civilization today is no longer played, and where it still seems to play it is false play," or Fredric Jameson's insistence that "play . . . may also no longer mean very much as a reminder and an alternative experience in a situation in which leisure is as commodified as work. . . . Play once meant children, who were in an older society the stand-in for those more distant representatives of nature like the savage. But where children are themselves taken in hand and organized, integrated into consumer society, childhood may have lost its capacity to suggest or project ideas like play, which were thought to convey freedom in motion, as a form of active self-invention and self-determination."[8] I propose for the time being to remain agnostic about such large-scale narratives; for now I wish only to observe that Jameson's account exemplifies, to return to Michael Taussig's formulation discussed in my preface, "the adult's imagination of the child's imagination" and doubles that imagining insofar as it juxtaposes an image of the free and inventive premodern child at play with his or her cramped and regulated modern counterpart. Jameson's claim provokes numerous questions to which I will return: what is, and has been, the relation between the child and the savage as cultural categories? Was there an era when children were *not* "taken in hand and organized"? When was this supposed age in which play existed as "freedom in motion"? The overall trajectory of this narrative—toward iconoclasm and away from play—significantly raises the stakes of interpreting moments in which iconoclasm and play converged and became one and the same action. We must be concerned not only with specific historical instances of iconoclastic play but with the place of both iconoclasm and play in the organization of history.

If the children who play with formerly holy things in Edgeworth's narrative assume a special resonance, as I have been suggesting, this is because their activity lies at the intersection of two categories—play and iconoclasm—that have assumed pivotal roles in narratives of emerging modernity, without being explicitly connected with one another. The iconoclast is viewed as the arch-disenchanter, the one who wields the hammer that banishes the spirits or the meanings supposed to inhere in the object and reduces it to mute materiality—and banishes play in the process. There are, however, two tensions in these narratives that we need to acknowledge—the first concerning the morality of iconoclasm, the second its efficacy. Concerning morality: some later figures are happy to describe themselves as iconoclasts, insofar as iconoclasm is construed as the continuation of an Enlightenment project of liberation from the tyrannous bonds of authority and superstition. Without the violent shattering of past error there could be no enlightened future: in 1765 Diderot wrote, "If we love truth more than the fine arts, let us pray God for some iconoclasts," suggesting that only via the sort of pious breaking practiced in the preceding centuries could truth be found.[9] On this model iconoclasts are heroes of reason, at the vanguard of the struggle for rationality against the benighted superstitions of the medieval church. Yes, they were violent in their actions, but their violence was necessary to dispel the sheer clutter of late medieval religion. As Bruno Latour has pointed out, iconoclasm is an integral part of the self-image of modern intellectual achievement. Even if the idols to be destroyed are the very Enlightenment ideals whose defense Diderot and his ilk demanded, the assumption that worthwhile achievement involves the unveiling and destroying of phony absolutes remains a widespread and often unacknowledged assumption: as Latour puts it, "Iconoclasm is an essential part of what it means to be a critique."[10]

This feting of iconoclasm as an intellectual strategy has, however, been accompanied by general horror when it is carried out in practice. In the nineteenth and twentieth centuries in England, it became common to flaunt one's own aesthetic refinement by lamenting the damage done by zealous Protestants in the sixteenth century. In the preface to *Culture and Anarchy* Matthew Arnold dubbed the Puritans responsible for iconoclasm: "incomplete and mutilated men" who "have developed one side of their humanity at the expense of all others."[11] If, as Michael Camille magisterially showed, idolatry in the Middle Ages was invariably something that *other people* did—a way of displacing anxieties regarding the valid and proper ways of revering images and objects onto safely stigmatized "Others"—then the iconoclast has become the idolater for the modern age, a retrograde figure whose imputed barbarism safeguards and underpins the civilized self-image of the West.[12] Nowhere is this clearer than in Western responses to the acts of iconoclastic violence that have recently been undertaken in the name of Islam. In 2015–16 a series of videos were released on the internet that showed members of ISIS or the Islamic State destroying an array of ancient statues in the Mosul Museum in Iraq with sledgehammers and power tools, while they also inflicted terrible degrees of damage on the ancient cities of Nimrud and Palmyra. The condemnation of these acts was swift and absolute, with the heads of prominent organizations including UNESCO and the Metropolitan Museum of Art denouncing those responsible as enemies of all humanity and of the universal values expressed in its art. While I instinctively share much of this horror, these acts also accentuated a tension between denunciation of this iconoclasm as barbaric and retrograde, and recognition of these iconoclastic acts as "no betrayal of universal values" but rather "driven by the same iconoclasm as Western imperialism," or of early modern Protestantism itself.[13] I am not interested either in further condemning or exonerating the perpetrators of these recent and horrifying actions: what interests me are the conflicting stories that we tend to tell in the West, and especially in the Anglo-American world, about our own iconoclastic past, and how we relate to it. Are we happy or ashamed to see ourselves, intellectually or practically, as the heirs to sixteenth-century breakers of images and holy objects?

This is a difficult enough question when we acknowledge, with James Simpson, that the fury, the hatred, and the violence of iconoclasm are "buried deep within Western modernity," but it becomes both stranger and potentially richer when considered in relation to iconoclasm as child's play.[14] By suggesting play as potentially equivalent to symbolic violence, Edgeworth's scene illuminates not just the ways in which modern thinkers have struggled to reconcile themselves to the iconoclasms of the past but the vexed relationship between iconoclasts and the objects of their activity. The child playing with a holy thing illuminates with unique clarity one of the central tensions of iconoclasm. In theory the disenchanting aim of most iconoclasm is to stress the meaningless, hollow, dead nature of its object, in diametric opposition to the immense significance with which it was formerly imbued. Nonetheless, iconoclasts tend through their actions implicitly to reassert the dangerous potency and deep significance of the object. This occurs in part through the rage that the object inspires and through its sheer ability to provoke such vigorous desecration. The covert reassertion of significance occurs through the forms that destruction typically takes, as when the hands or eyes of statues and images are targeted: such objects are treated most like real persons in the very moment that their personhood is emphatically denied.[15] In these ways the iconoclasts' behavior risks recapitulating and reinforcing the very errors that they putatively seek to overcome.

This possibility has been explored by Michael Taussig, who discusses the potential for the "defacement" of particular objects, as he calls it, to create rather than dissipate shadowy forms of power and holiness. In such moments "a strange surplus of negative energy is likely to be aroused from within the defaced thing itself. It is now in a state of *desecration*, the closest many of us are going to get to the sacred in this modern world."[16] Taussig begins with the compelling and hilarious instance of two concrete statues of the nude Queen Elizabeth II and Prince Philip that were exhibited in Canberra in 1995, prompting widespread outrage and eventually their violent destruction by a sledgehammer-wielding mob. He notes the range of negative responses that the statues provoked, which went beyond violence: "There was ridicule as well, the attempt to define the work not so much as filthy and sickening but, because of its filthiness, as childish." This seems to resemble iconoclastic child's play, which implies that an object is both dangerous—because it needs to be disenchanted—and childish, hence fit only for play. But, as Taussig notes, this double implication grants a curious ambivalence to the iconoclastic stance itself, which must descend to the level of the childishness that it denounces. One opponent of the statue is quoted as saying that the sculptor should be treated like a naughty child and ignored rather than having his bottom spanked; but, Taussig asks, "is there not an awkwardness to iconoclasm, paradoxically privileging its target by virtue of ridicule? And does not iconoclasm justify and even insist on violent, childish, debased, filthy, revolting, rotten, disgusting, filthy, insulting, profane, and so on, counterreaction[?]"[17] Taussig intuits an instability lurking within the actions of iconoclasts. They often seem to want to charge their enemies with childish inanity, even as their own apparently grim and somber stance seems to verge, in practice, upon a range of actions easily characterized as infantile, from petulance to actual play. The attribution of childishness to the object provokes—or covertly permits—a form of childishness in response, which seems almost like a cover-up, a pretext for playing inanely even as inane play is decried. What if, following Taussig, we begin by seeing the transformation of holy things into playthings in the sixteenth century not as an act of successful desecration but as the covert realization of the iconoclast's own desire to play?

Part of the reason for which I argue that iconoclastic child's play has a significance far beyond its occurrence as a local phenomenon, then, is the conflicting set of roles that iconoclasm and play have been assigned in various influential narratives of modernity. In addition to these wider narratives of disenchantment as the iconoclastically induced termination of cultural playfulness, I now want to turn to a related and more specific set of narratives that have frequently deployed both iconoclasm and play, concerning not disenchantment in general but the emergence of the category of the aesthetic. It has frequently been asserted that iconoclasm was necessary to liberate objects from the sphere of religion in order to free them for the disinterested contemplation proper to art.[18] These narratives, I would argue, significantly change and raise the stakes of interpreting iconoclasm as child's play. We can begin by postulating four potential trajectories for the objects at which iconoclasts took aim, objects that must have been intended to be symbolically equivalent or equally efficacious: such objects might be destroyed altogether, adapted for humdrum use, transformed into playthings, or liberated as artworks. But, I will argue, these should not be understood as self-contained and opposed alternatives; regardless of the category into which a transformed object was supposedly placed, it was shadowed by the possibility that it might belong in one of the others. If an artwork and a plaything were two possible outcomes of the iconoclastic process, the question of the relationship between these two categories of object inevitably surfaces. What can each tell us about the other? In the chapters that follow I will argue that understanding iconoclastic child's play encourages us to triangulate holy things, playthings, and art-things and thereby to unravel the parallel forms of engagement and revulsion, of attachment and detachment, that these three categories of object might inspire.

The claim that Protestant iconoclasm facilitates the emergence of art as an autonomous domain has been made by Hans Belting, who writes that, after the removal of sacred objects from churches in the Reformation, "images, which had lost their function in the church, took on a new role in representing art. . . . The

new presence *of* the work succeeds the former presence of the sacred *in* the work."[19]
We may have lost much in terms of the gorgeous fabric of the medieval church,
on this account, but there is a compensatory gain in the stepping forward, for the
first time, of the artwork as an autonomous object in its own right. Just as iconoclasm has been depicted as both the essence and the enemy of modernity, however,
here, too, matters are not so simple, for we find exactly the opposite claim in Hans-
Georg Gadamer's important essay "The Relevance of the Beautiful." "The rejection
of iconoclasm," Gadamer writes, "a movement that had arisen in the Christian
Church during the sixth and seventh centuries, was a decision of incalculable significance. For the Church then gave a new meaning to the visual language of art
and later to the forms of poetry and narrative. This provided art with a new form
of legitimation. . . . The great history of Western art is the consequence of this decision which still largely determines our own cultural consciousness."[20] Although
Gadamer's chronology is vague, his claim is rich with implications.[21] Iconoclasm
and art are for him natural enemies: it is only because the church turned away
from iconoclasm that there is Christian art at all, and on this account art emerges
smoothly from—and potentially continues to overlap with—the world of holy
objects rather than needing to be wrenched violently from it. Gadamer goes on
not only to oppose art and iconoclasm but to claim that "play's excess" is "the real
ground of our creative production and reception of art."[22]

Gadamer links his account of the aesthetic play enabled by the eschewal of
iconoclasm to "the co-operative play between imagination and understanding
which Kant discovered in the 'judgement of taste,'" which, he insists, is "a *free*
play and not directed towards a concept."[23] Before saying more about the Kan-
tian grounds of his narrative, I would like to spend a moment with the word that
Gadamer chooses to stress: *free*. So far I have discussed play, which Maurizio
Bettini justly calls "that impossibly difficult word," without defining it, and I will
persist in this strategic avoidance throughout this book, engaging with persistent
traditions and recurrent characteristics in the history and nature of play rather
than making claims that I consider true in every instance.[24] Gadamer's account,
however, illuminates one of the most common and least disputed claims in modern accounts of play: that play, if it is to be an activity worthy of the name, must
be free. The phrase "free play" sounds almost pleonastic to modern ears. Here is
Huizinga, for example: "First and foremost, all play is a voluntary activity. Play to
order is no longer play: it could at best be but a forcible imitation of it." In fact,
he goes even further: play is not only free; it "is in fact freedom."[25] More recently,

Martha Nussbaum lists "Play" among what she labels "central human capabilities that society must allow freely to flourish": "Being able to laugh, to play, to enjoy recreational activities."[26] This claim seems intuitively right—I would have difficulty playing in manacles or with a gun to my head—but it is nonetheless one that my interpretation of iconoclasm as child's play leads me to question. Let us return briefly to Edgeworth's sermon with which I began my preface. The children are already playing when the adults enter—"dauncynge them after their childyshe maner"—in a manner that seems spontaneous and chosen. But they are quickly compelled to attach to their play a particular meaning and message: "I haue here myne ydoll," after which "the father laugheth and maketh a gaye game at it." The children may still be playing once this happens, but they clearly are not playing a game of their own choosing, nor are they free to play exactly how they choose.

I will argue that this is another feature of Edgeworth's scene that makes it symptomatic of significant patterns of thought and action rather than a quirky anomaly. There have been many ways and contexts in which child's play has been subjected to different forms of adult scrutiny, intervention, guidance, and compulsion. In fact, I will contend, the playing of children has frequently provoked fear, horror, and disquiet on the part of adults: this is one recurrent way in which the adult's imagining of the child's imagining has functioned. Because we often only know of child's play via adult recollections and descriptions, the history of such play is in large part the history of the anxiety that it provokes among adults, their attempts to shape it, and the despairing realization that the control that they seek over play and its meanings is impossible to exert definitively. Viewed from this perspective, when it comes to children, "free play" is not a pleonasm, historically speaking, but practically an oxymoron. I will expand on these claims in what follows, but I want for the moment to emphasize the stakes of using iconoclastic child's play to question the wide acceptance of the claim that play is and must be free. Though Huizinga barely acknowledges the fact, lurking behind his account is perhaps the most influential of play theories, developed by Friedrich Schiller, who presented the *Spieltrieb*, the play-drive or drive to play, as the only way for the human to mediate between the conflicting demands of freedom and necessity, and therefore as the pinnacle of human capability: "man only plays when he is in the fullest sense of the word a human being," Schiller writes, "and he is only fully a human being when he plays."[27] This equation of freedom and play found

its way into other influential twentieth-century theories of play, like the phe-
nomenological account by Heidegger's student and collaborator Eugen Fink,
who wrote that in play humans experience "an almost limitless creativity" and
claimed that because it is virtually unlimited, play is "an eminent manifestation of human freedom."[28]

Schiller links his account of play as the realization of human potential
integrally to aesthetic experience, insisting in a phrase of supreme poise that
"with beauty man shall only play, and it is with beauty only that he shall play."[29]
Like Gadamer, Schiller built upon while departing from the aesthetic philosophy of Kant, who had written that in the presentation of a beautiful object
"the cognitive powers brought into play by this presentation are in free play."[30]
Paul Guyer has described "the idea that our pleasure in beauty and perhaps
in other aesthetic qualities as well is a response to the free play of our mental
capacities" as one of the "great ideas of modern aesthetics," showing that Kant
adopted and adapted it from his predecessors, provoking a response not just
from Schiller and Gadamer but from practically every subsequent writer on
the nature of aesthetic experience.[31] What is notable in Schiller's adaptation
of Kant's argument is his nervousness about elevating play to such an extent,
leading him to imagine the resistance of his reader: "But, you may long have
been tempted to object, is beauty not degraded by being made to consist of
mere play and reduced to the level of those frivolous things [*frivolen Gegen-
ständen*] which have always borne this name?"[32] He was all too aware that play
is not a straightforward vessel for the highest forms of human significance but
one vulnerable to diminishment.

In introducing Kant, Schiller, and Gadamer in this fashion, I might seem to
have drifted far from my opening in sixteenth-century Bristol, but I do so to begin
disentangling the curious and uneven place that play seems to occupy in contemporary discussions. Even in the present moment, no discussion of aesthetic
experience can avoid attention to playfulness. Take, for instance, Sianne Ngai's
important recent work, in which two of the three terms that she identifies as "our
aesthetic categories" (zany, cute, interesting) are defined via the ludic: "There is no
experience of the cute without playfulness"; zaniness involves "a strenuous relation to playing."[33] Yet just as Schiller seemed able to *idealize* play only by fending
off the imagined objection that to invoke play is to *trivialize* art and humanity,
play continues to hover between being seen as the highest thing—the freest, the
loftiest, the most dignified—and the most lowly and inconsequential. The tension

between these two possible valuations has rather warped and haunted the role of play in later aesthetic debate. The risks of making an idealized and dehistoricized *Spieltrieb* the distinguishing and dignifying feature of humanity have been stressed by Marxist thinkers, in the wake of Marx's blunt insistence in his *Grundrisse*: "Labour cannot become play."[34] Writers in this tradition have generally insisted that, even if the gap between play and labor were to narrow, the latter remains the inescapable horizon of human self-realization. This reproach was modified up to a point by Herbert Marcuse, whose Freudian rethinking of Marx was leavened with a Schillerian hymn to "the freedom to play" as the essence of "freedom itself," but more typical and decisive for this tradition was Theodor W. Adorno's denunciation, near the close of his *Aesthetic Theory*, of "the obstinacy of aesthetic comportment, which was later ideologically glorified as the eternal natural power of the play drive."[35] This skepticism toward Schiller's idealized grounding of the aesthetic in play was advanced from an alternative perspective by Paul de Man, for whom the problem with Schiller's account is not its ideological mystification but its unapologetic humanism: "*Spieltrieb* . . . becomes the determining principle of the human. The human is determined by this possibility of free play—'I play therefore I am,' or something of this sort." Schiller is comparatively uninterested in the carefree playing of animals or the play of light on the surface of water; for him we call each of these play only by analogy with true play, which is solely human. But, de Man insists, to define the human absolutely in this fashion is "a principle of closure," which "is to assume a control of man over language, which in all kinds of ways is extremely problematic."[36] The implicit postulation of a clear divide between human and animal play is particularly noteworthy: much recent work has emphasized the complexity of animal play and its propinquity to human forms.[37] Already in the early modern period, Michel de Montaigne stressed the way in which such play blurs human and animal natures and roles: "When I am playing with my cat, who knows whether she have more sporte in dallying with me, than I have in gaming with her? We entertain one other with mutuall apish trickes."[38] For Montaigne such play is a delightfully vertiginous experience, which, far from confirming his human distinctiveness, leads him to see himself as an object for another, barely knowable form of subject, a plaything in a chiasmic game beyond his knowledge and control.

There is no room for this undercutting of human distinctiveness in Schiller's account of play, which makes it all the more striking that recent years have seen concerted attempt to recuperate his account of the aesthetic and the *Spieltrieb*.[39]

I see this resurgence of interest as deeply symptomatic of a feeling among scholars and critics of various stripes that play might have something attractive to offer them, even if they cannot straightforwardly lay claim to it as either a focus or model for their own work without reckoning with these powerful forms of earlier skepticism about its ultimate value. This is the serious and symptomatic bind in which we find ourselves today: it seems impossible to think about the value of modern experience, and preeminently the valuable experience of art, without invoking play, yet to do so risks idealization (is play really as free as Schiller claims?), mystification (what are we really saying when we say that aesthetic experience is like playing?), and trivialization (does play really provide a firm ground for some of the most powerful experiences that we might have? Do we want to stake everything on mere play?). My own contention in what follows is that iconoclasm as child's play can both clarify these debates and offer a new way through and beyond them. Play in the iconoclastic scene seems at once free and compelled, instrumental and resistant, joyous and workmanlike, richly significant and emphatically trivial. Iconoclasm as child's play becomes a testing ground of sorts for investigating the stakes that those involved in it had in the meaning (or lack of meaning) of play, and the cultural and intellectual stakes that we might have in it today. Having made clear my own skepticism toward the Schillerian insistence on aesthetic play as entirely free, let me modify this skepticism via Adorno's account of the artwork, which, despite his own dismissal of the *Spieltrieb*, allows it to persist in revised form: "The freedom of artworks, in which their self-consciousness glories and without which these works would not exist, is the ruse of art's own reason. Each and every one of their elements binds them to that over which, for their happiness, they must soar and back into which at every moment they threaten once again to tumble."[40]

This construal of aesthetic freedom is one that I am far happier to endorse, and it is one that both illuminates and is illuminated by the holy object that becomes a child's plaything. This object, too, is both bound to certain meanings—the meaning that the object once held as a ritual or liturgical object, the meaning that the adults now try to impose on it—and has a propensity to soar above them. It is neither totally tethered to any one of these meanings nor freed entirely from all of them. It soars, but it soars precariously, and it is both this levitation and the tumbling to which it is perennially prone that make its status as an object of play a uniquely useful illumination of the play that might be both provoked by and aimed at an artwork.

Having written in my preface of the scene of iconoclastic child's play described by Roger Edgeworth as a startling anomaly to which I feel a deep and curious attachment, I have now suggested some of the reasons for which it resonates with me so profoundly. Iconoclasm and play seemed at first like strange bedfellows, utterly different and even opposed ways of relating to an object. I have tried to show, instead, that they are two activities that keep recurring, in curious but unthought proximity to one another, in various narratives of modern experience. This preliminary investigation leaves me not with conclusions but with a proliferation of unanswered questions. Can we bear to see ourselves as the heirs, culturally and intellectually, of early modern iconoclasm? Why are we both drawn to play as a distinctive and valuable human characteristic and skeptical of what it offers? What do we want iconoclasm to be and to mean, and what do we want from it? What do we want play to be and to mean, and what do we want from it? And what do we want the children who play to be and to mean, and what do we want from them?

These are the questions that will drive and animate the chapters that follow, though I want to end this introduction with the identification of one further set of symptoms. The desire to salvage something of value from Schiller's paean to human playfulness is far from the only place in recent critical writing where play has undergone a mini-renaissance. A notable shift across the humanities in recent years has been the tendency, shared by thinkers of differing theoretical commitments, to narrow or reject the distinction between subjects and objects, between human and nonhuman, and to attribute agency and vitality to a whole range of things. Bill Brown wittily conjures up the spooky sensation, induced by these various strands, of previously inert objects twitching to life: "Things quicken. What you took to be the inanimate object-world slowly but certainly wakes."[41] The intellectual and political implications of these strands of thought vary markedly, but the symptomatic fact that I wish to identify is the frequency with which writers across this spectrum turn to children's toys, the playing of children, and the world of childhood as the best analogy for the enlivened or agential object-world that they wish to evoke. This is true of Brown himself, whose work on "thing theory" was preceded by his remarkable analyses of toys in American literature and consumer culture, and who returns frequently to toys as paradigmatic of thinghood: "Do you grant agency to inanimate objects because you want to unburden yourself of responsibility?" he asks the reader;

"Or is it simply because you're lonely? Because, unlike a child, you don't have a toy to talk with?"[42] It is true also of Barbara Johnson, whose book *Persons and Things*, informed by psychoanalysis and deconstruction, has chapters titled "Toys R Us" and "Real Dolls."[43] One might also mention Bruno Latour's frequent invocation of the puppet as the best image of the imperfect relationship between an agent's intentions toward an object and the actual consequences (to be discussed in Chapter 3); or Jane Bennett's endeavor to allow "a *vital materiality* [to] start to take shape. . . . Or, rather, it can take shape again, for a version of this idea already found expression in childhood experiences of a world populated by animate things rather than passive objects."[44] Again and again these writers invoke childhood and its toys, and the yearnings to return to these relations integral to childhood, as both the subject of their studies and a model for their studies. This critical tendency represents a particularly intense manifestation of the adult's imagination of the child's imagination, and the frequency with which it recurs adds to my own sense that iconoclasm as child's play has the potential to speak to our current fascinations both with objects and with children. C. S. Lewis had been quite bold in juxtaposing artworks with toys and sacred objects, only to distinguish the artwork from "the ikon and the toy" on the basis that the purpose of each of the latter two is "not to fix attention on itself, but to stimulate and liberate certain activities in the child or the worshipper," whereas appreciation of the art-object is an end itself.[45] Alfred Gell pushed this possibility to a more provocative extreme in his book *Art and Agency*, where he baldly refuses to acknowledge any strict differentiation between the forms of action carried out by religious believers, iconoclasts, art lovers, and playing children. He rejects any distinction between the supposedly disenchanted modern mind and the superstitious belief-systems of earlier periods or of non-Western peoples, arguing that the ascription of agency to inanimate objects involves neither simple misguidedness nor naive animism but is rather an accurate reflection of the very real social efficacy that these objects frequently assume and exercise: "in relevant theoretical respects," he claims, "art objects are the equivalents of persons, or more precisely, social agents."[46] His example of the routine ways in which objects assume agency merits quoting at length:

The immediate "other" in a social relationship does not have to be another "human being." . . . It just happens to be patently the case that persons form what are evidently social relations with "things." Consider a little girl with her doll. She loves her doll. Her doll is her best friend (she says). Would she toss her doll overboard from a lifeboat in order to save her bossy older brother from drowning? No way. This may seem a trivial example, and the kinds of relations small girls form with their dolls are far from being "typical" of human social behaviour. But it is not a trivial example at all; in fact it is an archetypal instance of the anthropology of art. We only think it is not because it is an affront to our dignity to make comparisons between small girls showering affection on their dolls, and us, mature souls, admiring Michelangelo's *David*. But what is *David* if it is not a big doll for grown-ups? This is not really a matter of devaluing *David* so much as revaluing little girl's dolls, which are remarkable objects, all things considered. They are certainly social beings—"members of the family," for a time at any rate.[47]

This is a particularly daring example of the bold conflations that make Gell's work so generative. He refuses to assume in advance a firm set of distinctions among religious, aesthetic, and ludic experiences or to distinguish those (grown-ups, rational beings) who consistently deny agency to objects and those (children, naive non-Westerners) who naively ascribe it. His refusal can help us understand the fact that, in certain contexts in the sixteenth century, iconoclasm and child's play intermittently became one and the same. I have begun to describe the separate but constantly juxtaposed or intersecting roles that iconoclasm and play have assumed in various narratives of modernity, religious change, and aesthetic experience, and to argue that we must appreciate the potential for forms of reverence and irreverence to become troublingly indistinguishable if we are to understand these actions and their implications. The strategic conflation that Gell effects among holy thing, art-thing, and plaything is a strikingly bold move, but it is one that reflects the way in which at least some artists conceive of their work and its outcomes. Describing his work *Free Object*, a humanoid figure constructed from stacked cubes of rusting steel, Antony Gormley has said that "with this work, it's like a child playing with wooden blocks, seeing how this unstable thing might become stable. In fact, apart from the head, everything in this works as a stack of unfixed blocks. The head is the least stable bit and would fall off if it were not cast into the form, but for me this is a play."[48] Gell's and Gormley's remarks, that strikingly juxtapose the making and the apprehending of art with a child's toy, are unusually explicit formulations of a much longer set of traditions in which these categories have frequently intersected and been defined both by analogy with and opposition to one another. It is with this longer history that the next chapter begins.

1 TRIFLE

IN 1566, seven years after Elizabeth I ascended to the throne, royal visitors were sent into the county of Lincolnshire to ensure that it had been thoroughly cleansed of the vestiges of traditional and unreformed religion that had been brought back under Queen Mary. The previous year, the archdeacon of Lincoln, John Aylmer, had been appalled while undertaking a routine visitation by widespread evidence that the restored paraphernalia and practices had survived into the early years of Elizabethan reform. He appealed successfully for a special commission "for reforming this church and diocese . . . for undoubtedly this country [sic] hath as much need of it as any place in England."[1] The commissioners duly made their way through Lincolnshire, casting their beady eyes over the liturgical apparatus of the parish churches and grilling priests and parishioners to determine the precise fates of the holy things that they were supposed to have expunged. They compiled long lists, itemizing every previously holy object that each parish had once possessed and detailing the properly iconoclastic fate that these items had ultimately met.

The lists that the commissioners compiled have survived, and they have periodically been examined by historians of the English Reformation for the remarkable glimpse that they offer into the practicalities of iconoclasm.[2] Reading them, one finds it impossible not to be struck by the diverse forms that iconoclastic actions might take. Burning or breaking an object was one obvious way to abolish its holiness, but it was far from the only way. Many of the items were adapted for new purposes, and the phrase "put to prophane use" echoes like a refrain throughout the lists.[3] The commissioners were told of "the covering of the pix"—the container for the consecrated Host—"sold to John Storr and his wief occupieth yt in wiping her eies."[4] More than one item was given to a tinker, and vestments were donated to the poor.[5] Other objects were put to still lowlier uses: a holy water vat was used to make "a swines troughe"; a sacring bell was redeployed as "a horse bell therof to hange at a horses eare."[6] Altar stones were now used as "paving as to the townes behofe," and parishioners could routinely undergo the daring experience of placing their profane buttocks onto a rood loft, converted into "seates . . . for people to sytt in," or even fornicating and sleeping in another rood loft converted into a bed.[7]

Amid these diverse iconoclastic forms, however, the lists include several entries that cannot easily be grouped either with those objects that were burned and broken or those put to profane use. The commissioners were told of two pyxes "defacid and geven away . . . vnto a child to plaie with all." Later, it was reported to them that "three banner clothes" had been "geven awaie to childerne to make plaiers cotes of."[8] Some holy things, it seems, did not meet their fate on the pyre or beneath the hammer, nor were they refashioned for emphatically humdrum purposes. Instead, like the objects described by Roger Edgeworth in the 1530s, they were placed in the hands of children, to be desacralized by being made into toys.

The appearance of these entries on the Lincolnshire lists is significant for a number of reasons, not the least of which is it confirms that Edgeworth's scene of iconoclastic child's play from the 1530s was not a unique or isolated instance: three decades later, making holy things into playthings remained a viable way of, in theory, demeaning them and reducing them to insignificance. The context in which we encounter this evidence is, however, strikingly different. Edgeworth described iconoclastic child's play from the point of view of an appalled adherent to traditional religion. He depicted a scene in which an image was treated as a plaything in the interior of an irreverent household, but he did not suggest that this was a reflection of official policy—only that it encapsulated the ungodliness inherent with the program of reform as a whole. In the case of the Lincolnshire lists, though, matters are very different. The fraught position in which the parishioners of the county were being placed merits further consideration. They knew that these men were coming to inspect them with the most suspicious of attitudes, sharply attentive to any suggestion of lingering traditionalism or failure to act as thoroughgoing iconoclasts. These parishioners could be sure that if a formerly holy object was found to have remained among them unobliterated, they would have to be able to explain why. This meant that they must have been confident that the visitors would accept placing an object in a child's hands as an adequate strategy for ridding it of its holiness and its numinous force.

If the presence of the entries on these lists provides further evidence for iconoclastic child's play as a wider phenomenon, then, it also indicates some important challenges to my attempts to interpret it. I ultimately want to argue that iconoclasm as child's play is replete with the possibility of multiple meanings and that the nature and extent of the transformation that a holy object undergoes when it becomes a plaything is open to serious question. If this is the case, it must be asked: why did it not worry the Lincolnshire visitors, who apparently accepted it as a straightforward form of iconoclasm? To this I must add a caveat leading to a second, parallel question. It is important to stress that I have by no means *discovered* that iconoclastic child's play took place: Edgeworth's sermon, and the entries on the Lincolnshire lists, have been discussed by numerous historians, but they have tended to mention it only in passing, folding it into the large and varied repertoire of iconoclastic activities rather than considering it as a distinctive phenomenon in its own right.[9] Why, if it seems to be so distinctive to me, has it not seemed so to them?

The answer to both of these questions, I believe, lies in the relationship between the practice of iconoclastic child's play and a prominent and frequently discussed strand in Protestant polemic, which sought to demean and diminish Roman Catholic ritual by eliding it with the mere playing of children. In this context a particular cluster of words emerged that were used again and again to effect this deliberately insulting juxtaposition. A good example is the *New Catechism* written by the incessantly vituperative Thomas Becon, which presents a dialogue between father and son, in which the former proclaims: "How unmeet a schoolmaster a blind idol, a dumb mawmet, a popish puppet, a dead image is to teach us any good thing."[10] Later in the century we see the ways in which such polemical strategies found their way into poetry. In the "Maye" eclogue of Edmund Spenser's *Shepheardes Calendar* (1579), the shepherd Piers (who, the "Argument" tells us, represents a Protestant minister) tells a fable of a "false Foxe" who fools a kid by dressing

> . . . as a poore pedler . . .
> Bearing a trusse of tryfles at hys backe,
> As bells, and babes, and glasses in hys packe.

In case the reader misses the implied denigration behind these words, E. K's gloss explains that "by such trifles are noted, the reliques and ragges of popish superstition, which put no smal religion in Belles: and Babies .s. Idoles: and glasses .s. Paxes, and such lyke trumperies."[11] Nor was this polemical strain confined to England but emerged in comparable German contexts: in one of the sets of reformed church statutes compiled by Johannes Bugenhagen, the "child's play of the papists" [*kinder spel der Papen*] is derided as "idle deception and doll play" [*poppen spel*].[12] We see beginning to emerge in these moments a cluster of words that seem strongly related to child's play—*mammet, puppet, baby*, and especially *trifle*—which are compared to the workings of "popish superstition" in order to confirm its equally empty triviality.[13] Indeed, in Lincolnshire we find some parishioners sufficiently aware of this emerging polemical strand that they used it to describe earlier acts of destruction that they could not prove had taken place: the people of the Isle of Axholme insisted that "the Rest of such triflinge toyes and tromprie apptayninge to the popishe masse and popishe prelate was made awaie and defacid in Kinge Edwardes tyme."[14] The iconoclastic child's play in Edgeworth's sermon or in Lincolnshire has therefore seemed quite comprehensible (both to the Elizabethan visitors and to recent historians) as the actualization—the putting into practice—of this polemical strain. The playing children merely confirm the supposedly holy object to be the inane plaything that, in the iconoclasts' eyes, it always already was. This is the claim made, for example, by Amy Knight Powell, who outlines the polemical dismissal of popery as mere child's play and notes in passing that "other reformers made the same point by *simply* giving the images they removed from churches to children."[15] But was it quite that simple?

Although the practice of iconoclasm as child's play is clearly linked to this polemical strand, I argue in this chapter that they should not be conflated too swiftly. To do so is to mistake a strenuous attempt at simplification for something that was, in fact, simple in practice. My central claim is that there is nothing at all simple about trivialization strategies, which involve powerful and complex processes. It is no great surprise that they have not typically been recognized as such, however, since such strategies function not only by denying power and complexity to that which they trivialize but by concealing their *own* power and complexity in the process. "*This object is straightforwardly banal and trivial; my claim that this is so is itself an equally simple reflection of this object's uncomplicated and patent triviality*"—so runs the implicit logic of strategic trivialization. There has been significantly more attention to the processes by which value is created and reinforced than to those by which it is removed or diminished, but the latter is a potent social force with, I would argue, a crucial role to play in the formation of social, religious, and aesthetic communities. One way to understand such communities in practice might be not so much in terms of their shared commitments or beliefs but a common (and often tacit) agreement as to what they will and will not risk trivializing. Discussing the section of *Homo Ludens* that sees the spoilsport as the true enemy of play who "must be cast out as a threat to the play community," E. H. Gombrich writes that "the more one reads Huizinga, the more one comes to the conclusion that it was this character of common consent, *the agreement to refrain from certain questions*, that constituted for him an important condition of civilization."[16] The power of this tacit agreement is immense and underrated. *Belief* can be debated, but ritual *practice* relies on a common willingness to accept *this* particular set of embodied acts as at least potentially significant; there is little to convince those who reject them, and this makes such acts intrinsically, not accidentally, prone to ridicule and trivialization. If such practices are seen as ridiculous and trifling, this judgment seems to draw on the ceaseless potential for ludicrousness that comes with the human predicament of being an embodied agent in the world. The language of trifling cuts to the heart of how values actually function in specific communities and the deep fragility of this functioning, based as it is on a mixture of collective practices and a concomitant collective willingness to refrain from asking certain questions about why we do what we do. As Webb Keane puts it, "the fact of *not* being talked about can be an important part of the power and persuasiveness of certain aspects of a culture."[17] This is how, outside iconoclastic contexts, culturally essential trifles continue to function.

There is a specific reason that the practice of iconoclastic child's play illuminates the complexities of these processes of attempted trivialization better than mere polemic: here the object lingers, potentially able to accrue further meanings in its own right, rather than disappearing as it is mocked and reviled. The polemical disparagement of an object as a mere plaything dismisses it with a wave of the hand, insisting that it *obviously* never really was and never could be the appropriate focus for a genuine act of piety: it is banished by virtue of its supposedly patent frivolity. By contrast, the retaining of the object as an actual plaything causes it to hang around even as it is dismissed as trivial and inane; it integrates the object into the reformed household, making it a potential focus for other kinds of actions still to come. Its retention in this form might indicate not just contempt for the past but, as Margaret Aston puts it, "faith in the future."[18] It is as a descriptor of this curious object—the object that lingers after it is trivialized, as a locus both of the immense value that it once held, now theoretically cancelled, and its newly and repeatedly performed worthlessness—that I propose to retain and adapt the polemical term *trifle*.

The most basic problem with taking this polemical strand (and iconoclastic child's play as its actualization) at face value is that, in doing so, we assume that to compare a given practice to child's play is necessarily to demean it. The cluster of terms that we have begun to encounter along with trifle—*mammet, puppet, baby, toy*—are piled together in these polemical texts, just as the objects are piled together in the Lincolnshire lists, in order to emphasize their common and interchangeable inanity. But each of these terms has a complexity and a history of its own that needs disentangling. Far from referring straightforwardly to empty child's play, each of these words shimmers between the worlds of children and adults and between the worlds of play and religion: they are co-opted by Protestant polemicists, not just to tame the power imputed to holy objects but to tame the ambiguity of the words themselves and ultimately of child's play itself. To call Roman Catholic worship mere child's play is certainly to make an argument about the nature of religion, but it is also to make an implicit argument about the nature and worth of such play, which we should not ignore or take as inevitable.

Let us first pay more concerted attention to the word *trifle*. We saw it used above both by Spenser's E. K. and by the Lincolnshire parishioners. Its prominence is confirmed by its recurrence in a hugely influential text, the English translation of Jean Calvin's treatise against relics, which begins by denouncing purveyors of phony fragments of saints as "trifle bearers" and goes on to denounce repeatedly "small trifles and vayne trifles," linking them to the manner in which ordinary Christians have been "abused in setting their mindes rather on childishe playes, than on the true worshippynge of God."[19] The *OED* suggests that *trifle* arrived in Middle English from an Old French word meaning to lie or deceive. Its meaning developed from a false or deceptive tale, to an idle or frivolous one, to a more general sense of any "matter of little value or importance," to a more concrete sense: "A small article of little intrinsic value; a toy, trinket, bauble, knick-knack." One can see why this combination of deception and worthlessness would make it an attractive term for the denunciation of Roman Catholicism.

What if, however, in line with my account of the intrinsic vulnerability of embodied social practice, we read this language of trifling not as a statement of assertive
self-confidence but as the warding off of anxieties, as a *defensive* act of deliberate
simplification? What if we see the designation of something as a trifle in the sixteenth century not as a way of mocking it because it is already meaningless but as a
way of taming and fixing its possible meanings, precisely because they are potentially
so threatening and so various? In reading the word in this way, I mean to rethink
its use in relation both to holy things and to children, who were seen as particularly
prone to its dangers: one medieval conduct poem warned children, "Tryfle thou
with nothing," while Ben Jonson wrote in his *Discoveries* of "children that esteem
every trifle."[20] Patricia Fumerton has argued that within the mode of "trivial selfhood" that she finds characteristic of the English aristocracy in the sixteenth century,
children were seen as "living trivialities. . . . The role of children was to be 'little,' 'toylike,' 'pretty,' 'trivial,' and yet also socially 'precious.' . . . Children were trifles whose
circulation 'finished' them in the way an artwork is finished."[21] Fumerton's account
is relevant not only for aristocratic models of selfhood but also as one of a set of
early modern strategies for the taming of children—they are relegated to the status
of trifles, while their eventual "finishing" is both outsourced and ensured. To label
the child as a trifle is to imagine the child as empty, devoid of significance rather
than brimming with it. Reading this labeling as a defensive act resonates with Bill
Brown's discussion of the manner in which mundane objects can make and mark
the most profound differences: "the 'trivial thing,' " he writes, "is in fact a sublime
thing, irreducible to the physical object; it is at once physical and metaphysical, sen-
sible and suprasensible."[22] The trifle, I argue, is not the object that straightforwardly
lacks value: it is the object that *must* be labeled as lacking in value precisely because
its significance is potentially so unstable and opaque—because it seems to have a
transformative significance in excess of its seemingly inconsequential status. The
trifles of iconoclasm as child's play—by which I mean both the playing child and
the once-holy object with which he or she plays—cause the sublime and the trivial
to collide and converge: the mere thing, verging on no-thing, must be tamed and
demeaned precisely because it has the potential to change everything.

We saw a glimmer of these alternative possibilities—absolute significance and
insignificance—in my introduction, where Alfred Gell juxtaposed a little girl's
doll and Michelangelo's *David* as "remarkable objects": his defensive language—

"This may seem a trivial example. . . . But it is not a trivial example at all"—show him (like Schiller) both recognizing and trying to fend off the iconoclastic assumption that a comparison to child's play can only be demeaning. This is necessary because the strategy of trivializing an object by comparing it to child's play has a long history and was used in earlier Christian contexts by various writers who sought to distinguish their own, viable religious practices from those that they reviled. In his *Life of Constantine*, for example, written in the fourth century CE, Eusebius wrote:

> In all these undertakings the Emperor worked for the glory of the Saviour's power. . . . The sacred bronze figures, of which the error of the ancients had for a long time been proud, he displayed to all the public in all the squares of the emperor's city. . . . The city named after the emperor was filled throughout with objects of skilled artwork in bronze. . . . To these under the name of gods those sick with error had for long ages vainly offered innumerable hecatombs and whole burnt sacrifices, but now they at last learnt sense, as the emperor used these very toys [*athurmasin*] for the laughter and amusement of the spectators.[23]

This passage would seem to anticipate the polemical discourses of the Reformation: what had once been worshipped is now to be derided as a mere toy, a trifle. Once again, however, it is instructive to peer behind the facade of obviousness that this polemic has assumed, for more is at stake here than the straightforward labeling of once-sacred bronzes as toys. The word that Eusebius deploys—*athurma*—was one of the standard terms in Ancient Greek literature for a child's plaything.[24] It was also used, however, in a series of famous literary moments to refer specifically to the playfulness of divine beings. In the Homeric hymn to Hermes the infant god's tortoiseshell lyre is described as a "fine plaything" (*kalon athurma*) and a "lovely plaything" (*erateinon athurma*), and in Apollonius of Rhodes's *Argonautica* Aphrodite promises to give Eros, if he will fire one of his arrows at Medea, "that lovely toy [*perikales athurma*] of Zeus which his dear nurse Adrasteia made for him when he was still a babbling baby in the Idaian cave."[25] When Eusebius contemptuously labeled the bronzes mocked by Constantine as mere *athurmata*, he was not applying a demeaning label but seeking to effect a transformation on the word itself parallel to that which the emperor effected on the pagan statues. For the polytheistic Greek worldview there was no intrinsic contradiction in the idea of a divine player or plaything: Hermes brandishes delightful toys, and Zeus himself had a favorite childhood trifle. In labeling the reviled bronzes as *athurma*,

Eusebius was seeking to trivialize not merely the objects themselves but the entire theology that lay behind them, which was content to picture gods at play.

Eusebius's attempt was not an isolated phenomenon; it was part of the large-scale and profound reorientation of the nature and significance of childhood undertaken in the early centuries of Christianity. There was an apparent and vexing disparity between St. Paul's words in 1 Corinthians 13—"When I was a child, I spake as a child, I understood as a child, I thought as a child: but when I became a man, I put away childish things"—and the account from the Gospel of Matthew, in which Christ insisted, "Except ye be converted, and become as little children, ye shall not enter into the kingdom of heaven."[26] Childhood is described by Paul as a transitory phenomenon to be overcome and consigned to the past as one reaches spiritual maturity, but Christ seems to suggest that it is divorced from temporal specificity within a life and instead names a state toward which Christians can and must aspire. To polemicize against pagan religion as child's play is exclusively to stress the Pauline verse, to see pagan religion as inanity that the Christian must overcome, but this leaves the question unanswered of just what it means, in that case, to "become as little children": can this not involve pious play?

This tension was rarely acknowledged; instead, it was drowned out by a series of patristic writers who stressed the cruel playing of the pagan gods, and the empty playing of the pagans themselves, as a way of validating the opposed beliefs and practices of Christianity by implicit contrast with these forms of superseded trifle.[27] In the homilies of John Chrysostom the identification of paganism with the playing of children becomes a refrain, as the Greeks are persistently denounced as triflers, unable to put away childish things. Chrysostom, however, expands at length on this analogy rather than taking it for granted and explains just what makes these recalcitrant pagans like children in his eyes. In his fourth homily on 1 Corinthians he writes:

Do we not see when little children being borne in their father's arms, give him that carries them blows on the cheek, how sweetly the father lets the boy have his fill of wrath, and when he sees that he has spent his passion, how his countenance brightens up? In like manner let us also act; and as fathers with children, so let us discourse with the Greeks. For all the Greeks are children. . . . Now children cannot bear to take thought for anything useful; so also the Greeks would be forever at play; and they lie on the ground, grovelling in posture and in affections. Moreover children oftentimes, when we are discoursing about important things, give no heed to any thing that is said, but will even be laughing all the time: such also are the Greeks.[28]

This vivid vignette encourages Chrysostom's auditors to assume a tolerant and understanding stance toward their pagan contemporaries, who know not what they do. The Greeks are like playing children in their mood swings, in their eschewal of all that is useful and properly serious and dignified, and above all in their taste for play. Elsewhere, however, in his twenty-third homily on the Gospel of Matthew, Chrysostom reverses the comparison and encourages his Christian brethren to see themselves, not their pagan neighbors, as children at play. "Life is not a plaything [*paignion*]," he writes:

> Or rather our present life is a plaything, but the things to come are not such; or perchance our life is not a plaything only, but even worse than this. For it ends not in laughter, but rather brings exceeding damage on them who are not minded to order their own ways strictly. For what, I pray thee, is the difference between children who are playing at building houses, and us when we are building our fine houses? What again between them making out their dinners, and us in our delicate fare? None, but that we do it at the risk of being punished. And if we do not yet quite perceive the poverty of what is going on, no wonder, for we are not yet become men; but when we are become so, we shall know that all these things are childish.
>
> . . . Let us therefore become men. How long are we to crawl on the earth, priding ourselves on stones and stocks? How long are we to play? And would we played only! But now we even betray our own salvation. . . . But while these things shall all pass away, the torment ensuing upon them remains immortal and unceasing; which sort of thing indeed takes place with respect to the children as well, their father destroying their childish toys [*paidika athurmata*] altogether for their idleness, and causing them to weep incessantly.[29]

I have quoted Chrysostom at length to illustrate the detailed and dynamic role that the playing of children could assume in this tradition of Christian thought.[30] It is not enough to condemn the trifling of pagan religion as mere childish play; all of mortal life is subject to the same deflationary comparison. The putting aside of childish things ultimately demands the putting aside of earthly life itself as a vast plaything. We are exhorted not to "become as little children" but to "become men," which means enduring a violent reversal of the worth that we typically invest in worldly matters, and having them wrenched from our hands, even if this is as painful for us as it is for the child whose toys are pitilessly broken by its father to signal that the time of childhood has come to an end.

My account so far might seem to provide no more than a partial genealogy for the emergence of iconoclastic child's play in the sixteenth century. The deriding of popish trifles and trinkets by early modern iconoclasts might seem, via this account, to make all the more sense when seen as a late stage in a long-standing tendency among Christian writers to label opposing forms of religion as mere child's play. Yet in putting forward these examples, what strikes me again, but has already begun to seem somewhat stranger, is their common assumption that the comparison to children and their playthings is necessarily deflationary. It does not need to be explained: even John Chrysostom, who delves into the actions and emotions of playing children in considerable detail, does not specify what makes them trifling; merely to make the comparison is enough. It does not need to be argued or shown that true piety and child's play are mutually exclusive; it is repeatedly and shrilly stated as obvious and self-evident.

The frequency and vehemence with which play has been denounced in these traditions has led, understandably, to the modern claim that Christianity is thoroughly and intrinsically antipathetic to playfulness. In the most recent attempt to formulate a comprehensive anthropological account of play, for example, Roberte Hamayon characterizes the history of Christian attitudes as "an enduring tide of condemnation."[31] There is certainly ample evidence for this grim mind-set. In another of John Chrysostom's homilies on the Gospel of Matthew, for example, Chrysostom imagines one of his listeners thinking, "Far be it from me to weep at any time, but may God grant me to laugh and play all my days," and, he fulminates, "What can be more childish than this mind? For it is not God that grants to play, but the devil."[32] Yet, what if we return to my opening hunch that claims of this sort might be defensive rather than simply offensive, that they willfully take a great deal for granted, that they might be a way of taming and containing not just enemy religions but children and their play? What if consigning play to the devil in this fashion is a way not of confirming its trifling status but of placing it at a safe distance? My suspicions are prompted in no small part by the fact that the absolute distinction between true piety and play turns out to be by no means stable or obvious—a fact that many Christian thinkers knew all too well. For a notable cluster of Christian thinkers, rather than play being attacked as a mere trifle suitable only for pagan polytheists, it was an entirely fitting model for the true believer's relation to God. Rather than seeing "the rejection of amusement," to use Jean Delumeau's phrase, as a constant in Christian history, we should see it as a periodic strategy that frequently vied with other possibilities for play.[33]

Before I trace the earlier stages and foundations of this alternative tradition, I would like to start with an example from none other than Luther, since it adds weight to my claim, contra the claims by Baudelaire and Weber discussed in my introduction, that Protestantism cannot be seen as intrinsically antipathetic to play. Luther did, indeed, help to give wide currency to the attacks on popery as mere trifling, but, in doing so, he offered a glimmer of alternative values for child's play. Lecturing on Zechariah 8:5—"And the streets of the city shall be full of boys and girls playing in the streets thereof" (ASV)—Luther observed: "Note too that the children's activities, such as the playing and dancing of the young world in the streets, are not an evil thing but are well-pleasing to God. For He praises also these things here as His gifts, though to us they may seem to be something wasted and useless." This seems like a sharp warning against judging any set of actions as *obviously* trifling, since certain forms of apparently inane play can be valuable to God. Despite this warning, Luther then speaks of the monasteries and asks: "How will they stand the test . . . when Christ will say that the singing and dancing of the children in the streets are dearer to Him than all their howling and mumbling in their churches, and that the little girls' wreaths and dolls, the boys' hobby-horses and red shoes please Him much more than all their hoods, tonsures, surplices, chasubles, and adornments? For although their activities also are nothing but child's play, still, because they are without God's Word, they are not to be compared to real child's play but rather to buffoonery and fool's play."[34] This is a fascinating and deeply equivocal moment, in which Luther seems divided between the dignity that the scriptural verse accords to child's play and the long-standing polemical contempt for it. The playing of children is more pleasing than the inane trifles of the monks with which it is juxtaposed; and strikingly, at the close, Luther contrasts "real child's play," which he does not define but which has potential dignity and value, with the foolish play of the monasteries. Citing scriptural precedent, Luther, in fact, refuses the conflation of child's play and phony religious trifling that was so rife among earlier Christians and sixteenth-century reformers alike. Child's play here is not vacuous but potentially brimming with divine approbation; we cannot take its meaninglessness for granted.

There are other scriptural precedents for a higher valuation of play, but what makes Luther's pronouncement so unusual is his unapologetic derivation of this higher valuation specifically from the playing of children and their "wreaths and dolls . . . hobby-horses and red shoes." There is, beyond this moment in Luther's writings, a persistent counterpoint in Judeo-Christian thought to the dominant tone in which playing is condemned as inane, childish, devilish, in which it is seen instead as lofty, dignified, a proper activity for the human in relation to God. Usually, however, this viewpoint can be maintained only by emphasizing a conception of play from which children and their toys have been largely expunged. Play can to some extent avoid being seen as a trifling matter if it is dematerialized, placed at a distance from the child's lived encounter with objects. The crucial scriptural inspiration for this tradition was Proverbs 8:30–31, in which Wisdom describes being with God at the Creation. As these verses read in the Vulgate:

Cum eo eram cuncta conponens. et delectabar per singulos dies. Ludens coram eo omni tempore. Ludens in orbe terrarum, et deliciae meae esse cum filiis hominum.

I was before him forming all things: and was delighted every day, playing before him at all times; Playing in the world; and my delights were to be with the children of men.[35]

This account resonated with another crucial verse describing a ludic relation to God, 2 Samuel 6:21, in which David is mocked by Saul's daughter Michal for dancing before the Ark, and responds: "et ludam, et vilior fiam plus quam factus sum" (therefore will I play before the Lord).[36] For all the discussions of the God of the Jews as an austere, terrifying figure to be displaced by the loving Christ, these verses became no less authoritative bases on which a far more positive, laudatory understanding of play could be developed. This possibility was further increased when this scriptural strand was read alongside a passage from another text, Plato's *Laws*, which came to assume an enormous authority of its own. The Athenian who speaks in this late dialogue—and who was typically seen during the Renaissance as expressing Plato's own views—describes religious life as an ongoing process of reciprocal play between the human and divine realms. "I mean we should keep our seriousness for serious things," he claims, "and not waste it on trifles [*mē spoudaion*], and that, while God is the real goal of all beneficent serious endeavour, man, as we said before, has been constructed as a toy [*paignion*] for God, and this is, in fact, the finest thing about him. All of us, then, men and women alike, must fall in with our role and spend life in making our play as perfect as possible—to the complete inversion of current theory."[37]

Rather than true religion and play being strictly opposed, piety is, according to these scriptural and Platonic moments, not only a form of play but the progressive refinement of play. The Athenian's initial division between *mē spoudaion* and matters of seriousness seems to anticipate reformed attacks on popish inanity and irreverence, but instead it strikingly produces an account of play as the only proper response to the human's status as divine plaything. Rather than a conflation of trifling and playing, the Athenian pronounces: let us not trifle; let us instead play. Taking their lead to different degrees from these scriptural verses and from Plato's words, a variety of later Christian thinkers described piety and play as potentially one and the same. Sometimes they commented directly on one of the verses, as with the sermon on *The Song of Songs*, discussed by Mary Carruthers, in which John Forde pronounced: "The Wisdom of God played before the Father's face over the whole expanse of the earth, and plays also before the face of those who learn how to join in Wisdom's play by rejoicing and feeling wonder."[38] Other resources that buttressed this more positive valuation of play were found, such as the Book of Sirach, known as Ecclesiasticus—accepted as canonical by Roman Catholic and Orthodox Christians but rejected by Protestants—which pronounced: "First run into your own house . . . and there play [*et illic lude*] and work out your conceptions." St. Thomas Aquinas glossed this verse by explaining that "the contemplation of Wisdom is suitably compared to play on two counts, each of which is to be found in play. First, because play is delightful and the contemplation of Wisdom possessed maximum delight. . . . Second, because things done in play are not ordered to anything else, but are sought for their own sake, and this same trait belongs to the delights of wisdom."[39] A similar conviction took a different and more ecstatically expressed form in mystical writings. Meister Eckhart went so far as to construe the structure of the Trinity in terms of an intertwined, trifold playing: "There has always been this play going on in the Father-nature . . . [and] from the Father's embrace of his own nature there comes this eternal playing of the Son. This play was played eternally before all creatures. . . . The playing of the twain is the Holy Ghost in whom they both disport themselves and he disports himself in both."[40] Several centuries later, Eckhart's compatriot Jakob Böhme continued the tradition of conceiving of the divine-human relation as ludic: "As God plays with the time of this outward world, so also should the inward divine man play with the outward in the revealed wonders of God in this world," he wrote.[41] While this strand was prevalent in mystical writers, however, it was by no means exclusive to them. As Paula Findlen has demonstrated, the mathematician and astronomer Johannes Kepler "presented the order of the universe as a divine game," whose order was revealed to him "in a moment of ludic ecstasy."[42] "For in the act of making,"

Kepler proclaimed, "God played, arranging therefore in the adorable image of the Trinity."[43] "Just as God the creator played," he wrote elsewhere with a sideways glance at the verses from Proverbs, "so he has taught Nature, his image, to play, and indeed to play the same game that he has played before her."[44] In these various works from diverse periods and contexts, play is salvaged and described as far from a trifling matter; it is rather an action potentially of the highest worth when directed in a fitting way toward the divine. But, as I have suggested, and in contrast to Luther, this is no longer specifically *child's* play: it is distant from the material reality of children and their playthings, as if these trifles must be banished from the scene for play to be redeemed as properly pious.

The material basis of play reasserts itself in complex fashion, however, within a parallel but distinct trajectory that can be traced among Byzantine theologians, who drew more clearly on a combination of scriptural and Platonic precedents for their valorizing of play. Notably, Gregory Nazianzen wrote in one of his *Poemata moralia* that "the high Word [*Logos*] plays in every kind of form, mixing, as he wills, with his world here and there." This statement was taken by Maximus the Confessor as the basis for the seventy-first of his *Ambigua ad Joannem*, in which, rather than simply extolling play, he developed a complex account of exactly why it could be taken as the action of the *Logos*. Maximus related Gregory's words to "the great and dreadful mystery in the flesh of the divine descent to the human level of God the Word"—which is to say, the Incarnation—and sees them as equivalent to St. Paul's discussion of "the foolishness of God and his weakness" (1 Corinthians 1:25). When Paul says this, and when "the great and divinely minded Gregory [Nazianzen]" says that the *Logos* plays, Maximus argues that these terms, "by privation of what with us are most powerful attributes, point to what the divine possesses, and by negations of what is ours makes affirmation of the divine. For with us foolishness, weakness and play are privations, of wisdom, power and prudence respectively, but when they are attributed to God they clearly mean excess of wisdom, power and prudence."[45]

What distinguishes Maximus's account within the long traditions that I have been tracing is his sharp and subtle awareness that Gregory's discussion of play as an attribute of the divine is a *problem*, a puzzle to be solved, a tension to be reconciled. He does not—in the differing manners of Aquinas, Eckhart, Kepler, and Böhme—simply echo scripture by stating in general terms that God plays and that the human must play along. In keeping with the incarnational bent of his theology, his mind takes him immediately to the corporeal Christ. In making this move, he has already leapt from the highly abstract claim in Proverbs that the *Logos* somehow plays to a more concrete conception of a corporeal creature engaged in a playful act. Having done so, he (like Luther) immediately construes play as a trifling matter, aligning it with foolishness and weakness; but, whereas Luther was willing to praise "real child's play" as fittingly divine in contrast to foolish monastic play, Maximus tries to salvage the truth of Gregory's verses by inverting their meaning with an extraordinary piece of mental gymnastics. Play for humans is an intrinsically imprudent act; it is the negation of prudence. But, he insists, "What with us counts as privation, with God is certainly rightly taken to mean possession; while what with us counts as possession, with God is most fittingly taken to mean privation by excess."[46] Hence, in saying that God plays, Gregory can only be exactly reversing the meaning that play possesses in the human realm: what seems to be an assertion of some congruity between the human and divine realms—God plays, and the human can therefore play along—is reinscribed as a statement of absolute difference and incommensurability. In saying that God plays, we, in fact, attribute to him a shattering excess of prudence, which is precisely what we, in our play, lack.

What we witness in this virtuosic piece of last-gasp reasoning is a moment in which two traditions threaten to come together that must, at all costs, be kept apart. Maximus takes for granted that play is a piece of human imprudence—a claim very much in keeping with the long-standing (though by no means unanimous) Christian denigration of play as a pagan frivolity, a trifle, that I outlined above. To be acceptable as a description of God's action, play must be radically distinguished from its human and material significance, especially its association with children, which is annihilated as it crosses into the divine realm. The tradition of polemical trifling that eventually reemerges during the Reformation, as I have suggested, focuses on play*things*, *athurmata*. It is the bronze idols that are akin to toys, and concrete objects of worship that are denounced as trifles. Conversely, the more laudatory account of play gleaned from the Old Testament is useful for these later Christian thinkers precisely because it refers to the far loftier and more abstract God of the Hebrews, who lacks any corporeal form. In what sense does God or the *Logos* play in this conception of the divine? It is helpful here to turn to the account of play by Hans-Georg Gadamer, who, as we saw in my introduction, linked the eschewal of iconoclasm with aesthetic play. In *Truth and Method* Gadamer develops an ontological account of play, which, he claims, "has its own essence, independent of the consciousness of those who play." There is for him a "being-of-play," separate for its incidental manifestations: he cites as evidence for this the "many metaphorical usages" of the term *play* (*Spiel*): "If we examine how the word 'play' is used and concentrate on its so-called metaphorical senses, we find talk of the play of light, the play of the waves, the play of gears or parts of machinery, the interplay of limbs, the play of forces, the play of gnats, even a play on words. In each case what is intended is to-and-fro movement that is not tied to any goal that would bring it to an end. . . . The movement of playing has no goal that brings it to an end; rather, it renews itself in constant repetition."[47]

If Schiller saw play as the activity definitive of, and most proper to, the human, here we encounter play at its opposite extreme, used to describe a flowing and repetitive motion that seems most proper to the inanimate and the mechanical—but also, perhaps, to God. The account of Wisdom playing with God in Proverbs 8:30–31 resonates with the very opening of Genesis, in which, hauntingly, "the Spirit of God moved upon the face of the waters." This kind of highly abstract, liquid motion—like the motion of the waves mentioned by Gadamer—seems like the easiest, the safest kind of play to attribute to God, and to the believer before God, since it hints at a form of agency akin to the human while also allowing it to be dissolved. My discussion of these two traditions of play, the trifling and the laudatory, has suggested that the split between them reflects a deep tension within the idea of play itself as it has operated in Western thought. This tension was neatly encapsulated by Roland Barthes in an interview, when it was put to him that language itself is "related to the idea of play." "I wholeheartedly support the notion of play," he responded. "I like this word for two reasons. Because it evokes a properly ludic activity, and also the play of an apparatus, a machine, that tiny extra movement possible in the fitting together of its various elements."[48] Like Gadamer, Barthes both distinguishes between and connects the playing of concrete human individuals—"a properly ludic activity," perhaps what Luther calls "real child's play"—and a far wider set of senses of play from which the human is entirely absent: forms of play that are entirely natural or mechanical or, in the earlier writings that I have been discussing, divine. It is in the absence of the human, and alongside light, waves, gnats, and machinery, that God can be allowed to play and that we can, perhaps, play in return.

The history of Christian attitudes to play as I have sketched it here is bifurcated, with its two parts seemingly opposed to one another but in fact existing as two sides of the same coin, in that each is a radical simplification that must exclude the other in order to function: play must be obviously and entirely trivial and obviously and entirely worthy in different contexts. This becomes clear from the occasional attempts to resurrect the defense of play as a model for piety in the twentieth and twenty-first centuries, made by both Catholic and Protestant theologians. Most notably, Romano Guardini, a prominent voice in early twentieth-century Roman Catholicism, described liturgical activity as a form of pious play: "The liturgy has laid down the serious rules of the sacred game which the soul plays before God."[49] Yet what these defenses of play have in common, regardless of their theological orientation, is a disinclination to acknowledge that play is or can be anything other than pure, free, and delightful. These modern accounts combine the rhapsodic mood of Gregory Nazianzen or Meister Eckhart with a Schillerian paean to play as the apex of human self-realization: "the world of play," writes Walter Ong, "is the world of freedom itself—of activity for its own sake, of spontaneity"; for Hugo Rahner "play is a human activity which engages of necessity both body and soul . . . the kind of rhythmic, essentially beautiful exercise that forms the body," and he describes "the Christian ideal of the serious-serene human being at play in his fine versatility."[50] Similarly, when Gerard van der Leeuw derives aesthetic experience from the experience of "holy play," he does so on the basis of their shared and delightful coherence: "the meeting of God with man, of man with God, is holy play, *sacer ludus*. . . . Thus life is given consistency, and happiness guaranteed."[51] Conversely for Jürgen Moltmann, writing in a Lutheran tradition, works undertaken for the sake of God "are done spontaneously, unselfishly, as if playing."[52]

Nor do such conceptions survive only among trained theologians: T. M. Luhrmann's study of American Evangelical Christians has shown that they frequently conceive of their relationship with God as a play relationship, as a way of making the divine personal, apprehensible, and present.[53] In each of these various accounts a play relationship is an ideal relationship—one solely founded on, and productive of, freedom, joy, and delight. Play here cannot describe a relationship with the divine that is difficult, fraught, or volatile. Even if we periodically admit that we play with the things that matter to us most, these various Christian voices implicitly agree, we do so in a manner that differs fundamentally from the way in which we imagine the child, the miniature trifler, at his or her play; this is the same reassuring fiction that underpins iconoclastic child's play. It is woven deep into our ways of understanding it, this chapter has argued, that play must be either totally worthless and inane or entirely joyful and dignified; but whichever it is, we cannot allow it to drift between these two extremes, and it must continue to mean only what we want it to mean. This is the deep split that the language of trifling helps to maintain in order to evade the harder questions of why we (and children) value the objects and practices that we value and why we sometimes play with them.

In the next chapter I will move from the abstract to the concrete and discuss the ways in which these contrasting narratives of play tend to converge and interfere with one another both in specific playthings and in the figure of the incarnated deity. I will end this chapter, having spiraled from the specific discourse of trifling during the Reformation to much broader narratives of trivialization, by returning to the sixteenth century and the richly complex emphasis on trifles and trifling in the writings of Thomas More. More is a fitting figure with whom to end this narrative, since he was prominently involved in debates surrounding reform, iconoclasm, and the proper use of images and was critical of certain aspects of the established church while striving to remain within its confines; furthermore, he was fully aware of the classical, scriptural, and patristic traditions of writing about play that I have outlined. More's well-known emphasis on *serio ludere*, or serious play, appears differently, I argue, when read against this longer history of tensions surrounding the status of play and its trifling, childish tendencies.

The difficulties and opportunities created for literary production by the language of trifling come to the fore in More's letter of 1516 responding to Bishop Cuthbert Tunstall's praise of his *Utopia*: "I feared that when the learned works of so many other authors could not engage your attention," he wrote, "you would never willingly descend to my trifles [*ne nunquam fieret ut libenter ad meas nugas descenderes*]."[54] As Jeffrey Knapp observes: "nothing, of course, is more traditional than this low estimation of a literary work. . . . More nevertheless embraces this standard insult in a surprisingly thoroughgoing manner."[55] The term translated here as "trifles"—*nugas*—was a standard term in classical Latin for an object of little value, and it is tempting to dismiss More's use as a standard *topos* of modesty, a protective form of self-deprecation. When we read the letter against the text to which More is referring, however, one particular use of the word *nuga* stands out. It occurs when More's narrator, Hythloday, describes the manner in which children in this imagined realm are taught not to place excessive value in material things. The Utopians, he writes, gather also pearls by the seaside, and diamonds and carbuncles upon certain rocks; and yet they seek not for them, but by chance finding them, they cut and polish them. And therewith they deck their young infants. Which, like as in the first years of their childhood they make much and be fond and proud of such ornaments, so when they be a little more grown in years and discretion, perceiving that none but children do wear such toys and trifles [*cum animadvertunt eiusmodi nugis non nisi pueros uti*], they lay them away even of their own shamefastness, without any bidding of their parents, even as our children, when they wax big, do cast away nuts, brooches, and puppets [*nuces, bullas et pupas abiciunt*].[56]

The status of this description, like the whole of More's text, is crucially, playfully, ambiguous: a learned humanist reader would recognize and be expected to approve of this critique of a human tendency to overvalue gold and material objects; at the same time, it seems highly unlikely that More genuinely sought to overturn the basis of the mercantile economy, to envisage a world in which gold and other precious substances are held to have no value at all. The reader seems to be encouraged to oscillate between smug, complacent laughter and bracing self-criticism. These tensions, present in the text and provoked in the reader, have been brought out in various readings of *Utopia* as the embodiment of the humanist ideal of *serio ludere*; they are integral to Louis Marin's rich account of the "spatial play" of More's text.[57] Yet play in these discussions is conceived in rather vague, generic terms: Marin considers it principally as the "give" of a mechanism (much like Barthes), writing that "the topographical, political and economic spaces of utopia play in the way that we say that 'there is play' when the pieces of a mechanism, the elements of a system, or the parts of a whole are not perfectly adjusted to one another."[58] "There is play" in the text, but it is not connected to concrete acts of playing. Alternately, the play-impulse is recognized but sentimentalized in proto-Schillerian fashion, as when Walter M. Gordon writes that "the playful literature of both Erasmus and More develops as an extension of friendly and witty engagement of minds," or when Michael Holquist claims that "Utopia is play with ideas."[59] Even Stephen Greenblatt's rich account of the "brilliant playfulness that issued in *Utopia*" quickly links this feature of the text to More's theatrical approach to political life, making play subordinate to the stage-play world of Tudor politics.[60] I would like, by contrast, to note the verbal link between More's descriptions of his text as a whole in the letter to Tunstall and the objects with which the children are adorned; both are *nugae*, trifles. This suggests that this moment, in which the children set aside potentially valuable objects as they cast aside their trifling playthings, operates as a node of self-reflection on the value of the text itself.

When Ralph Robinson rendered this passage into English, his choice of "toys and trifles" for the single word *nugis* in the original was a deliberately emphatic hendiadys, and it was a decision made several decades after the work's composition, by which time the language of trifling had assumed its new prominence in the language of iconoclastic reformed polemic. More, however, had already used the very phrase that Robinson chose for this translation in his own polemical writings: in his *Apology* he described a heretic who ended up in Bedlam and who "used in his wandering aboute, to come into the chyrche, & there make many madde toyes & tryfles, to the trouble of good people in the dyuyne seruyce."[61] In this text "toyes & tryfles" are not to be tolerated as harmless diversions or the proper pursuits of childhood but are to be recognized as having the potential to genuinely subvert the orderliness and values of the traditional church and must be violently stamped out, the perpetrators whipped or imprisoned.

Another of More's texts, however, brings out the ambivalent status of child's play—and the adult's imagination of the child at play—most clearly. In the preface to the third book of his *Dialogue of Comfort Against Tribulation*, written in 1534 while he was imprisoned in the Tower of London, More presents a conversation between the elderly Hungarian Anthony and his younger relative Vincent, who has brought news of the Turks' imminent invasion, an impending terror that Vincent sees anticipated in ominous "tokens," "like as before a greate storm, the see begynneth sometyme to worke & rore in hym selfe ere euer the wynd waxeth boystuouse." Anthony responds by elaborating on the forms that such portents take:

I am of such age as you see | & verely from as farre as I can remember, it hath been markyd & often tyme provid trew, that whan children haue in Bowda [Buda] fallen in a fantasye by them selfe to draw together, & in their playing make as it were corsis [corpses] caried to church | and sing after their childish fasshion the tewne of the dirige, there hath greate deth there shortly folowid after | And twyse or thrise I may remembre in my dayes, when children in diuers partes of this realme haue gatherid them selfe in sundry companyes, & made as it were parties & batayles | & after their batayls in sport wherin some children haue yet taken grete hurt, there hath fallen very batayle & dedely warr in dede.[62]

This moment encapsulates the difficulty of deciding just how serious children's play is and the tendency for its relationship with reality to slip and shift. The children seem almost possessed by the sudden desire to play at funereal games—"fallen in a fantasye by them selfe"—and the anecdote, insofar as Anthony endorses the eerily predictive force of such playing, seems to emphasize the tendency for children's play to escape from and horribly overflow its carefully delimited status as mere trifling. The children's practice of making "as it were corsis" and "as it were parties & batayles"—the *as if* mode that Kendall Walton has identified as the structure of playful make-believe and artistic mimesis alike—spontaneously and horrifyingly gives way to real-life cadavers and fights to the death.[63] Play here is no trifle, separate from the realm of significance; it is both useful and unsettling in its dark foreshadowing of reality.

As Walter M. Gordon observes, however, the upshot of More's account becomes still less clear when it is read in relation to its likely ancient sources—texts that offer differing perspectives on the divinatory power of children and their play. Several Greek writers wrote of Egyptian beliefs in such powers. Dio Chrysostom, for example, described "the prophetic utterances of Apis," where "lads at play [*paides paizontes*] announce the purpose of the god, and . . . this form of divination has proved to be free of falsehood." And Aelian similarly wrote of Apis: "a man prays to this god, and children without, who are playing and frisking to the music of pipes [*paides de athurontes exōkai pros aulous skirtōntes*], become inspired and proclaim in time with the music the actual response of the god."[64] These credulous accounts support the ominous readings of child's play by More's Anthony, in which it really does have oracular force and children have a privileged position in relation to the divine.

It becomes impossible to sustain this straightforward reading of More's passage, however, once we relate it to a more likely direct source: Plutarch's "Isis and Osiris," parts of which More's friend Desiderius Erasmus translated into Latin. In this work Isis asks a group of "little children" whether they have seen a chest containing the body of Osiris, and they point her toward the coast, where his murderers "had launched the coffin into the sea": "Wherefore," Plutarch comments, "the Egyptians think that little children possess the power of prophecy, and they try to divine the future from the portents which they find in children's words, especially when children are playing about in holy places [*paizontōn en hierois*] and crying out whatever chances to come into their mind."[65] Plutarch does not describe the truly divinatory powers of children but gives an etiology of the processes by which they come mistakenly to be attributed such powers. The children simply happen to have the knowledge to help Isis, but this comes to be taken as a sign of privileged knowledge; later, any random exclamation by children "playing about in holy places" tends to be read as dripping with opaque significance. For Plutarch, then, such tales testify not to the powers that children possess but to the peculiar ways that adults find themselves imagining children, especially children at play. In this instance there is no possibility that this play is trifling or that the children who engage in it are "living trivialities," in Fumerton's phrase; the problem is not that their play lacks meaning but that it might (or might not) brim with it. It seems to invite rampant overinvestment and overinterpretation from adults who see in its opaque operations the shape of things to come.

Anthony's credulity in *A Dialogue of Comfort* reads very differently against this background; so, too, I would suggest, does the language of *nugae* and the playing children of Utopia once they are situated within More's oeuvre as a whole. The common currency of the phrase *serio ludere* has perhaps reduced the need for attention to just what play is doing in these humanist texts; while More employs the deprecatory and self-deprecatory language of *nugae*, toys and trifles, seeming to diminish or limit what such playfulness can achieve, I would suggest that he combines this tendency with attention to child's play itself as at once trifling and transformative, potentially both devoid of meaning and prone to accrue a startling degree of significance. It is precisely this combination that allows these moments in his texts to resonate so profoundly with the scene of iconoclastic child's play, which shares this curious combination of vacancy and fullness of meaning.

As I argued above, the trifle should not be mistaken for a category of simplicity; it is precisely the means by which threatening complexity is disguised, or disguises itself, *as* simplicity. More's deployment of the language of *nugae* in his ludic texts draws on the ambiguity of child's play and the way that a child treats an object in playing with it. On the one hand, he suggests that such play is *mere* play and that the Utopian child will come to realize this naturally; he or she will set aside childish things, almost like a good Christian, and move on to the next stage in life through an embarrassed repudiation of "toys and trifles." On the other hand, More's description can only have its effect on the reader because of the genuinely transformative potential of child's play—its ability to accrue the sorts of unstable cultural efficacy described by Plutarch. The moment from *Utopia* similarly relies on the child's ability, precisely through his or her trifling, to establish forms of value that invert and disturb those that prevail and that structure the world in and for which More wrote. Detritus can be valued as the most desirable of stuff; gold and pearls can be treated as mere trifles. The description may be laughable, but it can only succeed in its unsettlingly ludic function if the playing of children really might have the potential to transform and invert the values of adult readers. Rather than simply endorsing the logic in which certain people, actions, and objects—namely children, play, toys—are obviously trifles, More's text points toward what Susan Willis calls a "politics of the trivial"—an awareness that dismissing certain elements of "daily life" as "trivial, fragmented" (and, as I suggested above, the no-less-powerful act of *refraining* from viewing or acknowledging them as trivial and ridiculous) is one way that an order of value sustains its putative self-evidence.[66] Categories of imputed triviality such as the trifle operate precisely by way of distraction or misdirection, insisting—a little too vociferously—that there is literally *nothing to see here*. I suggest that we should rethink the trifle, in light of both iconoclastic child's play and the interconnected traditions that I have explored in this chapter, not as a name for a genuinely worthless or trivial object but rather as a way of designating the trivial thing that might also be the sublimely transformative thing, the object on whose putative meaninglessness everything somehow hangs, the object that is not merely meaningless but *extravagantly* meaningless, its flouting of its own triviality forcing us to recognize how much children at play commonly invest in the apparently trifling, and how much we invest in them, both as triflers and as trifles.

2   DOLL

IN 1536 A MAN in Cologne was reported to have pulled the arms from a crucifix and given it to his children to use as a toy.[1] Of all the acts of iconoclastic child's play that I have encountered, this one intrigues me the most. The examples I have considered so far, from Edgeworth's sermon and from Lincolnshire, provide only the barest of information about the objects that were given to children as playthings. They are referred to only as "Images" in the former instance, and, in the latter, while we know it is pyxes and banner cloths that were used in this way, it is not clear how precisely they were treated. In Cologne, however, we know something of the precise actions to which the crucifix, that pivotal Christian symbol and object, was subjected: in this instance the act of iconoclasm was a two-part process, a sequence of actions extended through time rather than a single and decisive moment of destruction. The arms were broken off before the object became a toy. The holy thing could not be handed to the children unscathed but first had to be marked in some way, severed symbolically from its previous role while still remaining recognizable. Iconoclasm of this sort takes time: it is a process with discrete stages, but its terminus is neither the total abolition of the object nor simply its exemplary lingering in broken form. The crucifix is neither obliterated nor placed on a pedestal as a static and salutary reminder of error successfully overcome. It remains to be played with.

So I begin this chapter with the tantalizing story from Cologne—tantalizing not least because I have no way of discovering any further details about it. Robert Scribner reports the event on the basis of documents from the Historisches Archiv in Cologne, which collapsed in 2009. But, as with Edgeworth's sermon, I see the paucity of available information about this scene not so much as an obstacle to understanding but as a stimulus to imagination. What did the adult feel who wrenched the arms from a crucifix that had, presumably, once been considered among the most sacrosanct of objects? Were the children aware of the potentially shocking nature of their subsequent play, and if so, did they enjoy it all the more for its frisson of transgression, or did the object's power ultimately overshadow and set limits to their play?

To ask this in another way: if the former status of the object had to be perpetually recalled, on some level, in order for the play to have its iconoclastic meaning, in what sense had its power to endure truly been overcome? As well as wondering what this play meant for the adult who snapped off its arms and the children who played with it, then, I find myself wanting to ask, What did it mean for the crucifix? Is it still a crucifix once it is broken? If not, what name would we apply to it? I am going to assume for now that this crucifix was not bare wood but was adorned with a figure of Christ and that cross and suffering figure were snapped at one and the same time. Do we have a name for this armless deity, for the category of object into which it crosses once it becomes a plaything?

I would like, somewhat speculatively, to propose one, by returning to Edgeworth's near-contemporaneous scene, discussed in my preface. The objects that he describes, as I have just mentioned, are referred to only as "Images"—and while Nicholas Orme speculates that they may have been "small wax votive offerings" rather than "large wooden images," on the basis that they must have been small enough for the children to carry and handle, there is no way to be certain.[2] Let us recall, however, that a specific term does come to be applied to these objects as the scene of play unfolds: when the adult asks "what haste thou there? the childe aunsweareth (as she is taught) I haue here myne ydoll. . . . So saithe the mother to an other . . . where haddest thou that pretye Idoll?" Ydoll, Idoll: although redescribing a revered object as an idol was the most basic aim of iconoclasm, it is difficult for the modern reader of English, confronted with these sixteenth-century spellings, to ignore the word *doll* that seems to leap out from them. Are we justified in thinking of these objects in these terms—to understand the polemical intent behind iconoclastic child's play as the transformation of an idol into a doll? Does the Christ-figure attached to the crucifix in Cologne become a doll once his arms are snapped off and he is placed in a playing child's hands?

The possibility of a punning connection here has rarely been considered by historians of religion or childhood, and when it has emerged, it has been given short shrift.[3] It does seem to wither before philological scrutiny: the use of the term *doll* is usually explained as an abbreviation of the name *Dorothy*, which gradually migrated from a generic name for a girl to the standard designation for, as the *Oxford English Dictionary* defines it, "an image of a human being (commonly of a child or lady) used as a plaything," a meaning to which the *OED* attests only at the very end of the seventeenth century. In the sixteenth century these playthings were simply known as "babies": the toy is straightforwardly equated with the living child that it resembles. Keith Thomas observes that "many Tudor writers refer to 'the babies that children make,'" and we encountered the term in the previous chapter from Spenser's *Shepheardes Calendar*, with its description of "Belles: and Babies .s. Idoles."[4] The terms *baby*, meaning a human figure used as a child's plaything, and *idol* are tightly juxtaposed here, as if there is a magnetic attraction between the two categories. It is this blurring that tempts me to hold on to the possibility of a punning resonance between *doll* and *idol*—or at least to believe that the wide currency of the latter term might have helped the former emerge as a standard term for such a plaything during the course of the early modern period.

Notably, in Ancient Greek and Latin, the most common terms for a doll— *korē* and *pupa* respectively—are also words for a little girl. The names for toys of this sort therefore seem, in several languages, to blur with the children after whom they are often modeled and for whom they are often intended. This linguistic evidence itself suggests that a doll is rarely reduced to the status of a mere thing: when an object is designated as a doll, it is being described as the kind of object that, through the ways in which it is manipulated and animated in play, blurs and blends with the child who is doing the playing. The doll resembles the idol because both hover unsettlingly on the cusp of agency: as Maurizio Bettini puts it, "the doll is an image/nonimage living on the margins of a world of movement and sound, ready to participate in that world if she should ever choose to do so."[5] If we interpret a doll as an object imbued with the potential to become an agent, then we can better understand the anxiety that hovers around the cheerful scene that Edgeworth depicts. To make an object into an "Idoll" in a scene of play risks not confirming its deadness but instead granting it new forms of life.

This chapter will continue to develop the questioning begun in the previous chapter as to whether playing with an object is necessarily to trivialize it. I propose the doll/idol—the "idoll"—as a hybrid figure that, like the trifle, is neither obviously valuable nor worthless, neither obviously alive nor dead, obviously deserving of neither pure reverence nor pure revulsion, neither tentative care nor violent breaking alone. The idoll as an object materializes the conflicting valuations of children and their play discussed in the previous chapter into a concrete form of encounter. It confirms the object of iconoclastic child's play as the distillation of our vexed and shifting encounters with children and with objects and the ways in which we do and do not want them to mean.

———————

The snapping of the arms from the crucifix and the giving of it to the children is trivialization in practice. The object is supposedly relegated from holy thing to trifle, but, as I argued in the last chapter, there was nothing intrinsically wrong with imagining the relationship with the divine as a play-relation; there was, in fact, good scriptural precedent for doing so. Nonetheless, this play-relation could generally be embraced only by distancing the form of action envisaged from the playing of children and by idealizing it as entirely delightful and free; we saw Maximus the Confessor struggling to reconcile this conception of play with "the great and dreadful mystery in the flesh of the divine descent to the human level of God the Word," the incarnated Christ, and doing so only by inverting the significance of divine play. The crucifix that passes into a child's hands, however, raises the question that Maximus ultimately avoids or inverts in a new and difficult way: what kind of plaything can Christ become? Is subjecting a material representation of Christ to play—reducing it to an idoll—necessarily to demean and trivialize it? This was certainly the claim made by numerous reformers, and the polemical strain in which paganism or popery were compared to mere child's play often focused specifically on dolls. Lactantius, writing in the second and third century CE, quoted Persius's dismissal of the dolls that young girls dedicate to Venus: "Perhaps [the poet] despised them for their tiny size. He failed to see that the very images and statues of gods all made of gold and ivory by the hands of Polyclitus, Euphranor and Phidias, were no more than big dolls [*nihil aliut esse quam grandes pupas*], dedicated not by girls at play, which can be excused, but by bearded men. . . . So it is that they bring to these great silly decorated dolls [*his ludicris et ornatis et grandibus pupis*] ointments, incense and perfume . . . and precious clothes."[6]

Lactantius's words became well known to the populace of early modern England, since they were repeated in the official homily against idolatry that was read from pulpits across the land during the reign of Elizabeth I. This polemical strand was also resurrected in Reformation Germany by Heinrich Bullinger, who asked, "In our places of worship, what are representations of the Virgin mother and the other gods and goddesses but huge dolls [*puppae grandes*]?"[7] In these texts, to describe a supposedly holy object as a doll is automatically to deflate its claim to significance. If this was the case in religious polemic, similarly deflationary claims can be identified in artistic contexts: when Giorgio Vasari wanted to minimize the achievements of the minor Florentine painter Nunziata, he called him "*dipintore di fantocci*," a mere painter of dolls.[8] Whether in religious or secular contexts in the sixteenth century, it would seem, no doll could be worthy of true reverence.

This history of Christian devotional practice suggests, however, that this was not necessarily the case. Indeed, the decision to make a crucifix into a doll throws into sharp relief the deeply challenging imaginative poles between which the pious imagination was often compelled to move, simply by virtue of Christ's two most important and commonly represented manifestations: being an infant and a tortured, broken body. Representationally speaking, these forms could hardly have been more different, but they were facets of one and the same deity, such that the innocent infant was already the crucified man *in nuce*.[9] The proliferation of images of the infant Christ might seem to invite play as a form of physical encounter with a divinity materialized as a tiny child, but since this child was already in a meaningful sense the crucified adult, it is impossible in principle to draw a sharp distinction between such ludic devotion and the iconoclastic playing of the children in Cologne: both play with an image of God. Moreover, medieval piety did not always in practice cordon Christ's suffering body sharply off from play: a fourteenth-century Book of Hours juxtaposed scenes of the Passion with exuberant games undertaken by "seemingly irrelevant hybrid figures and clowning animals," while a follower of the Cistercian Gertrude of Helfta described her "placing a small crucifix in a sepulchre at Thursday Vespers, as if in play [*quasi ludendo*], in memory of the Passion."[10]

It was precisely this possible conflation of play and piety—in relation not only to the Christ child but to his lacerated adult body—that infuriated reformers, who were challenged and unsettled by forms of late medieval piety that strikingly resembled doll play. Bullinger's scornful rhetorical claim—that such images were huge dolls—is one with which at least some Christians who devoted themselves to these images through pious play might have been happy to agree. While the Christ child was not equally available for pious play in every context, from the thirteenth century onward he emerged with increasing frequency as a figure who both played and could be played *with*, and sporting with the infant Christ might be one way to honor him in popular piety.[11] A medieval carol on the nativity scene described the Virgin playing with her son:

> On her lap she him layde,
> And with her pappe he playde,
> And euer sang the mayde,
> "Come basse [kiss] thy mother, dere."

Another carol suggested that even the animals in the manger joined in the fun:

> In a cracche was that chylde layde;
> Bothe oxe and asse with hym playde
> With joye and blisse.[12]

As numerous scholars have shown, this conception of a playful infant Christ was also reflected in visual representations, such that a distinct category of image, "the Virgin with the playing child," has been identified, first appearing in a Serbian Gospel also from the thirteenth century.[13] There was a massive proliferation of statues of the Virgin and Child, in wood, stone, and ivory, that depicted playful forms of relation between the two or in which Christ's mother gazed adoringly at him as he played with a bird or ball.[14] Yet as well as these objects, now typically categorized as "medieval art," others were produced to which this label seems harder to attach without further thought. These representations of the Christ child, often roughly life-sized, look remarkably like dolls. Some had articulated limbs, others were entirely rigid; some were richly adorned with clothing, others seem to have been stark and bare; some stood in miniature pedestals, seemingly designed to be propped upright, while others lay recumbent; some are sleekly idealized infants, others have the chunk and heft of a relatively newborn baby. For all this variety, scholars have had little hesitation in identifying these objects as a recognizable set and in dubbing them "holy dolls."[15]

To borrow Gell's description of Michelangelo's *David*, however, these objects were not children's playthings but "doll[s] for grown-ups," principally nuns and beguines. Numerous scholars have shown the integral role that holy dolls played in the visions of late medieval women, and there was a fluid back-and-forth between the material object and the ecstatic experiences that it inspired, and by which its potency as an instantiation of the divine was demonstrated.[16] Handbooks for meditation urged these pious women to "kiss the beautiful little feet of the infant Jesus who lies in the manger and beg His mother to offer to let you hold Him a while," and the Dominican nun Margaretha Ebner in the fourteenth century was just one of many women for whom the child came alive in a vision in just this fashion: "one night," she wrote, "the Child granted to me that I could see him play in the cradle with joy and full of life."[17] Jacqueline Jung comments that the infant Christ often exhibited "*viel spiel*" (great play) when appearing in this fashion and suggests that "the *kindli* of women's visions were, in essence, immaterial, imaginatively generated versions of the sculpted Baby Jesus dolls that populated conventual chambers from at least the fourteenth century onwards."[18]

While it may have been grown women who played with the holy dolls in this fashion, Jeffrey Hamburger observes that later writers, in a continuation of iconoclastic polemic, expressed contempt for these practices by comparing them to the playing of children. He quotes a German periodical from the late eighteenth century, which claimed that "even at the age of fifty, the nun remains herself a child who plays with a holy doll just like a three-year-old girl with a secular effigy."[19] Modern scholars have debated whether the actions of the nuns "reveal a confusion of attitudes toward the sacred and toward play" and whether the dolls "threaten to reduce religion to recreation, piety to play," but even to phrase the issue in this way is to beg the question.[20] The nuns who played with these holy dolls did not *confuse* piety and play or *reduce* the former to the latter; rather, in line with my argument in the previous chapter, their actions revealed the extent to which piety and play are perennially prone to overlap, to blur and to be confused with one another. The modern assumption that they must be separated is testament not to the realities of late medieval religion but rather to the long-term success of the iconoclastic polemic that insisted that play must be antipathetic to true piety. The nuns who played with holy dolls joined the chorus of eminent and everyday voices surveyed in the previous chapter—from Gregory Nazianzen to St. Thomas Aquinas, from Meister Eckhart to modern American Evangelicals—who were and are happy to conceive of their relationship with the divine as a form of play. Where their actions differed from these writers was in their willingness to give their play a material form—to insist on it as an encounter with the Incarnated Christ—and thereby to court the comparison with playing children that most accounts of pious Christian play kept firmly at bay. Nor were such objects always confined to nunneries; they were capable of wide peregrinations. Margery Kempe, on her pilgrimage to Rome in 1414, met a woman who carried with her a chest containing an image or effigy of just this sort: "And the woman the which had the ymage in the chist, whan thei comyn in good citeys, sche toke owt the ymage owt of her chist and sett it in worshepful wyfys lappys. And thei wold puttyn schirtys thereupon and kyssyn it as thei it had ben God hymselfe."[21] With holy dolls like this at loose in the world and available for pious play, how could it be certain that to play with a crucifix, another image of the incarnate deity, was inescapably to ruin and demean it?

———————

The argument that I have been developing might seem to support a certain narrative shift from the Middle Ages into the Reformation: piety and play were joyously interchangeable in the former, part of a seamlessly integrated whole embodied in the "holy dolls" that catered to the needs of ordinary Christians, but were cruelly wrenched apart in the iconoclastic years, when holy objects and play alike were disenchanted and reduced to the merely trivial. A narrative of this sort is too simple, however, if we want to understand the status of holy things before they became objects of iconoclasm or to disentangle the status of those that were placed in the hands of playing children. There is a risk here of nostalgically idealizing the Middle Ages as the time when free, naive, and pious play was the norm—in the manner of Henry Adams, who wrote at the start of the twentieth century that to understand the Gothic, one must "grow prematurely young. One can do it, as one can play with children. . . . One need not take it more seriously than one takes the baby itself. Our amusement is to play with it, and to catch its meaning in its smile."[22] To sentimentalize the pious play of the Middle Ages is another form of reduction, of trivialization, dissimilar in intent but not in effect to that which the iconoclast intends.

Instead, I wish to step back from the category of the "holy doll" that I have been discussing and ask how clear, how self-contained, it actually is. The designation of this particular set of objects as dolls seems attractive and straightforward to modern eyes, but there are reasons to pause over this description. The giving of the broken crucifix to the children in Cologne is of such tantalizing interest to me precisely because it seems to involve an object moving from one category to another—it *becomes* a doll—and this process in turn provokes me to ask, What counts as a doll in the first place? This might seem like a strange question, but it has eminently practical implications. Numerous histories of dolls have been written, and they all trace a similar trajectory, from roughly humanoid figures produced in traditional societies to the ornate, eerily realistic and finally mass-produced figures familiar today.[23] Yet the decision to designate all of these objects as "dolls" raises fundamental questions of categorization. As Philippe Ariès observes, there is a perennial difficulty in archaeological contexts of "separating the doll, the child's toy, from all the other images and statuettes which the sites of excavations yield up in well-nigh industrial quantities."[24] When archaeologists encounter any small figurine that is even vaguely anthropomorphic, they are presented with a quandary concerning how it should be categorized: particularly when it is found in a child's grave, there is a temptation to designate it as a doll. While some archaeologists have discussed the interpretative challenges prompted by these discoveries, it is remarkable how many of them fall back on some set of criteria by which the two kinds of object—doll and cult figure—can ultimately and stably be distinguished from one another: dolls, they argue, have jointed limbs, whereas cult objects do not; or playthings have piercings to allow them to be pulled with a cord, which holy effigies do not, and these criteria are applied to ancient contexts as different as Roman Egypt, sixth-century Gaza, and Byzantium.[25] I will return to these fundamental questions of categorization in my conclusion, but some version of this presumptively clear distinction between varieties of figurine underpins many histories of dolls, and the opening page of Antonia Fraser's *Dolls* is revealing: "The oldest doll-like figures," she says, "were not dolls at all but religious images," but she quickly emphasizes that "obviously early dolls are not to be confused with prehistoric idols, ancestor images, or fetishes."[26] I would argue, by contrast, that these categories are perennially and significantly *confusable*. What if, using the crucifix that becomes an "idoll" as our guide, we reverse the logic of these narratives and consider the possibility that labeling an object as a doll is not a *reflection* of its fixed nature and function but precisely an attempt to *fix* its nature and function? What if we see the archaeological confusion between dolls and other, "doll-like" objects not as incidental and easily solved but as a crucial symptom of just how unstable the categories into which we place such objects, and the meanings that they are thereby assumed or allowed to possess, might be?

I am not arguing that there are no objects that can reasonably be labeled as dolls, in the sense that they were created specifically as playthings for children. Indeed, there was an emerging market for just such objects in early modern England, and they were imported with increasing frequency, especially from Holland, but they could also be fashioned more spontaneously from available material, including wax, clay, and old cloths.[27] Recall Keith Thomas's observation

that "Tudor writers refer to 'the babies *that children make*,'" with the emphasis
on their having been fashioned *by*, and not *for*, the children in question: doubtless these included many rough-and-ready, minimally humanoid objects that
would barely count as dolls as we tend to construe the term today.[28] Typically,
dolls are understood as objects designed to be played with; but I would suggest
that we take seriously the *OED*'s definition that I cited above—"an image of a
human being . . . *used* as a plaything"—and see such objects as defined in part
by the ways in which they are in fact treated, not the function for which they
were designed. In fact, I would go further and suggest that a doll might be seen
as an object that *comes to resemble the human when it is incorporated into play*
but might barely resemble a human to start with: *idol* is a provisional name for
what the object starts to become when it is used as a plaything and begins to
tend or arc toward the assumption of human form. This is one point at which I
disagree with David Freedberg's magisterial study *The Power of Images*, which
stresses "the resembling image" as the one most prone to come powerfully to
life.[29] In the case of dolls, I would argue, the most hauntingly alive objects can
be those that seem not to reproduce the human but somehow to mimic human
life, even though they seem barely to resemble it at first and are improvisation-
ally composed from scraps and fragments.

    The true heirs of the early modern "babies that children make," the modern
"idolls," might therefore not be the eerily verisimilar china and plastic figures
that populate toy shops and children's museums, the later chapters of histories of
dolls, and modern horror films but rather those uncategorizable literary creations
like Edgar Allan Poe's "Angel of the Odd," constructed out of utensils including a
small wine-flask, two bottles, a funnel, and a tobacco case "joined together in a
vaguely anthropomorphic manner," or Franz Kafka's Odradek, who "looks like a
flat star-shaped spool for thread. . . . But it is not only a spool, for a small wooden
crossbar sticks out of the middle of the star, and another small rod is joined to
that at a right angle." His sparse lineaments only hint at the structure of human
anatomy, but he nonetheless takes on a life of his own, lurking in corners and
chuckling happily at his perpetual homelessness with a laugh "like the rustling
of fallen leaves."[30] Odradek and Poe's Angel stand as reminders of the minimal
suggestions that children often need in order to transform a mute and meager
object into a version of the human, as well as the uncontrollable life that an object
can assume when it is so transformed; they seem simultaneously to fall below
and to transcend the figures that we typically describe as dolls or as humans.

I propose, then, to use the figure of the broken crucifix in Cologne, and of the "idoll" as it emerges in iconoclastic child's play, to open up the category of the doll to a whole range of objects that come to be incorporated into play, from those designed for this purpose to those that are only "vaguely anthropomorphic," in Poe's phrase; in doing so, I wish to revisit my discussion above, in which I drew a distinction between statues of the Christ child playing with the Virgin Mary and the "holy dolls" that nuns used in their pious play. How stable a distinction is this? If, as I have argued, we should define dolls as objects that are played *with* rather than as objects designed for play, does the line between statue and doll begin to break down? We are back to Alfred Gell's contention that Michelangelo's *David* is simply an enormous doll. But let us be more literal about his claim and ponder its implications: would any statue placed in a child's hand become a doll? How long would the child need to play with it before we agreed that it was now truly a plaything and not just a misappropriated or misused artwork? The question of what distinguishes a doll from a statue has been posed surprisingly seldom, as if even to acknowledge the potential for their confusion is to demean the artwork by acknowledging its contiguity with the realm of the irredeemably trivial. An exception is the careful discussion by Stanley Cavell:

The statue has aspects. By walking around it, by the changing light, in your changing mood, the figure can be seen as vulnerable, as indomitable, as in repose, as if in readiness. A doll has occasions. I am thinking of a rag doll. It can be happy or sad, fed or punished. In repose it has aspects, for example it can be seen as sleeping or dead or sunbathing. But only if you know which is true.—There is only one who knows which is true, the one whose doll it is. And that one cannot strictly be said to *know* it at all, except as a joke, or perhaps as a fiction.[31]

Cavell goes on to question his apparent certainty that the concept of "knowing" cannot be applied to the owner of the doll's understanding of the doll's "occasions." In characteristic fashion he draws a distinction and then quickly undoes it, picking away at his own desire to draw a firm dividing line. The statue has aspects, but so does the doll in repose: what, then, distinguishes the two? I mentioned above that some of the "holy dolls" of the Christ child were placed on miniature pedestals. Perhaps they became more statue-like in the process; perhaps statues remain static and can be circumnavigated, whereas the doll is there to be manipulated and to respond: we move the doll, and we move in relation to the statue. But even this distinction will not do. As the recurrence of what Kenneth

Gross calls "the dream of the moving statue" suggests, the history of the form
has focused obsessively on moments in which statues come to life, descend from
their pedestals, walk, breathe, and interact with humans.[32] I am suggesting, then,
that the transition from holy thing to plaything that took place when the crucifix
in Cologne was given to children, and the holy dolls that seemed to invite play
and worship interchangeably, ultimately confirm the same point from different
directions: there can be no absolute and stable distinction between the category
of objects that are suited or intended for play and those that are not. Any statue,
any holy thing, any artwork is a doll *in potentia.*[33]

I want to flesh out this somewhat abstract-sounding, speculative claim by
observing some instances of literal overlap of the categories of statue and doll at
an earlier point in the history of Christian worship. A striking moment of this
confusion occurs in the life of the ninth-century Byzantine emperor Theophilos,
retold by numerous historians and included in John Skylitzes's eleventh-century
Synopsis Historion. Theophilos was a committed iconoclast, but his powerful stepmother, Euphrosyne, and his wife, Theodora—whom Euphrosyne had encouraged him to choose as his bride in a much-mythologized ceremony—were both
iconophiles.[34] Theophilos would send his five daughters to visit his stepmother
at her home near the monastery of Gastria, where, in Skylitzes's account, "she
gave them various gifts which are attractive to the female sex":

Then, taking them aside, she would earnestly entreat them . . . to hold in abomination
their father's heresy and do homage to the outward form of the holy icons. Whereupon
she would thrust some of the icons (which she kept in a chest) into their hands, setting
them against their face or lips, to sanctify the girls and to stir up in them a devotion to the
icons. Now it did not escape Theophilos's attention that she was habitually behaving in this
manner, nor that she was kindling a favourable attitude to the sacred icons in her grandchildren. For he enquired what they had received by way of gifts from their grandmother
and what she had done that had pleased them. The daughters whose intellects were already
mature neatly sidestepped their father's inquiries as though they were statements made to
be refuted. But Pulcheria, who was still a little child, spoke of the kindness, the quantity of
fruits, and then she went on to mention the revering of the sacred icons, saying (her words
reflected the simplicity of her mind) that her grandmother had many dolls [*ninia*] in the
chest, "And she puts them to our heads and faces after kissing them."[35]

This response "put the emperor into a rage," but his respect for and devotion to
his stepmother meant that, in contrast to the brutal punishments that he inflicted

on some iconophiles during his realm, he merely prevented his daughters from visiting her there again. Skylitzes then follows this account with another anecdote regarding "a pitiful fellow living at the palace, a eunuch named Denderis, not unlike Homer's Thersites":

He said such odd things that people laughed at him; he was maintained in the palace to entertain people. Now one day he burst into the empress's boudoir and surprised her kissing the sacred icons. When the fool saw them he asked what they were, and he came nearer to find out. Speaking like a peasant, the empress said: "These are my pretty dolls and I love them very much."

The emperor, who was at table when this deformed young man came to him, asked him where he had been. The eunuch replied that he had been with "mama," for that is what he called Theodora; also that he had seen her taking pretty dolls from under her pillow in her chamber. The emperor took the point: in great wrath he left the table and went to her immediately. He hurled verbal abuse at her, calling her (with his unbridled tongue), among other things, idolatress, repeating as he did so what the deformed one had said. The empress, meanwhile, placating the emperor's wrath, said: "O, emperor, you have misunderstood; the truth is not as you perceive it. I was looking at myself in the mirror, attended by my handmaids. Denderis saw the faces reflected in it and, from that, he witlessly came and reported to you what you said." With these words, she assuaged the emperor's wrath. She condemned Denderis to a suitable punishment, convincing him never again to say anything about the dolls to anybody. So that once when Theophilos was infuriated with the Sovereign Lady, and asked Denderis whether "mama" was still kissing her pretty dolls, setting his hand to his lips, the fellow replied: "Hush, emperor, hush! Not a word about the dolls!"[36]

Historians of Byzantium have been concerned primarily with dating these events and determining whether they really happened.[37] I am less interested in the accuracy of these tales than in their plausibility, for they confirm the rich set of potential confusions associating doll, idol, and sacred statue for which I have been arguing in this chapter—the same confusions revealed, in a different manner, by iconoclastic child's play. The implications of these anecdotes from John Skylitzes are highly equivocal. They imply that dolls and icons are prone easily and persistently to be mistaken for one another. This mistake is, however, not dangerous or demeaning to those who love icons, but it has potential pedagogical advantages: if the daughters of the emperor can be convinced to love the icons as dolls, then they will have been inducted into iconophilia simply by

FIGURE 1. Coptic doll in the form of a cross. Benaki Museum, Athens. Reproduced with permission.

virtue of their natural childish proclivities, not as a result of theological argument. It effectively does not matter, from this stance, whether the icons are loved and cherished as playthings or as manifestations of the divine; the outcome is the same. The evidence from surviving Byzantine dolls suggests that such confusion was woven into certain of these objects: while some of them are nonspecific human figurines, one, a wooden doll from the Coptic period, is harder to classify (fig. 1). Similar in appearance to a modern gingerbread man, it resembles both a rudimentary human figure *and* a cross, while the three concentric circles on its "face" (if that is the right word) could be mere ornament or the suggestion of eyes and mouth.[38] As ambiguously person-like and thinglike as Poe's Angel of the Odd or Kafka's Odradek, this object is like a Byzantine duckrabbit, fluctuating as one looks at it between doll and crucifix, between the meager suggestion of the generically human and the very embodiment of divinity.

While the type of confusion embodied in this object is prominent in the icons mentioned in Skylitzes's text, however, it is presented as by no means unavoidable: the only ones who seem truly to make the mistake are the immature younger daughter, Pulcheria, and the imbecilic eunuch, Denderis. We encountered in the preface the grouping of children and the mentally ill—along with women and pagans—as those prone to conflate the image and the prototype that it depicts. Lactantius, shortly before he dismissed the statues of the pagans as giant dolls, quotes from Lucilius, who claimed that it is only the ignorant who tremble before such idols, "just as young children [*pueri infantes*] believe that all statues of bronze are alive and are people."[39] As

Freedberg comments: "It is peasants and children, then, who think these things; this is how we comfortably relegate orders of belief that make us uncomfortable and deny or upset our education. Peasants, children, and crazy people. But can we be sure that beliefs of this kind do not extend more widely; and if they do, how are we to talk about such beliefs?"[40] These are precisely the questions implicitly raised, and then quickly shut down, by these accounts from ninth-century Byzantium: statues and dolls are potentially indistinguishable, yes, but only to children and fools. The emperor himself does not even need to clap eyes on the objects in question: as soon as he hears them described, he knows they must be idolatrous icons and flies into a rage. He knows better. But the confusion is merely suppressed, not explained away. When, centuries later, a broken crucifix was placed in a child's hand, the message was supposedly the same: only a foolish papist or an ignorant child could conflate holy thing and plaything without seeing that one is as inane as the other. We adults know better. But we, too, cannot and must not plumb the depths of this confusion; we cannot ask what, in the end, makes dolls and idolls so meaningless. We can only keep playing with them, manically, as if they will perform and demonstrate their own triviality.

What, then, does the conflation of doll and idol conceal? I have argued in this chapter for a more capacious conception of the (i)doll that breaks down the distinction between it and other objects: it is not simply an object resembling a human designed for play but an object that becomes varyingly like a human once it is played with. For the remainder of this chapter I will offer an account of doll-play and of devotion to objects that suggests why they might frequently overlap with or be mistaken for one another—but not because they were equally trivial activities, as the iconoclasts would have it, nor because they were equally delightful and pure, as the owner of holy dolls would have it. Instead, I will suggest that piety and play are potentially convergent as forms of unstably oscillating response—alternating between reverent care and irreverent carelessness, even violence—to intrinsically ambiguous objects. Child's play is a compelling but unstable way of conceiving of the relation to holy objects precisely because, like devotion itself, it can contain, and swing abruptly between, extremes of ruination and care.

Sigmund Freud wrote famously that "in their early games children do not distinguish at all sharply between living and inanimate objects, and . . . they are especially fond of treating their dolls like live people. . . . Children have no fear of their dolls coming to life, they may even desire it."[41] As Barbara Johnson helpfully paraphrases this claim, "dolls are thus things the coming alive of which excites infantile desire rather than fear."[42] On this account, and as I have already suggested, dolls are not simply small, humanoid toys that happen to come to life for the child in play; their tendency to come to life is part of their definition as dolls. The life and agency that the doll seems always on the verge of assuming are reflected in the care and attention that the child often lavishes on it, as on a real person. This was noted in early modern England, with John Hall observing that "we shall finde girls . . . providing apparel and food for their Babies, with most high and great indulgence: as supposing they do hereby as really pleasure and benefit these as their parents do them."[43] It is notable here that it is *girls* who are identified as indulging their "Babies," in keeping with the central role that dolls have played in the socialization of girls and naturalization of their allotted cultural roles, from ancient Rome to today; this makes it all the more striking that in Edgeworth's account it is decidedly both boys and girls, and both mothers and fathers, involved in the scene of iconoclastic play.[44] In any case, in making an "Idoll" into a doll, iconoclasts were transforming it into just the kind of object with which children frequently formed strong affective attachments. A child playing with an idol is likely to begin to love it, talk with it, bring it to life. As I have suggested, however, we should be wary of sentimentalizing the child at play in this fashion. The doll is not simply a toy that comes to life for this child and is loved by the child in response. If these events occur, they are often part of a more complex and shifting set of interactions, one that has the potential to unsettle the desired meanings of iconoclastic child's play.

Here it is instructive to return to the scene from Roger Edgeworth's sermon. The parents in the scene that he describes need repeatedly to intervene and shape the play that is occurring: "What haste thou there?" they ask, reassuring themselves that the children know that these are idolls with which they play. Again, I am inclined to read this not as blithe confidence that they can straightforwardly ascertain and determine the meaning of the play in which the children engage; such play, as I argued in my preface, often forms a self-contained scene from which watching adults feel radically excluded. Instead, the parents feel the need to intervene precisely because children typically do *not* establish a stable and continuous relationship with their dolls: the doll does not necessarily come to life for the child and remain alive in the same, unchanging fashion. It is because the relationship is prone to change that the iconoclastic adults seek to regulate its meaning, but their scrutiny cannot be total: the play can always change and change again, assume another meaning once their backs are turned. Kenneth Gross writes perceptively, in relation to dolls, of "the mysterious roots of the child's relation to its toys, the nature of the impulse to play, what it means for the child to enter into [an] always changing relation to such objects (things often made and given to children by adults.)"[45] Both parts of his description are crucial: he quite properly refuses to specify whether the relationship to the toy is mysterious only to those adults who watch the child at play or to the child him- or herself; both of these may be the case, in different ways. He also rightly stresses the way that the relationship to such an object in play seems constantly to change, meaning that an object can be alive at one moment and dead the next, an intimate friend then suddenly a source of intense dread or an object of loathing, subjected alternately to the gentlest of care and the harshest of violence. Playing with a doll, then, is not a homogenous activity or the formation of a stable and consistent relationship. As Susan Stewart observes, "Once the toy becomes animated," it enters "an entirely new temporal world, a fantasy world parallel to (and hence never intersecting with) the world of everyday reality."[46] Doll-play is not temporally unchanging but has a *rhythm*, an alternating and undulating movement through time that can find room within itself for the most striking extremes of response. Temporal rhythm of a sort has been central to modern accounts of play thanks to the most theorized of all child's play scenes, the "Fort-Da" game played by "Little Ernst" and described by Freud, in which the unfolding rhythm of the disappearing and reappearing wooden reel allows the child to cope with the similarly fluctuating presence and absence of his mother.[47] Yet Freud's account also reveals the danger and temptation for the watching adult of reducing the child's playing to a single and self-contained function even as it occurs—Little Hans is "pressured into creating meaning," as Jonathan Lear puts it.[48] The specificity of both the game and the object dissolves, and it is presence and absence that, Freud insists, are truly (and indubitably) played with. I would modify Freud's reading to suggest that a child playing with a doll, rather than establishing a comfortingly stable relationship with the doll in this manner, engages in what the psychoanalyst Christopher Bollas describes as "an emerging rhythm of mindfulness, mindlessness, and mind objectified as an object of thought."[49]

If we are to adequately describe the child's playing with the doll, then we must acknowledge that it is not invariably pure and delightful; to see it in this idealized fashion is just another comforting way of imagining the child's imagination at work. On the contrary, the varied rhythm of this play with a doll can

without doubt include moments of violence and destruction. Dolls are objects
that are not only loved but hated with equal passion, and this does not diminish
but rather *confirms* their significance. If they are cared for by children as feeling,
breathing beings, then they are also attacked as feeling, breathing beings—just
as the rage aimed at the object by the iconoclast can reaffirm rather than evacu-
ate the life that it is held to contain. Acute in this regard is Baudelaire's account
of the doll: "The overriding desire of most little brats," he asserts, "is to get at
and *see the soul* of their toys."[50] For Baudelaire, when the child destroys its doll,
it does so not to prove that the toy has no soul but to find the soul that it knows
must be there. Baudelaire perceptively refuses to contrast caring for a toy with
destroying it; these are not necessarily opposed actions but can be two moments
in the unfolding rhythm of the child's response to the doll, two poles of the same
deeply felt attachment. It is because the doll is in some sense alive, ensouled, that
it can be treasured and treated as a beloved person; but the same conviction,
transformed into the desire to ascertain why the doll has the potential to mean
so much, prompts its desecration and mutilation. Likewise, for Rainer Maria
Rilke, even the eventual confirmation of the doll's deadness—its failure to possess the soul for which the child violently searches—does not end the affective
relationship that the child has with it: the "terrible, thick forgetfulness" of the
doll provoked his "hatred," aimed at "that gruesome alien body for which we
have wasted our purest warmth."[51] The doll's inertia is a provocation to a new
intensity of rage, a still more binding form of attachment.

   The thinker who best captures this capacity of the doll not merely to mean
different things to children and to adults but to mean different things to children
at different moments—and who thereby navigates most successfully between the
twin risks of trivializing and idealizing child's play—is Walter Benjamin. In his
review of Karl Gröber's *Kinderspielzeug aus alter Zeit*, Benjamin writes that "the
perceptual world of the child is influenced at every point by traces of the older
generation, and has to take issue with them. The same applies to the child's play
activities. It is impossible to construct them as dwelling in a fantasy realm, a fairy-
land of pure childhood or pure art. Even when they are not simply imitations of
the tools of adults, toys are a site of conflict." He criticizes Gröber's claim—that
"the child wants from her doll only what she sees and knows in adults"—because
it rules out the possibility that the child can play with the doll in any way other
than that which is expected of her; by contrast, he claims, "for the child at play,
a doll is sometimes big and sometimes little," involving a shifting rather than a

stable mode of relating to an object, as well as a shifting in the object itself.[52] It is not simply that the doll becomes a real person for the child, Benjamin insists, but that the uneven rhythms through which the child relates to the doll rehearse the uneven rhythms by which we relate to other people: "before we transcend ourselves in love and enter into the life and the often alien rhythm of another human being, we experiment early on with basic rhythms that proclaim themselves in the simplest forms in these sorts of games with inanimate objects. Or rather, these are the rhythms in which we first gain possession of ourselves."[53] This is a beautiful claim, but I am less convinced than Benjamin that the child's rhythmic play with the doll is all that simple or that we ever possess ourselves so securely. Such play is as much about an encounter with an object as recalcitrant and inscrutable other, which causes the child to oscillate between moments of self-possession and dispossession.

How can the rhythmic moments of love and rage that the doll sometimes inspires help to illuminate the precarious position of the "idoll" in the scene of iconoclasm as child's play? The account that I have been developing brings out the deep strangeness of this form of sixteenth-century activity, whose implicit attempt to reduce the object to a permanent state of insignificant triviality is at odds with child's play as an activity that unfixes rather than fixes the meaning of its object and one that can lurch between love and rage. Viewed from another perspective, however, the implicit argument of iconoclastic child's play *did* make sense—but not for the reasons that either those who engaged in it or those who decried it believed. They were united, as Edgeworth's sermon suggests, in their belief not only that to give such an object to a child was to demean the object but that such treatment contrasted emphatically with the forms of treatment to which holy objects had previously been subjected, whether properly or improperly. This, too, however, is a claim that crumbles under scrutiny, as I will argue in the next chapter: late medieval religion itself incorporated moments of tentative awe, violent rending, and manic ebullience, and it is in this sense—not simply in the more idealized form embodied in "holy dolls"—that piety and play truly were akin and prone to overlap. I would like, however, to end this chapter by again suggesting the practical implications of the arguments that I have been advancing about the "idoll" as a composite and ambiguous form that prompts an oscillating rhythm of response on the part of the child, and I will do so by attending to three objects from different eras and contexts that are illuminated by the arguments of this chapter and that point toward the concerns of the next.

The first of these objects is one of the "holy dolls" of the sort that I discussed above, which recently appeared in the *Madonnas and Miracles* exhibition, showcasing domestic devotion in Renaissance Italy, in the Fitzwilliam Museum in Cambridge (fig. 2). It was the first object that visitors encountered when they entered the galleries: unlike the upright figures on their miniature pedestals that I discussed above, it lay recumbent and unadorned, a relatively humble and roughly life-sized model of a baby, with nothing on the object itself to identify it obviously as the Christ child.

Dating from the end of the fifteenth century, this object was owned by the Marchigian mystic Camilla Battista da Varano, and the curators of the exhibition describe its function straightforwardly: "Camilla's divine encounters took place

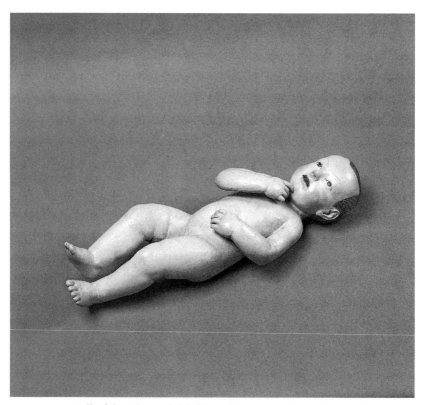

FIGURE 2. Doll of the Christ child, fifteenth century. Nuns of Santa Ciara, Camerino. Reproduced with permission.

through the agency of this wooden doll."⁵⁴ The object's original purpose and use was presented alongside the remarkable story of its more recent provenance. This holy doll had remained the most treasured possession of the nuns of the Poor Clares of Santa Chiara in Camerino: "From the late fifteenth century," note the curators, "the congregation of the faithful queued up to kiss it on the feast of the epiphany," and this practice has continued until the present day.⁵⁵ In October of 2016, however, the nunnery was destroyed by the earthquake that devastated the Marche region of Italy; remarkably, the doll survived. The mother superior took a photograph (fig. 3) showing the figure—not in the plain, bare form in which it was subsequently exhibited but adorned in considerable finery—lying amid the rubble, and, unsurprisingly, some were quick to label its survival a miracle.

Reading about its more recent history changed the way that I experienced this object. Encountering a once-holy item in a museum, I am often confronted by a vivid sense of the profound change of status that it has undergone in being detached from the sprawling universe of pious objects and integrated instead into an alternative system of artworks and artifacts, made part of the culture or heritage industries. In this instance, however, the exhibition was more akin to a temporary refuge for an object that had lost its home. Naked in its glass case, this holy doll seemed to be not so much frozen perpetually in time as waiting for a precise period of time to elapse before it could return to its proper place. The fact that the object was still, when in Italy, revered as a holy thing—publically at epiphany but, quite possibly, at other times by the modern-day nuns engaged in forms of pious play like their medieval predecessors—brought home to me the sense in which such an object in a museum has not necessarily undergone a decisive change of state from cult object to artwork. To a believer it is perhaps less an object that has lost its power than one in which power hibernates. It

FIGURE 3. Doll of the Christ child lying in rubble. Nuns of Santa Chiara, Camerino. Reproduced with permission.

brought to mind another of Alfred Gell's challenging claims: "I cannot tell between religious and aesthetic exaltation; art-lovers, it seems to me, actually do worship images in most of the relevant senses."[56] I found myself observing not just the object but the people with whom I was sharing the exhibition space, scrutinizing how they responded to the holy doll; it was indeed difficult to tell, as they impeccably obeyed the modern norms for discreet museum behavior, whether they were experiencing the doll as an artwork, a historical curiosity, or a manifestation of the divine. What electrified me in the presence of this object was precisely the realization that it might, even while it was in the exhibition, be provoking strikingly different responses from different people within the same space and at the same time. I experienced not the inevitable dominance of one of these possibilities of response but precisely the simultaneity of their potential.

There are times, of course, when Gell's words do not ring true and when the distinction between religious fervor and aesthetic appreciation is easier to draw. I recalled reading, after visiting the 2008 exhibition of relics in the British Museum, that museum staff had to clean lipstick from the cases each night, left there by pious visitors for whom the inaccessibility of the object behind glass was no obstacle to its radiating power. I thought, too, of a striking anecdote related by Michael Camille regarding his training as an art historian, when, in Santa Maria Novella in Florence, he was taking notes on the modeling and contrapposto of Brunelleschi's wooden crucifix, "enjoying in the crepuscular light the thrill of the 'presence' of an art object I had previously seen only in 'art' books." Suddenly, however, "an older woman, dressed totally in black, dragged forward a young girl by the hair and knocked her head, again and again, on the base of the sculpture, chanting all the while." Camille realized "that the image I was describing as a work of art was something else for this woman, something she was using to drive evil spirits from her daughter's mind."[57] I saw nothing so dramatic transpire in relation to the holy doll (behavior of this sort is frowned upon in Cambridge); but encountering this object in light of iconoclastic child's play made me acutely aware both of the potential indistinguishability of piety, play, and aesthetic appreciation—might they all be happening silently around me in the same space? Might one person be engaging in all three, successively and interchangeably? Might I, without even knowing it?—and the gulfs that potentially separate them. This is an object that might be played with reverently and joyfully; it might also be smashed to bits, whether in contemptuous rejection or to search for its soul.

My second object is the broken, armless figure of Christ known as the "Fiddleford Crucifix" (fig. 4) because it was
discovered in the derelict Great Hall of
Fiddleford Manor in Dorset in 1952.[58] It
is a modest object: a little more than six
inches high, it is light and fragile, constructed of sparsely decorated plaster of
paris. It would have taken no great effort
to break off the arms, and, since the substance from which it was made is almost
worthless, it could not be melted down or
sold for gain. The object probably dates
from the late fifteenth or early sixteenth
century, and there is no way of knowing
why it has survived or what sort of life it
lived in the centuries before it was rediscovered. Although there is no evidence
that it became a plaything, when I picture
the children in Cologne being given the
damaged crucifix, this is the object that I
imagine as their toy.

FIGURE 4. The Fiddleford
Crucifix, late fifteenth / early
sixteenth century. British
Museum, London. Reproduced
with permission.

This object captures the ambiguous being of the "idoll" that the object
of iconoclastic child's play becomes. As
we contemplate the object in the broken
form in which it has survived, two modes
of response suggest themselves, but they oscillate unstably rather than one domi-
nating and deleting the other. The broken, meager crucifix is a forlorn object. It
could easily seem faintly ludicrous—a trifle. Its missing arms have abolished its
symbolic silhouette, and it now looks like an implement to be handled rather
than revered from a distance: Christ's torso and legs look in outline almost like
the handle and blade of a simple toy knife. It is easy to imagine the forms of ordinary play that a defaced and lowly object of this sort might inspire, the range
of games into which it might be incorporated as it became a doll. Yet viewed
from another perspective, the snapping off of the arms seems less like the sort of

casual cruelty that might be directed at an alternately loved and reviled toy and more like the latest act of violence directed at the body of the suffering Christ himself. The gaunt abdomen, with its puncture wounds rendered more meticulously than the rather rudimentary daubing of the beard and mouth, and the resilient downward gaze seem to withstand the force of, and patiently to endure, this latest act of iconoclastic brutality: what is one more wound to a body already so lacerated? While iconoclastic actions directed against rejected deities from all religions have a paradoxical dimension—in that they seem to express belief in, and fear of, the very gods that they claim to deride—the strangeness of these acts becomes particularly apparent when they are directed against the already suffering and forlorn Christ: as Bruno Latour asks, "How could you destroy an image that is already that much destroyed?"[59] In fact, in the early modern period, Roman Catholics sometimes argued that the wounds inflicted on images of Christ by iconoclasts not only failed to diminish the sanctity of such objects but actually augmented them. Most famous in this respect was the statue of the Virgin and Child that came to be known as the *Vulnerata*, which was vandalized by the English sailors who sacked Cádiz in 1596 and mutilated Mary's face and arms and hacked off the infant Jesus. The members of the English College, however, insisted afterward that "the reverence which we shall do to the blessed virgin in this her image shall exceed all the trespasses and disloyalties which heresy hath been able to invent," and the statue was all the more revered for the assault that it had providentially survived.[60]

This example suggests the curious and equivocal effects that symbolic violence aimed at a representation of the divine might have. Whether or not the Fiddleford Crucifix survived as a holy thing that became a plaything, the fact that it can seem to embody both the violence of the iconoclast and the long-suffering endurance of the object exemplifies the tensions endemic to the "idoll," the idol that becomes a doll. The iconoclast would insist on seeing only the broken, humiliated, pathetic trifle, fit for child's play; a traditionalist like Edgeworth would insist on the object's undiluted holiness and worth, magnified rather than mitigated by its violent breaking. But in the actual treatment of such an object by a child, these options need not have been mutually exclusive. In the unfolding, rhythmic, discontinuous drama of child's play itself, the dual possibilities that we can still sense in viewing the Fiddleford Crucifix today might have been alternately present, as such activity lurched between the forms of reverence and violent irreverence that each of the two sides in the iconoclastic debate claimed as the only possible response to the object.

I will conclude by leaping into the modern world. In 2001 the Californian artists Shelley and Pamela Jackson launched a hypertext project titled "The Doll Games," in which they combined images of their childhood dolls and the objects associated with them, placed in various poses and surrounded by various skeins of text. The tone of their words lurches between the obviously tongue-in-cheek and the seemingly sincere, but the whole project seemed calculated to trouble the very distinction between seriousness and play. It also seemed designed to anticipate and nullify any attempt at scholarly analysis, since the project was framed with an introduction supposedly written by "J. F. Bellwether, PhD," which was both intermittently insightful and clearly a pastiche written by the sisters themselves: Bellwether cited one of his own publications, which appeared in the journal "*Post-modern Culture*, MDXIXVIIIIIX."[61] What distinguishes the project for me is its unusually acute grasp that what the Jacksons are investigating is, in a sense, not their childhood games at all but their (impossible) adult imagining of their own childhood imaginations. As Pamela Jackson writes: "What is a doll game? What is a doll? What are two kids playing? In the project we are archaeologists, voyeurs, utopians of doll games. Sometimes we're embarrassed. The doll games are inaccessible in a lot of ways—fundamentally baffling, no matter how much we scour our memories and pore over the doll box—but it still seems possible, as we assemble the fragments, that we might be able to recover them somehow or even bring them to some new life. We're curious what that new life would be."[62]

These opening questions, I have suggested in this chapter, are eminently real ones. It is the *nonobviousness* with which these artists approach not only their own childhoods but the very categories of doll, child, and doll-play—as enigmas that need to be unraveled rather than the most obvious and ready-to-hand of phenomena—that makes this project so compelling. The inaccessibility of their childhood does not lead the Jacksons to sentimentalize it as a pure realm of lost innocence or freedom; rather, the sense of inaccessibility drives the effort at recovery, which is understood not as a literal act of excavation but as an opportunity to spin further imaginings that are *enabled* by the fragmentary reconstruction of their childhood games, even if these games cannot be recaptured. Many of their texts treat the questions that are, without doubt, central to modern understandings of mass-produced dolls, mostly Barbies or similar: the versions of femininity and masculinity that they project and the ways in which, as girls, the Jacksons responded to the simultaneous foregrounding and erasure

of sexuality that these dolls embodied.[63] Most germane to my concerns, however, are the miniature character sketches that they provide alongside pictures of
many of the dolls. One, Phyllis, is "willowy, gentle, pretty but perhaps lacking in
depth"; another, Harvey, "originally a Little Red Riding Hood doll of unknown
make . . . was at once tenderly lyrical and crudely predatory, both a hapless Romantic with perfumed hair and a goatish lout." While on the one hand the dolls
seem to have remarkably clearly defined personalities, their bodies break down
into pieces that can be exchanged and overlap, and this increases rather than
diminishes their individuality, as is particularly the case with the pair of Laurie
and Jesse: "Sensitive, lithe, comely, with flowing hair . . . Laurie embodied the
Doll Games' romantic male ideal. Tragically mutilated during a makeover, the
circumstances of which remain shrouded in mystery," he lost his head. "Dreamy,
gentle Jesse," conversely, "entered the Doll Games as a disembodied head," plun-
dered from a Scandinavian costume doll: "Initially sharing Laurie's body and
taking turns with him . . . Jesse took over Laurie's body and his role at Laurie's
death." It is impossible to know as a reader or viewer of the project which of
these fine details are salvaged from childhood memories and which are spun
by the Jacksons as adults to fill in the gaps when confronted by an object that
they know once possessed such complex individuality for them but for which
they cannot reconstruct precisely what this was or how it operated. When the
dolls broke and frayed, they were folded into newly emerging and no less vivacious selves, just as when the memories of childhood now break and fray, they
are spun into new adult imaginings. The Doll Games embodies the mixture of
triviality and depth, of integrity and dissolution, of humanity and inhumanity,
of pleasure and anxiety that is, this chapter has argued, integral to the object that
emerges in iconoclastic child's play: the idoll.

The Jacksons seem to have intuited a version of this possibility, when sus-
pending one of their characters, the splendidly named Josh McBig, between
the sacred and the risible (fig. 5). Josh is The Doll Games' "archetypical 'manly
man,'" but he "had a vulnerable quality: his legs dangled weakly from his loosely
jointed hips and later began to loosen and fall off, as did his hands and even
eventually his left foot, making him a source of comedy, especially in the late
farces, but also transforming him, in the end, into what we can only see as the
Doll Games' sorrowful, suffering Christ." Not so much suspended between the
sacred and the ludicrous, perhaps, as an embodiment of the sacred emerging
amid the ludicrous, the sacred *as* ludicrous.

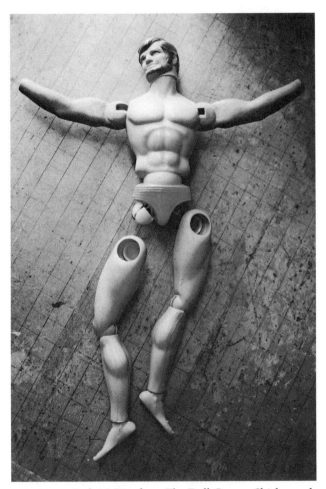

FIGURE 5. Josh McBig, from The Doll Games, Shirley and
Pamela Jackson. Courtesy of the artists. Reproduced with
permission.

3   PUPPET

IN THE SOUTHERN GERMAN TOWN of Biberach in the sixteenth century, it was reported, "many things" (*viel der Ding*) were taken from churches and religious houses and given to children as playthings. We saw in the previous chapter that this practice was not restricted to England in the sixteenth century, and this evidence suggests that it was not restricted to Cologne within Germany but occurred with some frequency in that country as well. Among these *viel der Ding*, as Albert Angele reports, the Holy Spirit sent at Pentecost was "broken by the children in their playing [*beim Spielen zerbrochen*]."[1] Unlike the crucifix in Cologne, which was subject to symbolic violence before it could become a toy, the dove seems to have been smashed in the course of the play itself.

What, though, was the precise nature of the transformation that the dove underwent when it became a plaything? To understand the nature and stakes of the change, we must understand something of its mode of action before it became a toy. While its trajectory into the children's hands may have been a new departure, this was an object that was already remarkably mobile. Presumably, it was one of the wooden doves, representing the Holy Spirit, that were often lowered from church roofs on Whitsun—sometimes accompanied by flaming scraps of paper representing the "tongues of fire" that the Spirit granted to the Apostles or by tiny wafers representing Christ's Real Presence in the Eucharist or, on occasion, showers of raisins and almonds.[2] The lowering in of the dove is described as part of a rich analysis by Robert Scribner of the "para-liturgical celebrations" that clustered around, and supplemented, the formal rites of the church calendar.[3] There was frequent overlap—sometimes unspoken and mutually supportive, sometimes fraught and contested—between official and popular religious forms. These paraliturgical practices frequently incorporated, or focused on, the playing of children—or rather, they were often actions undertaken by children in front of adults that were alternately justified and criticized as play.[4] In Franconia "a carved Christ-child doll was placed in a cradle on the altar and rocked by children, while others danced about in a ring, shouting and jumping with joy," and, strikingly, "on Ascension Thursday there was a performance representing Christ's Ascension, the battle between the Devil and the heavenly host, and the Devil's consignment to hell. A figure of the Saviour, again usually a crucifix or statue, was drawn up on a rope through a hole specially built in the church roof. In the roof were a number of youths, who created a rumpus with rattles and similar implements. Shortly afterwards, a doll or puppet coated with pitch was hurled down through the hole on to the floor below."[5]

These were precisely the practices at which reformers loved to howl with outrage and hurl derision. A well-known account by the antiquarian William Lambarde confirms that such practices were also known in England:

In the Dayes of ceremonial Religion, they used at Wytney to set foorthe yearly in maner of a Shew, or Enterlude, the Resurrection of our Lord and Saviour Chryste . . . chieflie to allure by pleasant Spectacle the comon Sort to the Likinge of Popishe Maumetrie. . . . The Preists garnished out certein small Puppets, representing the Parsons of Christe, the Watchmen, Marie, and others. . . . The like Toye I my selfe (beinge then a Chyld) once saw in Poules Churche at London, at a Feast of Whitsontyde, wheare the comynge downe of the Holy Gost was set forthe by a white Pigion, that was let to fly out of a Hole, that yet is to be sene in the mydst of the Roofe of the great Ile.[6]

Lambarde seems to describe a live dove rather than the movable figures mentioned by Scribner, yet he links it explicitly to a puppet show depicting Christ himself. Like the holy dolls discussed in the previous chapter, there was apparently no contradiction in the idea of capturing the divine in puppet form.[7] Nonetheless, by the time that Lambarde was writing (probably the 1530s, the same decade in which Roger Edgeworth delivered his sermon on iconoclastic child's play), "the puppet had become virtually synonymous, in the religious context, with idolatry," as Amy Knight Powell observes.[8] That said, it is often difficult to determine to just what kind of object the English term *puppet*, the German *Puppe*, or the Dutch *pop* referred; this was, after all, just what the iconoclasts intended in labeling holy things as playthings, which were interchangeably worthless and trivial, the differences between them of little import.[9] When Lambarde decried the "Popishe Maumetrie" of these "certein small Puppets," he made use of a pun particularly beloved of English reformers: thanks to the flexibility of sixteenth-century orthography, it was often pointed out that *popery* and *popetry* differed only in a single letter.[10]

Should these effigies of doves, devils, and Christs be described as puppets, as we understand the term today? Precisely because there has been considerable historical and theoretical attention to puppetry—both in general and specifically in relation to Reformation polemic—this chapter will keep this question open.[11] As will become clear, it is not the puppet per se that interests me (and I will ultimately question whether it is possible to talk of objects being dolls, puppets, idols, or toys *per se*). Rather, I use these figures to consider what it means to think of the object of iconoclastic child's play as *articulated*, in multiple senses: articulation as mobility of the kind that it assumes once broken or played with; articulated through language by those who shape its play; but, with precise relation to the puppet, articulated in the sense of being visibly and ostentatiously composed of parts that move and function in relation to one another. It is as a simultaneously *jointed* and *disjointed* figure, to echo Marjorie Garber's description, that the puppet most interests me, in that like the object of iconoclastic child's play it seems to combine functioning wholeness with already-brokenness.[12] I will therefore have more to say about marionettes and the like than about finger or glove puppets, and I will ultimately juxtapose these figures with other kinds of already broken objects, especially relics, rather than focusing on puppets as traditionally understood.

The value of Scribner's vivid account lies in the variety of artificial figures that he describes in motion—effigies of Christ, Satan, and the Holy Spirit as dove—that might or might not be dolls and puppets and that assumed their celebratory role in part through the children and youth who played with and around them. Once again, viewed from this perspective, the polemical intentions behind iconoclasm as child's play seem both obvious and deeply strange: if some of these objects were already used as playthings for children, including as puppets, in late medieval religious practice, then how truly transformative was it to place them in a child's hands?

––––––––––––––

If the involvement of children in iconoclasm was intended, on the one hand, to actualize the polemical claim that popery was mere puppetry, it also coheres up to a point with the frequent claim that the Reformation was principally a move-

ment of the young.[13] Charles Wriothesley, describing Bishop Barlow's denunciation of an image of Christ at St. Paul's Cross in the first year of Edward VI's
reign, observed that "after the sermon the boyes brooke the idolls in peaces."[14]
On the Continent iconoclasm broke out among similarly youthful groups: in
Geneva in 1535, Carlos Eire wrote:

> As the canons began to sing vespers, some boys interrupted them by staging a coun-
> terceremony of their own: Hooting and howling, they mocked the Latin chant of the
> service. Suddenly, the youths charged the sanctuary, overturned the chairs on which the
> canons usually sat, and cursed them for making images and having confidence in them.
> The priests stood frozen with fear as the boys, still shouting, waved the chairs at them.
> Outside the cathedral, others who heard the noise came running in, and, upon seeing
> what the children were doing, pounced on the images, knocking them to the ground
> and breaking them into pieces. The children dropped the chairs and joined in, collecting
> some of the debris and carrying it outside, where they chanted to passersby, "Here we
> have the gods of the priests; would you like some?" (*Nous avons les dieux des Prebstres,
> en voulles vous?*)[15]

In a sense this scene is the inverse of iconoclastic child's play; rather than objects
being placed in the hands of children who are directed to play with him, here
iconoclasm begins as spontaneous rebellion among the young, into which the
adults are then swept.[16] Most relevant is Eire's description of the boys' mockery
of the priests as a "counterceremony," which resonates with Scribner's claim that
iconoclastic actions "sometimes seem more like carnivalesque parody, a matter
of play rather than of ritual. However the disparity is only superficial, for play
(or carnival) and ritual can be seen as complementary and homologous forms
of metacommunication. Both are stylised forms of behaviour marking out a
distinctive 'set-aside' time and place. . . . When play appears as 'counter-ritual,'
it stands in close dialectical tension with the ritual it seeks to mock."[17]

Just as I earlier argued that iconoclastic child's play should not be conflated
with the trivializing polemical discourse of popery as mere play, however, I am
also not convinced that it should be folded quite so swiftly into these accounts
of public, ritualized, carnivalesque behavior—precisely because the object is
not finally cast out or destroyed but lingers on in the household, to be played
with once the fervor of destruction has passed; it assumes a private as well as
a public life. Nonetheless, Scribner's subtle account illuminates the similarity
of content, especially of *tone*, between pre-Reformation paraliturgical play

and iconoclastic play. The raucous mockery of Satan, the equally boisterous rocking of the Christ doll in its cradle, and the rowdy hoisting of Christ or the dove through the roof of the church are curiously replicated by the iconoclastic youth in London and Geneva. Consider another of Scribner's examples, from May of 1527, when "the annual cross procession in Frankfurt was mocked by persons who fashioned a carnival puppet in the form of a wolf, and as the procession went by, the puppet was waved out of a window and the procession mocked by cries of 'A wolf!, a wolf!'"[18] When reformers behaved in this way, they were not simply rupturing the solemnity of religious ritual with their anarchic puppet-play; rather than bringing a puppet into a sphere in which it obviously did not belong, they were entering one in which it might already have seemed quite comfortably at home.

By far the best known of these liturgical puppets in England was the so-called Rood of Boxley in Kent, the destruction of which was a prominent set-piece of iconoclastic reform in the 1530s. It was described by John Hoker of Maidstone as a figure of Christ that "nodded his head, winked his eyes, turned his beard, bent his body to receive the prayers of worshippers"—or, in the memorable terms of one ballad,

> He was made to joggle,
> His eyes would goggle,
> He wold bend his browes and frowne.

But it was revealed to be "worked by wire through little pipes" by the deceptive monks.[19] The Rood was destroyed but not before it was brought to court and "made to act amid the jeers of the courtiers"; then "the bishop of Rochester preached at London, with the image opposite him, when it performed again, and was afterwards cut to pieces and put in this fire."[20] It has been disputed whether this object, curiously vivacious and mobile up until the very moment of its immolation, can accurately be described as a puppet, though since the same ballad proclaimed

> But now may we see
> What gods they be,
> Euen puppets, maumats and elfes,

it was clearly conceivable in those terms.[21] My interest, however, is less in whether it truly was a puppet than in what the Rood of Boxley tells us about the place of such objects within the range of ways in which the divine was made manifest in late medieval religion.

The destruction of the Rood of Boxley was based on the implicit premise that no puppet could possibly manifest the divine—a claim that, as we have already seen, cannot withstand scrutiny. This is not only because there have been (and still are) numerous religious traditions in which objects identifiable as puppets were integrally involved in devotional practice.[22] Although medieval crucifixes were generally not moved by secret wires in the manner of the Rood of Boxley, there are numerous surviving instances from the Middle Ages of crucifixes with movable limbs that should, I would argue, be considered in a similar light. At Easter, some of these Christ figures were taken down from their crosses and paraded through the streets, their arms folded so that they could be laid into a sepulcher on Good Friday before being "resurrected" on Easter Sunday.[23]

What connects these movable crucifixes to the puppets that interest me, as I suggested above, is not just their kinetic propensity but the visibility of the joins and gaps that allowed them to move. It is the ostentatious articulatedness and jointedness of this kind of puppet, the making manifest of the relations among their autonomous parts, that make them both like and unlike living bodies.[24] In a seminal article by Gesine and Johannes Taubert on these movable Christ figures, the first image that they show is a magnified view of the gap at the shoulder joint of one of the figures: a dark line where the wooden pieces meet, a black void at the figure's armpit.[25] Such jointedness is characteristic of many puppet figures, divine and otherwise: the gaps and fissures so prominent in such figures contribute to what Matthew Isaac Cohen calls "the puppet's destructive ontology," the fact that it is often created to be broken apart in performance and return magically to life, a cycle of decimation and revivification that continues as long as the puppet remains in play.[26] If this is a general feature of articulated puppets, however, their constitutive brokenness takes on a new and unsettling significance in relation to these figures of Christ. In a fourteenth-century crucifix with movable arms from Swabia, recently discussed by Amy Knight Powell, the dark line at the joint that advertises the movability of the limbs echoes, even as it arcs physically away from, the horrifying and wider wound in Christ's side—another rift in the wood, but one from which sculpted and painted blood gushes down.[27]

The curve of the joint also seems to fade into the arc of Christ's pectoral muscle as it winds around his body, its dark course thereby paralleling and blurring into the series of lines made by his emaciated ribs. This object leads me to revisit the question, posed by Bruno Latour, that I cited at the end of my previous chapter: "How could you destroy an image that is already that much destroyed?" Elsewhere, Latour writes that "the historical differences between iconoclasm and iconophilia appear to be very small. . . . What can be done literally by destroying the image itself can be done figuratively *in* the image. In that sense, all Christian figures are born broken."[28] This claim is borne out particularly well by the broken disjointedness of the Christ puppet as an *articulated* form; it is the very obviousness and simplicity of its material constitution, the feature that reformers claimed to find so outrageously inappropriate to the manifestation of the divine, that seems paradoxically to *capture* the broken disjointedness of the crucified body. There is a sense in which even a pristine puppet seems proleptically broken or seems to invite a breaking that reveals, rather than ruins, its essence. Kenneth Gross, recounting the extraordinary episode from Cervantes's novel in which Don Quixote attacks and decimates a puppet show, comments that "the life of puppets does not just survive destruction; it feeds off it. . . . The domain of puppets is itself, at its most animated, a world of destroyed things."[29] Though Gross does not make the link, it is this feature that makes the connection between Christ and the puppet at once vexed and irresistible, a startling possibility that survived in certain corners into the eighteenth century. In Samuel Sharp's popular *Letters from Italy* (1767) Sharp reported a scene from the Largo del Castello in Naples, where "every afternoon, Monks and Mountebanks, Pick-pockets and Conjurors, follow their several occupations": "It happened one day, that Punch succeeded marvellously, and the poor Monk preached to the air, for not a living creature was near him: Mortified and provoked that a puppet-shew, within thirty yards of him, should draw the attention of the people from the Gospel, to such idle trash, with a mixture of rage and religion, he held up the crucifix, and called aloud, *Ecco il vero Pulcinella;*— 'Here is the true Pulchinello,—come here,—come here!' "[30]

This story might seem like the final victory of iconoclastic discourse, a confirmation that the monk's idol and the puppeteer's mammet are both "idle trash." But there might, I have suggested, be a very different side to the equivalence that the monk proclaims. Christ does not reveal the falsity of the puppet as a figure but incorporates and elevates its truth. The brokenness of the puppet illuminates and expresses, rather than demeaning, the brokenness of Christ; the lacerated lowliness of the puppet and of the crucified God are one.

———————————

By making manifest the brokenness and imperfection of Christ as a condition, rather than a diminution, of his divinity, the holy puppet foregrounds the challenges of knowing how properly to relate to a potentially forlorn and foolish God. I now want to move away from specific attention to holy puppets and explore the wider tensions within the very idea of a sacred Christian object that these beings crystallize. The holy puppet illuminates the complexities of what Caroline Walker Bynum has called "Christian materiality." Arguing that "the various types of holy matter . . . are not easily separated from each other," Bynum observes that "in the same period in which statues and wall paintings were thought to come alive in order to bestow benefits or protest desecration, other physical objects, such as relics, contact relics, and consecrated wafers, increased in prominence and began in new and more literal ways to announce the holy within them."[31] She suggests that late medieval religious discourse and practice fluctuated unstably between alternative and contested possibilities for understanding the materiality of the holy: "The sacred slips between animate and inanimate, bodily and heavenly, present and eternal, as if the poles were simultaneous, rather than dichotomous. . . . Distinctions between living and dead, body and thing, presence and mimesis, part and whole, animate and inanimate, tended to blur; all of creation could convey and reveal God."[32] Bynum briefly discusses holy dolls among the forms in which the holy was materialized, and I would like to build on her rich account and argue that the discourses around sacred puppets—and the iconoclastic transformation of the holy thing into a plaything—engage in different ways with the generative ambivalence of Christian materiality as she describes it. Rather than focusing on questions of materiality, I propose to return in a new way to the long and risky tradition of asserting the foolishness or silliness of Christianity and even of Christ himself. Bluntly put: the divine puppet was derided as foolish, absurd, and risible; but, for a certain strand within Christian thought, it was necessary to acknowledge that the entire notion of an omnipotent God reduced to and encapsulated in human form was, indeed, viewed from a certain perspective, foolish, absurd, and risible (this was the possibility that we glimpsed in a different way at the close of the previous chapter, with Shelley and Pamela Jackson's account of Josh McBig). To ask this in another way:

was it any more absurd to try and capture God in the wooden body of a puppet than in the fleshly, awkward, imperfect body of a human? We encountered this notion of divine foolishness briefly in Chapter 1, where, tellingly, Maximus the Confessor could attribute foolishness and play to God only by inverting and annihilating their human meaning in the process. Tertullian, arguing in the third century against heretics who sought to deny that Christ took on a truly human body, was bolder in his discussion of the words of St. Paul:

God hath chosen the foolish things of the world [stulta mundi], that he may put to shame the things that are wise [1 Corinthians 1:27]. What are these foolish things? . . . Can any of them be so foolish as belief in God who was born, born moreover of a virgin, born with a body of flesh, God who has wallowed through the reproaches of nature? . . . There are, I submit, other things too that are foolish enough, those concerned with the reproaches and sufferings of God. If not, let them call it prudence that God was crucified. . . . Wise you cannot be, except by becoming a fool in the world through believing the foolish things of God.[33]

Tertullian initially suggests that these *stulta mundi* are things that merely *seem* foolish to non-Christian eyes: the basis for this was Paul's claim that "the preaching of the cross is to them that perish foolishness; but unto us which are saved it is the power of God" (1 Corinthians 1:18). The ability to see beyond the surface of foolishness becomes here the mark of true Christian faith. Inverting the significance of foolishness in this way—to say that it is merely apparent—is a way to bypass the difficulties presented by St. Paul's words, but it does not entirely nullify them. It is still striking to find a series of Christian thinkers willing to make a most remarkable acknowledgment: that their central tenets, including their emphasis on a God in truly human form, not only can but *must* at least appear to be ludicrous, risible. What could be more apparently foolish than the Gospels, or the Crucifixion itself? M. A. Screech explains this view in cheerfully trenchant terms: "The Christian religion did seem particularly stupid and absurd to both the Jewish and the Gentile worlds in which it first appeared. Two millennia of existence, marked by long periods of dominance, have blunted this stark fact. For Jews and for Gentiles the three basic doctrines of Christian belief were not merely unlikely, unproven or distasteful: they were daft. These doctrines are the Incarnation, the Crucifixion and the Resurrection of the body."[34]

To be a practicing Christian, by this account, is to hold certain beliefs and perform certain practices while staring the fact of their manifest foolishness in the face rather than trying to justify them in terrestrial terms. The Incarnation does not, according to this strain of thought, *dignify* the human by making it a fit vessel for the divine; rather, the embodied Christ becomes extraordinary precisely as a convergence of the most magnificent, transcendent, and dignified with the most foolish, flimsy, fragile, and laughable. Accordingly, the Christian can only say to a nonbeliever: *you are right—I am a fool, my God is a fool, these scriptures are foolish, the liturgy is foolish.* Tertullian took this strand of thought to its furthest extreme in a famous pronouncement: "The son of God was crucified: I am not ashamed—because it is shameful. The Son of God died: it is immediately credible—because it is silly [*credibile est, quia ineptum est*]. He was buried, and rose again: it is certain—because it is impossible [*certum est, quia imposibile*]."[35] While it is the last of these phrases—often misquoted—whose paradoxical directness has attracted by far the most attention, echoed by Thomas Browne among others, I am more interested in the penultimate statement: the death of Christ is *ineptum,* a word with strongly negative meanings in classical Latin, including "unsuitable, impertinent, improper, tasteless, senseless, silly, pedantic, absurd, inept, without tact."[36] This conception of the divine both places extraordinary imaginative demands on a believer and grants him or her remarkable latitude: the Incarnation, and especially the Crucifixion, is to be apprehended as the highest, the loftiest, and the most majestic of phenomena; at the same time, it is to be recognized as—at least on worldly terms—silly, indecorous, laughable.

Although Tertullian did not link this foolishness to play directly, it is notable that the Christian thinkers who conceived of God's—and their own—action in ludic terms were often the ones most daringly willing to confront the challenging possibility of Christ's foolishness and lowliness. Most significant in this regard is Desiderius Erasmus, who proclaims the foolishness of Christ—at once boldly and elusively—in *The Praise of Folly,* in which the eponymous figure observes "that godlike Paul attributes something of folly even to God himself: 'The folly of God is wiser than men.' For Origen in his interpretation will not allow you to say that God is foolish only in the opinion of men, as you can for that other text, 'The doctrine of the cross, to those who are perishing, is indeed foolishness.'"[37] The daring of this claim can be gauged from the anxious and irate responses that it prompted. When Martin Dorp wrote a long letter to Erasmus in 1514, warning him that "your *Folly* has aroused a good deal of feeling," he singled out this specific aspect: "And then Christ, and the life in Heaven—can the ears of a good Christian endure to hear foolishness ascribed to him?"[38] In his reply Erasmus

insisted that he had said nothing unorthodox in this work but had simply presented the same Christology that he had advanced in his earlier *Enchiridion* but
had done *"sub specie lusu"* (as a joke), but literally "under the appearance of play."
While Erasmus's reply has generally been seen as setting right the misguided and
myopic Dorp, in fact he somewhat conceals the daring of his original account
of Christ's foolishness.[39] Referring back to the passage in *The Praise of Folly*, he
writes: "Nor is there any risk that someone at this point may suppose that the
apostles or Christ were foolish in the ordinary sense. . . . But this same folly of
theirs overcomes all the wisdom of the world." He goes on to insist that, having
framed holy folly or madness as "a *kind of* folly and madness," he has made clear
"that this is meant figuratively and is not literal." This is, however, an evasion: like
Maximus the Confessor before him, Erasmus falls back on the claim that since
all human meanings are superseded and inverted in the divine, such folly is not
truly foolish. As he put it in the *Enchiridion*, "see how many things are made new
in Christ and how the names of things change their meanings."[40]

This is, however, precisely the interpretation of divine foolishness against
which Folly specifically warned—that it only *seems* foolish, to undiscerning or
impious eyes. As Screech has compellingly argued, the reference to Origen at
this point—a characteristically risky decision on Erasmus's part, given the Greek
Father's reputation for unorthodoxy—is crucial to understanding it: in interpreting 1 Corinthians in his eighth *Homily on Jeremiah*, Screech writes, Origen

stresses that this text does *not* mean merely that God's wisdom seems foolishness, but
rather that all the wisdom which God actually vouchsafes to man is only, as it were, his
own "foolishness." Yet this divine fatuousness is greater than the greatest of all human
wisdom. Even the wisdom of Paul . . . is to be reputed folly when compared to celestial
wisdom as it is, to that perfect knowledge (*gnōsis*) which is God's. Eventual access to this
perfect knowledge is vouchsafed to man through God's baby-talk, so to speak, through
that "foolishness" which is all of God's wisdom that man can take. Such foolishness is
the wisdom of God revealed, in ways that man can grasp, in the Bible. The highest manifestation of that foolishness—that divine Wisdom made intelligible to man—is Christ:
God made man.[41]

Origen, like Erasmus after him, was more than aware that he was taking a risk in
making his claim: "If I speak of *the foolishness of God*, how the faultfinders would
misquote me! How they would blame me!"[42] In his *Homilies on the Song of Songs*
Origen nonetheless elaborated on this notion that the Incarnation encapsulates

divine foolishness: "We were empty: he emptied himself, taking on the form of a slave. We were a people foolish and lacking wisdom: he was made the foolishness of preaching so that the silliness of God [*fatuum Dei*] might be wiser than men."[43] As Screech shows, Erasmus not only put an echo of this idea into Folly's mouth but briskly endorsed Origen in his annotations to the New Testament, where he understood *kenosis*, the emptying out by which God became man, as a process by which Christ "made himself most humble and nothing [*humillimus et nihil*]." "If God lowered himself to our weakness to make us strong," he asked, "what is there new if he should lower himself to our foolishness, making wise men out of fools?"[44]

This has been something of a theological detour, but it is one that I have made with a specific purpose, for I do not believe that we can grasp the complex implications of either making Christ into a puppet or a holy thing into a plaything unless we understand this background. What does it mean for an iconoclast to ridicule an object, to describe it as obviously inane and ludicrous, when at least some thinkers had long been willing to proclaim that the Christian holy was a realm in which the unimaginably magnificent was necessarily embodied in the overtly foolish? While Erasmus was willing to follow Tertullian and Origen in emphasizing "the silliness of God," to repeat Screech's arresting formulation, what also emerges from his writings in a less comfortable way are the extraordinary challenges that this conception presents to a believer faced with a particular ritual practice or holy object. What is demanded is a remarkable species of double-think—an ability to see the object or practice in question as genuinely and irreducibly foolish and trivial, while also recognizing that it becomes meaningful in relation to the divine wisdom toward which it (ineptly) points. A tense mixture of reverence and cheerful contempt toward any given materialization of the divine would seem to be demanded of the believer—even in relation to the words of the Bible or Christ himself.

To return, then, to where I began: I want to suggest that a combination of loftiness and silliness, of magnificence and ineptitude, is embodied in the figure of the holy puppet. When reformers denounced the Rood of Boxley and similar objects as manifestly inane and inadequate to the divine, the follower of Tertullian, Origen, or Erasmus might reply that they were absolutely right but right in the wrong way or for the wrong reasons. Actual puppets of Christ, jointed and movable crucifixes, holy dolls—all of these should be seen not as anomalies, nor as expressions of merely "popular" as opposed to official religion, but as exemplary crystallizations of the conflicting demands that the sheer fact of the Incarnation as the silliness of God makes on the faithful. This also brings out the deeply equivocal nature of the iconoclastic rhetoric and attacks aimed at such objects: not only, as Latour ponders, how one can break an object already so broken but how one can reduce to the level of the ridiculous objects that seem already to flaunt, to revel in, their ludicrous triviality. To attack them as mere popish puppets is to amplify, not to alter, part of the overt and difficult claim that they invariably make on those who view them.

Ultimately, however, Erasmus's response to divine foolishness was equivocal, and even he was unable to embrace it as wholeheartedly as Folly herself—especially when it came to the question of whether the divine could be imagined as a play*thing*, like a holy doll or puppet, to which the individual believer might relate. It is here that the question of the foolishness of the divine intersected for him with the problem of the materiality of the holy. Erasmus's most striking exploration of this possibility came in a renowned section of his ever-expanding collection of *Adagia* concerning "Sileni Alcibiadis" (The Sileni of Alcibiades), a phrase used, Erasmus explains, "with reference to a thing which in appearance . . . seems ridiculous and contemptible, but on closer and deeper examination proves to be admirable. . . . For it seems that the Sileni were small images divided in half, and so constructed that they could be opened out and displayed; when closed they represented some ridiculous, ugly flute-player, but when opened they suddenly revealed the figure of a god, so that the amusing deception would show off the art of the carver."[45] Erasmus then refers to the most famous mention of such objects, the end of Plato's *Symposium*, in which Alcibiades compares the wise but homely Socrates to these figurines, making similar comparisons to the philosophers Diogenes and Epictetus.[46] "But," he continues startlingly,

is not Christ the most extraordinary Silenus of all [*An non mirisicus quidam Silenus fuit Christus*]? If it is permissible to speak of him in this way [*Si fas est de hoc ad cum loqui modum*]—and I cannot see why all who rejoice in the name of Christians should not do their best to imitate it. If you look only on the face of the Silenus image, what could be lower or more contemptible [*abjectius, aut contemptius*], measured by popular standards? . . . But if one may attain to a closer look at this Silenus-image, that is if he deigns to show himself to the purified eyes of the soul [*purgatis animi luminibus*], what unspeakable riches you will find there![47]

Erasmus is aware of the riskiness of what he is doing and that many will find the comparison that he proposes impermissible. He therefore vacillates here on whether the incarnate Christ is, or only seems, foolish. Having raised this shocking possibility, he then departs from the very comparison that he has introduced: whereas in the Silenus figure one level of material appearance gives way to reveal another, equally material but far more dignified level, this becomes instead a movement from seemingly contemptible appearance to the riches perceptible *purgatis animi luminibus*—a leaving behind of the material altogether for the spiritual. Having begun with a radical possibility—that Christ appears contemptible— Erasmus defends this claim by sliding toward a much more standard theological defense of images as valuable but imperfect representations that point toward a transcendent divine that they imperfectly embody. This becomes for Erasmus a movement in which the believer is jolted, repulsed, from the contemptible Christ toward the richness of the invisible divine. But, even as he effects this movement away from Christian materiality, the appearance of Christ himself is never described as anything other than foolish and repulsive.

———————

The possibility of a repugnant form of holiness intersected with the question of the iconoclastic puppet in the reception of Erasmus's most extended satirical engagement with the material practices of late medieval piety—his account of the cult of relics. As I have discussed elsewhere, Erasmus criticized the excesses of the cult precisely because it seemed to offer great reverence not only to the most mundane but to the most sordid and disgusting items, when it should be directed toward the genuine presence of Christ in the scriptures.[48] This attack provided ideal fodder for English reformers, who published a carefully edited translation of Erasmus's colloquy *Peregrinatio religionis ergo*. In this text Erasmus's mouthpiece, Ogygius, describes to his interlocutor, Mendemus, a visit to the shrine of Thomas Becket at Canterbury that he made with his friend Gratian Pullus, who expressed only revulsion toward the objects that he was expected to revere. Entering the sacristy, the pair were shown a chest containing, Ogygius explains,

some linen rags, many of them still showing traces of snivel. With these, they say, the holy man wiped the sweat from his face or neck, the dirt from his nose, or whatever other kinds of filth human bodies have [*aliaque corporis excrementa*]. At this point my friend Gratian again displayed something less than graciousness. To him . . . the prior kindly offered one of the rags as a gift, thinking he was making him a present that would please him very much. But Gratian was hardly grateful for it. He touched the piece with his fingers, not without a sign of disgust, and put it back scornfully, puckering his lips as through whistling [*et contemtim reposuit, porrectis labiis, veluti poppysmum imitans*]. (This is what he ordinarily did if he came across anything he thought contemptible.)[49]

When he described Gratian Pullus's squeamish response to these relics, Erasmus made use of a curious and arcane Latin word, *poppysma*, used only a handful of times by classical authors. A borrowing from Greek, it referred to a clicking or smacking of the lips, intended to ward off evil spirits.[50] When Erasmus's colloquy was translated into English, however, it took on an altogether different complexion: there Gratian

toke one of them betwene hys fingers, and dysdaynyngly layd it down agayne, made a mock and a mow at it, *after the maner of puppettes*, for thys was his maner, if an thing lykede hym not, yt he thought worthy to be despysede.[51]

This mistranslation is a case of brilliantly creative error. Erasmus, flaunting his Latinity with the obscure word *poppysma*, seems to have baffled the anonymous translator, who assumed from its spelling that the word must have something to do with puppetry. The translator made this choice because, thanks to the wide currency of the idea in iconoclastic discourse, it seemed eminently appropriate that to treat a relic with contempt might involve making "a mock and a mow at it, after the maner of puppettes." The comparison between a relic and a puppet is not in Erasmus's text, but it seemed apt, ready to hand. While the direct connection between relics and puppets is made by Erasmus's translator rather than by Erasmus himself, it is a juxtaposition that illuminates the peculiar affinity between these categories of object. As the English translator reimagines them, Gratian Pullus's actions attack the relics on two grounds at once: these objects, valued highly as *loci* of the sacred, are both too lowly to be of any true significance and too disgusting to be comfortably handled at all. His contempt is, however, at odds with the lowliness and foolishness of the incarnate Christ as Erasmus understood it, who was supposed to overturn worldly values, to topple flimsy human assumptions about the nature of worth, and to enthrone the seemingly lowest as the absolute highest—an alteration uncannily like the reversals of value enacted in the games of children. But the behavior of Gratian Pullus, faced with the fleshy relics of Thomas Becket, also highlighted a further parallel: just as the child wallowed cheerily in its own filth, the pious believer was expected at times not only to tolerate but to delight in the trivial, the fragmented, and even the disgusting forms in which the holy was materialized.

Erasmus's satirical account of the cult of relics and its excesses thereby reveals the difficulty that he had in reconciling his risky account of the foolishness of Christ with the material forms in which this foolishness might be made present. Defenders of the cult of relics did not deny that these objects were humble and disgusting; instead, they often insisted that this was proof of these objects' worth, their participation in the logic of inverted value inaugurated by the Incarnation itself. As Peter Brown asks, regarding the diminutive size of many relics, "How better to express the paradox of the linking of Heaven and Earth than by an effect of 'inverted magnitudes,' by which the object around which boundless associations cluster should be tiny and compact?"[52] The relic and the puppet are alike, I would suggest, precisely because both can take the form of seemingly inconsequential and conspicuously broken objects "around which boundless associations cluster," for the believer or for the playing child. It was often crucial to emphasize, in order to disseminate holiness as widely and effectively as possible, that, as Theodoret of Cyrus insisted in the fifth century CE, "in the divided body the grace survives undivided and the fragments, however small, have the same efficacy as the whole body."[53] This meant that for the relic—as for the toy, on Baudelaire's account—breaking could augment its significance as an object rather than reducing it, precisely by making it portable.[54] As Paulinus of Nola wrote of this process around the same time as Theodoret:

This, then, was the means by which the faithful and zealous escorts of the relics were afforded a chance at the prompting of faith to break off some keepsakes from the holy bones as their deserved reward. . . . As a result, the sacred ashes have been scattered over living areas like life-giving seeds. Wherever a drop of dew has fallen on men in the shape of a particle of bone, the tiny gift from a consecrated body . . . the drops of ashes have begotten rivers of life.

From this source Christ's abundance, so rich in its tiniest forms, has fallen [*stillauit copia Christi / diues et in minimis*] on us also; for we, too, have received, in the form of a fragment of dust [*puluere parvo*], the sacred tokens of the apostle's flesh.[55]

Paulinus here stresses the collision, in the relic, between the unimaginable magnitude of the divine and these objects' diminutive size, making clear the quasi-Incarnational logic underpinning the cult of the saints: "*diues et in minimis.*" The relic is an object whose mode of being in the world profoundly challenges the distinctions between part and whole, large and small, subject and object, animate and inanimate—as well as that between breaking and making. Only by grasping these collective challenges can we understand its peculiar affinity with the puppet and the plaything. Any "fragment of dust" can be a vessel for the holy—*spirantis . . . pulueris* (living dust) Paulinus calls relics elsewhere—but the very tininess of these fragments emphasized that they were doubly part of a larger whole: part of the body that had been thus fragmented but also part of the entire chain of holy things that irradiated and held together Christendom.[56] Hence, for Gaudentius, as Brown notes, the indistinguishable relics of the Forty Martyrs of Sebaste were "the perfect image of a group indissolubly fused together" precisely *because* they were a heap of amorphous matter: these were "tiny fragments around which the imaginative associations of a very special kind of death could cluster undisturbed."[57] The fact that such fragments in no way resembled the whole saint did not diminish their agency or efficacy. Each time a shard of bone or a speck of dust behaved in this fashion, it reiterated a deliberately scandalous logic akin to that of the Incarnation: it was all the more wondrous that an object so apparently lowly could effect such power.

Indeed, as if in anticipation of Gratian Pullus's reproach, some of the objects proved their holiness by being not only humble but actively disgusting: while few thinkers dared address this idea directly, the inverted logic of the relic tended always toward the abject, the excremental—"the saint as rejected turd," as Julia Reinhard Lupton bluntly puts it.[58] Gratian Pullus, as we saw, came close to this conjunction when complaining of rags supposedly stained with Thomas Becket's snot, sweat, "aliaque corporis excrementa," thereby euphemistically posing a question that he did not dare ask directly: would a saint's shit be as holy as any other lowly part of him or her?[59] Becket's shrine may not have confronted worshippers with this particular unpleasant dilemma, but it did contain one set of relics intended to impress viewers because of, and not despite, their provocation of disgust: the hair breeches worn by the saint and discovered only after his death as a sign of his exceptional piety. These unprecedented garments caused open wounds in his flesh that teemed with lice and maggots and may have been displayed and venerated during the later Middle Ages—their very harshness and loathsomeness testimony to both the piety of the saint and the sanctity of the shrine.[60] While such objects, at once holy and repulsive, came to the fore amid the later development of the cult of relics, it is notable that as early as Tertullian's treatise on the Incarnation, he anticipated objections not only to the impossibility of this central doctrine but its vileness, a vileness centering not on the excremental but on the processes of gestation and birth: "Beginning then with that nativity you so strongly object to, orate, attack now, the nastiness of genital elements in the womb, the filthy curdling of moisture and blood. . . . You shudder, of course, at the child passed out along with his afterbirth, and of course bedaubed with it." Tertullian does not deny this disgust but makes it ineradicable from the nature of the human, asking his foe, "Yet how were you born? You hate man during his birth: how can you love any man?" Accounting for the true fleshliness of the Incarnation led Tertullian, I would suggest, toward an implicit and daring claim parallel to "*credo quia imposibile est*": "*credo quia turpi est*" (I believe it *because* it is disgusting). The broken, forlorn relic, like the puppet, not only mirrors the barely expressible notion of the foolishness of Christ but points toward the literally unsayable but nonetheless unavoidable idea of the loathsomeness of a God in a human body, with all its attendant messiness.

Most believers' encounters with these meager or actively stomach-churning materializations of the holy were, however, not direct or straightforward. As Brown emphasizes, although pilgrimage was driven by "a yearning for intimate closeness, the shrine at the end of the journey comprised "closed surfaces" behind which "the holy lay, either totally hidden or glimpsed behind narrow apertures."[61] Whether or not the relic itself was wholly or partly visible or its presence was conspicuously occluded, the composite of relic and reliquary functioned according to a deliberately paradoxical logic that both transformed and pointed beyond the nature of the object itself. This composite object was composed of matter—typically bone or hair; dried skin, breastmilk, or blood—that would be valueless and perhaps revolting in any other context, but here, only here, it lay beyond worldly value and was worthy of reverence. Conversely, what seems at first glance to be the majesty of the object, its golden and jewel-encrusted veneer, is ultimately subordinated to the lowly fragment embedded within it; these ornate surfaces curiously delete themselves, pointing away from themselves toward the objects that they occlude and the higher, divine truth that these objects embody.[62] The relic in its reliquary, then, echoes the logic of the Incarnation through its deliberately challenging conjunction of the obviously lavish and splendid with the conspicuously lowly and foolish, even disgusting. Cynthia Hahn discusses a pendant reliquary containing a tiny door (fig. 6a), surrounded by a broken surface, in which "the jagged holes reveal bits of matter, perhaps once or still saturated with the holy *myron* and blood. When one finally opens this interior door, another figure of the saint in his grave appears [fig. 6b], this one gold but too small to detect if a smile lingers on his lips. Again, the feeling is intimate and evokes a toy, but this is an educational toy, the manipulation of which prolongs pious thoughts and brings great comfort to its viewer."[63]

The analogy with a toy is, I would argue, acute and appropriate, but Hahn is too quick to conclude that such an object can provoke only "pious thoughts" and provide only "comfort," even if this was its educational intent. Having wandered some distance from the Tudor translator's decision to compare Gratian Pullus's mockery of the relics to the dancing puppets, I would like to loop back to my earlier arguments and suggest that polemical juxtapositions of this sort—the same juxtapositions that lay behind iconoclasm as child's play—reveal different sorts of affinity between holy thing and puppet or plaything that neither the iconoclasts nor their foes were happy to acknowledge. This reliquary is toylike not (or not only) because of its intended and piously educative function, as Hahn suggests, but because, like a children's plaything, it does not comfortably fit into prevailing systems of value. As its cover pops open, puppetlike, the person who opens it should no longer ogle the glistering gold but be overwhelmed by the way that this gilded surface is broken, ruptured, warped, seeming almost to be swallowed by the dark fissures through which the holy matter appears to push, as if the tiny and fragile image of the saint at its center is being engulfed by the lingering fragments of his actual body. Just as children were believed not to value the right things in the right way—to prefer toys and trinkets to their worldly or spiritual inheritance—the viewer

FIGURES 6A AND 6B. Pendant Reliquary, Byzantium, eleventh century. British Museum, London. Reproduced with permission.

of this relic is to be drawn to it by its initially dazzling outer case, but each time it is opened, the glistering gold is superseded by the holiness of the dark, the lowly, and the strange that is captured within. Insofar as this object is doubly articulated, jointed, hinged—both in its opening mechanism and in the material disjunction that is thereby revealed—it evokes not just an educational toy but a holy puppet.

———————

The salient feature that brings this reliquary, and relics in general, into enthralling tension with the figure of the puppet is that such objects both testify to and open up the further possibility of violent *dis*articulation. I have suggested that it is the way that the features of this object—its conspicuous brokenness, the obvious articulation of its multiple surfaces and parts—chime, awkwardly but resonantly, with the broken body of Christ that makes the idea of a divine puppet both shocking and compelling. If holy things, including relics, resemble playthings, they do so not least in the various ways in which, and reasons for which, they both seem *already* to be broken and can subsequently be violently broken; this can make it difficult to determine whether such acts bespeak loathing or reverence (much like Baudelaire's brat, who might rip his toys apart because he reviles or reveres them). The logic of pious fragmentation, according to which the part was as efficacious as the whole, had the extraordinary effect of enabling a parallel logic, in which snapping a piece from a relic or dividing it into parts bespoke faith in its power and determination to disperse it ever further: I destroy it *because* I believe in it.[64] There were moments at which, when they failed in their protective duties to a community, relics might be ritualistically rebuked, cursed, or placed on the ground or on hair shirts in order to humiliate or prick them into action.[65] Again like toys, the breaking or chastising of such objects confirmed rather than denied their significance; this is not true only if the relic responds with miraculous liveliness, resisting partition or dividing itself spontaneously into pieces like the tooth of Thomas More, owned by the Jesuit uncles of John Donne, that "fell asunder and divided of itself" when the two were forced to part company.[66] Even in its mute materiality, the relic (like the puppet) might possess what Gell calls "passive agency," possessed by both dolls and sacred objects, in which an awareness that the child does everything for the doll (and the devotee for the object of devotion) "does not prevent them having the liveliest sensation that the doll is an alter ego and a significant social other."[67] Sacred objects in the Middle Ages could, as Philippe Buc stresses, be highly mobile, with new turns of events able to "create new readings which superimposed themselves on the original ... intentions" of those who approached them; iconoclastic play might be seen as perpetuating, rather than dispelling, the medieval object's preexisting mobility, the "spectrum of meanings" that it might "potentially summon."[68]

The relic's potential to be significant because of and not despite its brokenness was a feature, as well, in a related but distinct way, of the Eucharist, which was the preeminent manifestation of the divine as an emphatically fragmented, everyday, and—insofar as it tended miraculously to bleed or turn to flesh—potentially abject thing.[69] It is notable in this respect that the Eucharist, too, was mocked as a puppetlike plaything. There is a notable moment in John Foxe's *Acts and Monuments* in which the examination of Bishop Ridley by the Marian Bishop of Lincoln is recorded, and Ridley seeks to distance his own sermons delivered at St. Paul's Cross from those who rail indiscriminately at the sacrament of Communion, "terming it Jack of the boxe, the sacrament of the halter, round Robin, and like unsemely termes."[70] The *OED* gives this as the first instance of the phrase "Jack-in-the-Box" in written English, not as a description of the puppetlike plaything itself but of the solemn ceremony that this form of toy was invoked to mock.[71]

While puppets might be mocked in this way as obviously inane, however, they were also recognized as objects to which children might form genuine and enduring attachments. The translation of Philippe Mornay du Plessis's *A Woorke Concerning the Trewnesse of the Christian Religion*, begun by Sir Philip Sidney and completed by Arthur Golding, observes: "I pray thee how often hast thou taken from thy Childe a puppet or some other toye that he played withall, to see whether he be stubborne or no: How oft haste thou plucked the knife out of his hand, even when he cryed to have it still."[72] Attachment to a puppet was easy to mock but harder to overcome. The derision of a puppet God had to reckon with these powerful attachments, which echoed some of the deliberate challenges of late medieval piety: the believer, I suggest, was *expected* to experience and wrestle with the difficulty of encountering certain objects, especially relics, as *at once* the absolute highest and most foolish, prone to leap suddenly to life and prove their holiness, and at the same time as objects verging on the foolish, the trivial, even the disgusting. Amid these ways of materializing the divine, including the emphatically disjointed figure of the holy puppet, there is a fluctuation between reverence and disgust, brokenness and wholeness, violence and reverence. The iconoclasts who made holy things into playthings perpetuated these ambiguities by other means rather than dispelling them.

The scene of iconoclastic child's play therefore captures a different version of the volatile and fecund oscillations already present in late medieval religion between violence and reverent care, between foolishness and significance. If these richly conflicting possibilities are encapsulated in certain late medieval practices, and especially in holy puppets, they are by no means consigned solely to the past. I discussed in my opening chapter the way that iconoclasm and play recur in modern accounts of aesthetics, and I would like to end this chapter by arguing that the holy puppet, at once radiant and foolish in its brokenness, sheds important light on the aesthetics of objecthood in the present day. While there has been considerable interest in puppets in modern thought, these tend to take their inspiration from a limited set of traditions, circling in one way or another around Heinrich von Kleist's 1810 story "Über das Marionettentheater," especially Kleist's claim near the close: "Grace appears most purely in that human form which either has no consciousness or an infinite consciousness. That is, in the puppet or in the god."[73] The divinity of the puppet derives from its lack of self-consciousness—a blithe self-forgetting of which the human is incapable. Kleist was perpetuating a longer tradition, not of embodying the divine as a puppet but of understanding human-divine relations on the model of puppetry, most importantly formulated in Plato's *Laws*. "We may imagine," the Athenian claims in that dialogue, "that each of us living creatures is a puppet made by gods, possibly as a plaything, or possibly with some more serious purpose. That, indeed, is more than we can tell, but one thing is certain. These interior states are, so to say, the cords, or strings, by which we are worked; they are opposed to one another, and pull us with opposite tensions in the direction of opposite actions, and therein lies the division of virtue from vice."[74]

This seems to place humans at the mercy of cruel and whimsical gods—akin to Gloucester's lament in *King Lear*, "As flies to wanton boys, are we to the gods, / They kill us for their sport"—but, as Mihai Spariosu notes, for Plato being a divine puppet "is a cause for joy rather than for tragic lamentation."[75] This is partly because, as we saw in an earlier chapter, elsewhere in this text Plato insists that since the human is a toy for the gods, the best thing to do is to learn to play piously along: if the human is a puppet, we might say, she is apparently one possessed of some agency, some ability to grab and move the puppeteer's strings in response.[76] While this account might seem to point toward later living puppets such as Pinocchio, it can be read a different way. Plato's puppet might be an image not for total control but for the limits of control, a way of considering the tendency of objects shaped and yanked into certain forms of meaning (including children) to offer resistance, to assume a reciprocal agency of their own. Bruno Latour, describing what he sees as a modern fantasy of mastery over objects and materials, writes that "the marionette image is justified here, as long as the puppeteer is asked a few questions. She will tell you, as will everyone else—as will any creator and manipulator—that her marionettes dictate their behaviour to her: that they make her act; that they express themselves through her; that she could never manipulate them or mechanize them. And yet she holds them, dominates and masters them. She will straightforwardly admit that she is slightly outstripped by what she controls."[77] This account allows us to amalgamate the Platonic account of the puppet, in which the strings are pulled in both directions at once, with the account I have been developing, which sees the puppet as a fit vessel for the divine thanks to its very brokenness, its forlornness, its foolishness. The two are not mutually exclusive, nor are they as different as they seem: both suggest how the puppet can be divine because of, not despite, its wondrously forlorn material recalcitrance.

If the articulated puppet is, as I have argued, akin to relics and the Eucharist in its conflation of reverence and violence, of brokenness and cohesion, then these earlier forms of pious object can illuminate not just Kleist and other later avant-garde understandings of puppetry but wider aspects of the materiality of modern art-making.[78] Some of the apparently boldest experiments in twentieth-century art sought to trouble the distinction between creation and destruction, between breaking and making, and they sought to provoke a connected amalgamation of, or oscillation between, wonder and disgust. I am thinking, for example, of Lucio Fontana's works in which he slashed the canvas rather than daubing paint on it—the point being not to oppose creation to destruction but to amplify the destructive aspects of creation and the creative potential of destruction. The canvas becomes a new kind of thing when it is split asunder, just as a worshipper who snaps one relic into two or more pieces makes holiness radiate ever more intensely; just as the iconoclast who strikes at a statue with a hammer, or who places a holy thing in the hands of a playing child, tends not to abolish the object but to make it afresh; and just as the child, in turn, often does not ruin the toy by breaking a part of it but creates a new object to love and hate in turn. Richard Wollheim, in a classic essay, opposed the creative, romantic vision of the work of art-creation to another kind of work, "which is at once destructive and yet also creative, [and which] consists in the dismantling of some image which is fussier or more cluttered than the artist requires."[79] The artist removes, subtracts, and scrubs out, as well as patiently adds.

As Matthew Bown has noted, perhaps the works that most teasingly chime with the relic cult, in its periodic courting of disgust, not just the brokenness of its objects, are Piero Manzoni's cans purporting to contain "artist's shit"—as with a golden reliquary, the abject remainder of the charismatic figure who grants the object its power is present in its absence, concealed behind a metallic veneer that simultaneously foregrounds and erases itself as it is subordinated to the material remnant that may or may not lie within.[80] To return to my opening example from Biberach: if sacred puppets like the images of the Holy Ghost lowered through church roofs were indeed given to children as playthings, then, I would suggest, these objects of iconoclastic child's play belong not only to the history of early modern religion but to the prehistory of modern art. Such an object, like the contemporary artwork, has the capacity to be valuable even as it flaunts its mundanity and its capacity to disgust; it can be whole even as it manifests itself as definitively broken; it can captivate even as it parades its triviality and its foolishness. Patrick Collinson, discussing the long-term implications of Reformation iconoclasm, writes: "Thanks to the sixteenth century, it is clear to us that to speak of 'Our Lady of Walshingham' is not at all the same as to speak of Michelangelo's *Moses*. And yet, on the far side of that critical divide, an object of devotion, a work of art and a kind of animated doll or puppet might be all one and for any practical purpose the same thing as the saint who was represented and adored."[81] This is an acute account of pre-Reformation piety, but I would suggest that, in fact, the supposed clarity of separating holy thing, play thing, and art thing in modernity remains anything but clear. Any encounter with an object that might fit into any one of these categories can become both haunted and enlivened by each of the other two and actively informed by the difficulty that we have in keeping them apart.

Suggestive though these modern parallels are, let me return at the last to my point of origin, Roger Edgeworth's account of iconoclastic child's play in action. Edgeworth does not mention puppets, although the children holding the objects and "dauncynge them after their childyshe maner" do behave rather like Erasmus's Gratian Pullus with his puppets-in-translation. It is not here I want to look for a parallel, however, but rather, again, at the treatment of the children themselves by the parents, who enter and choreograph the play that transpires, anxiously shaping its meaning. This is the more important parallel—for the parents effectively want to treat the children as their puppets, determining and defining the meaning of their actions as if pulling strings to which they are attached.[82] The children are intended to become a version of the "kind of animated doll or puppet" described by Collinson—for the benefit of the adults. It is notable in this respect that one book of fifteenth-century school exercises included a warning against the manner in which "all the richest menys Childrenn everywher be lost nowadais in their youghe [youth] at home, and that with ther Fathers and mothers," specifically because "the mothers must have them to play withall stede of puppetes, as childrenn were borne to japes and tryfullys [trifles]."[83] Setting aside the patronizing misogyny of this claim, it is notable how easily the language of trifling and puppetry asserts itself when considering the adult's desire for control over the life and the meaning of the child.

As Plato and Latour suggest, however, the puppet is both an attractive metaphor for total control and imposition of the will in this manner and an imperfect one, precisely because the puppet, in its awkward, disjointed heft, tends to reassert its own agency, to dictate to the puppeteer as well as being dictated to, just as the playing of children often proves to be less amenable to adult control than the adults would wish. Just as iconoclastic child's play itself seems initially comprehensible but becomes ever more strange once one asks just what it was intended to prove and to achieve, the designation of a reviled object as a puppet has taken on a similar strangeness for me in the course of my discussion. Magnificently broken things in their disjointed foolishness, puppets and children are alike not in their triviality and the crafty ease with which they can be manipulated but precisely because they exemplify the collision between the utmost desire for (adult) human control and its recalcitrant limits.

4 FETISH

IN THE LATE SEVENTEENTH CENTURY a Dutch woman named Margrieta van Varick established a textile shop with her husband, Rudolphus, in Flatbush, which today is a neighborhood in Brooklyn. Margrieta had previously lived in Malacca (modern day Malaysia), and in the course of her peripatetic life she gathered objects from Europe, East Asia, and her North American surroundings, compiling a remarkable collection, the inventory of which came to light just a few years ago. The catalogue of the exhibition based on Margrieta's collection contained a discussion between Peter N. Miller and Natalie Zemon Davis, which included the following exchange:

PNM   One of the inventory items that has been a challenge for us to figure out is listed as "Indian Babies."

NZD   Indian babies?

PNM   So we are thinking . . .

NZD   Dolls? Baby dolls?

PNM   . . . small ceramic figures, probably from China but that are called "Indian," probably for "East Indian."

NZD   Of gods. Of divine figures. Well, yes, that's an interesting thing in the household of a Reformed minister's wife. Unless we are going to see this as an early example of ecumenism. That is interesting. They might be small statuettes of Indian gods, divinities. Hindu divinities.

PNM   Entering her collection, they might simply have been aestheticized or perhaps viewed as toys for the children.

NZD   Yes, yes, yes.

PNM   As they shift contexts, they also shed meaning. . . .

NZD   Yes, but if they were divinities, it would be quite a step for them to become toys for the children. I could imagine their becoming exoticized and then becoming a curiosity, but . . . This is really a fascinating puzzle. First of all, if it really were a statuette of an Indian divinity or a Hindu god, how would she have obtained it? Is this the kind of thing that would have been sold by some Indian merchant to a Dutch woman? Maybe it would be collected, or collected and then given as a gift. But you wouldn't think that an Indian believer would make a gift of an Indian statuette divinity to a nonbeliever.

PNM   Perhaps in a market stall where the husband or uncle is going to buy something else and picks it up on the side?

NZD   Then it could be picked up. And profaned. I would wonder about it being made a plaything for one's children, however, even if you completely de-exoticize and de-sacralize it and so forth. You know, there were still witchcraft beliefs in the late seventeenth century world, and in North America. And I would wonder more about its setting in a cabinet of curiosities than its becoming a toy, but perhaps I am wrong.

PNM   This is a question we have thought a lot about. . . .

NZD   . . . I would wonder what the term "Indian babies" was in the original Dutch. If I were making a film about it, it would be fun to imagine this colonial Dutchman turning to an African slave woman and saying "What is this?" And she says: "Well, that is an Indian baby." Or something that she knew from a connection with the Indians, or something of this kind.[1]

I have included this exchange at some length because it crystallizes and compresses many of the concerns that I have been developing but locates them in a significantly different world—an alternative region of collisions and possibilities. The examples of iconoclastic child's play that I have considered so far have been scattered, but within a relatively small area—Bristol, Lincolnshire, Cologne, Biberach—whereas the example that Miller and Zemon Davis discuss apparently involves objects moving across three continents, from East Asia back to Europe and thence to North America. Zemon Davis perfectly captures the baffling but intriguing suggestions of this all-too-brief mention in yet another list, a fact recorded in passing that seems to pulsate with manifold possibilities. In fact, the mention is so opaque that it is not even clear if we can categorize this as another instance of iconoclasm as child's play, since we know even less than in the other instances I have discussed of the reasons for which it took place; it was not part of a wider program of reformed iconoclasm from which it might derive its significance even as it swerved in new directions. Nevertheless, the outcome appears similar: objects that might once have been revered, representations of the divine in some sense, are dislodged from their prior location and end up as playthings for children—"babies," dolls, like those discussed in my second chapter. Miller identifies possible reasons for which the migration of these objects might have taken place— "they might simply have been aestheticized or perhaps viewed as toys for the children"—but concludes that "as they shift contexts, they also *shed* meaning." This is to identify the shifts involved as akin to the aims of iconoclasm—disenchantment, the reduction of the object to mute matter—but, as I have suggested, shedding an object's meaning is not as easy as it seems, just as I would again query Miller's use of "simply" to describe the object's aestheticization or becoming-toy: to transform a holy thing into either an art-thing or a plaything is also to open it to the possibility of new forms of meaningfulness neither reducible to, nor easily distinguishable from, its former state. Indeed, Zemon Davis is struck by the peculiar nature of the transition involved, insisting that it remains "a fascinating puzzle," and she finds herself both emphasizing the challenges of achieving total de-exoticization or desacralization and imagining the curious and tense domestic scenarios in which these objects might have been lodged, the interactions that might have continued to revolve around them.[2]

We might not be able to discover any more about what these objects were exactly or where and how Margrieta van Varick acquired them, but what is certain is that iconoclastic child's play of the sort that I have discussed in preceding chapters did take place in Dutch-colonized Malacca, the place in which she probably acquired these objects. The Dutch had tried to capture Malacca and its valuable trade routes since the early seventeenth century and finally succeeded in 1641, ousting the Portuguese, who had colonized it in the early sixteenth century. They set about ridding the region of the practices and material traces of Roman Catholicism, but their iconoclastic actions (like those carried out in Europe in the sixteenth century) often involved the ambiguous inversion and repetition of earlier rites rather than their outright abolition. While the Portuguese Jesuits had organized public processions of images on saints' days and other special occasions, as Tara Alberts observes in her fascinating account,

sporadically, [the] Jesuit Pedro Mesquita reported, the Dutch would demonstrate their disdain for popish images by confiscating pictures and ornaments. The continuing importance of these objects was thus tacitly acknowledged by their subsequent treatment: following a mocking public parade, the objects were disposed of, with those of less value given to children, "to play with them like dolls" [*para brincarem com ellas como bonecas*]. Their sacral power was thereby denied and undermined. Yet the futility of such ceremonies was demonstrated, according to Jesuit accounts, by the conversions won, achieved through prayers directed through images, or by non-believers coming into direct contact with Catholic objects.[3]

Alberts notes elsewhere that the Jesuit willingness to combine holy processions with drinking and dancing that had broad public appeal led to "accusations that missionaries were merely 'playing' at religion, attracting people to church with baubles without instilling true faith."[4] As in the European context, the decision to give these objects to children as dolls is clearly intended to actualize such criticisms. But the Jesuits' counterclaims suggest the same fragility of such practices for which I have been arguing throughout, since there was no guarantee that the contact with such objects facilitated by play would assure their continued ridicule. Margrieta van Varick may or may not have been aware of such practices in the milieu in which she acquired the "Indian Babies" that she would eventually bring to Flatbush, but that is not why I introduce these examples here. The cultural and geographic placement of these practices is a significant consideration in how we should understand them: what changes is not so much the objects themselves, or the play to which they give rise, but the number of communities potentially present when such play takes place, the divergent forms of understanding that converge on such actions, and the meanings that they can thereby accrue. To put it straightforwardly: in the European examples that I have thus far considered, iconoclastic child's play took place within a set of Christian communities that were in the process of splitting, fragmenting, and redefining themselves in relation to one another. But the stakes change when these actions are transplanted to Dutch Malacca and into a contested missionary and mercantile context. What we find here is not a binary relationship between two competing forms of Christianity but a complex triangular relationship, in which Jesuits and Dutch Protestants simultaneously seek to assert the superiority of their own religion both to that of their Christian enemies and to the religions of the local people whom they hope to convert.[5] In a disputed colonial context, then, the implicit polemical meaning of iconoclastic child's play is doubled: childishness is imputed by the Dutch simultaneously to the Jesuits and to local religions. If iconoclasm as child's play becomes a potentially potent form of polemical activity in this context, it also becomes yet more unstable and fraught with ambiguity, since the object that is played with finds itself suspended in a complicated force field of possible meanings and interpretations, capable of being read differently by different groups at different times. The unstable status of these objects—exemplified in different ways by Zemon Davis's perceptive uncertainty that the "Indian babies" could straightforwardly be aestheticized or desacralized by becoming toys and by Pedro Mesquita's insistence that playing with Catholic objects might lead to conversion rather than ridicule—suggests that iconoclastic child's play was particularly fraught and complex in the context of these triangular relationships.

In this chapter I continue my investigation of iconoclasm as child's play from a different kind of starting point. Whereas the words that have formed the title of my previous chapters have been everyday words drawn from the world of play that I have then sought to explore and rethink, in this chapter I begin with a well-known historical and theoretical category—the fetish—that is less obviously linked with child's play.[6] I do so in part because, as Willem Pietz showed in a series of seminal articles, the fetish emerged in a polemically loaded triangular context structurally similar to that which I have been describing, in which the Dutch and the Portuguese fought one another for both religious and commercial control over an indigenous population—not in the East Indies but on the west coast of Africa, from the fifteenth century onward.[7] I will not retrace many of the well-trodden paths of thought surrounding the fetish but hope to show that the word does, in its own distinctive way, stand at the crossroads of iconoclasm and child's play, or at least appears in a new light when placed at this crossroads. Webb Keane, expanding on Pietz's account in his discussion of more recent cross-confessional encounters in Indonesia, offers a useful general account of the scope and stakes of the fetish, broad enough to be applicable both to its first emergence and its later theoretical elaboration by Marx, Freud, and many others. "Talk about fetishism," Keane writes, "arises in the encounter between an observer and some sort of Other. To impute fetishism to others is to set in motion a comparison, as an observer recognises that someone else is attributing false value to objects."[8] This observation is particularly useful for my purposes because, just as I have sought to reorientate attention from the historical reality of the children involved in iconoclasm as child's play to the cultural force of the meanings *imputed* to the playing of children, Keane's account allows a parallel shift in regard to the fetish; rather than asking what a fetish is or what function it serves for the people to whom it matters (whether psychological, economic, or otherwise), we can ask what processes are at work when an object is described as a fetish or when fetishism is *ascribed* to a person or an entire people. As Keane observes, "To speak of fetishism is by implication to assert that one views the desires and acts of others with a clear eye."[9] Generally speaking, to designate fetishes or fetishism—very much like designating a given set of practices as mere, trifling child's play—is not only to denigrate their significance but, in the process, to assert that one has a perfect grasp of what they are and what they mean: this despite the fact that, in the psychoanalytic sense of the term, the fetishist is unusual in being, unlike the hysteric or the narcissist, perfectly happy, muddling along quite nicely in the midst of his or her pathologies.[10] Hence there is an initial and perhaps surprising connection between accounts of fetishism and descriptions of both iconoclasm and child's play: such accounts are often defensive, seeking to fix and to stabilize that which is troublingly unstable. As Keane puts it, "the discourse of fetishism, in its several varieties, is concerned in part with the true distinction between subjects and objects. . . . Talk about fetishism is especially concerned about the misattribution of agency, responsibility and desires to objects, to what the observer knows to be dead matter."[11] This "misattribution of agency" is what the idolater is invariably accused of by the iconoclast, but such "misattribution" is also, as we have seen, the everyday practice of the child at play.

If we begin by understanding the language of fetishism simply as a way of describing the wrong object valued in the wrong way and for the wrong reason, then criticizing these "other" forms of action and valuation becomes a way of negatively justifying the forms of value that obtain in the West without having to probe their basis too deeply. The fetish stands for a form of desire, belief, or conviction that can be labeled abnormal or aberrant; the fetishist becomes a scapegoat whose vilification ensures that the normalcy of prevailing desires and values goes unquestioned. As numerous scholars have valuably shown, the construction of fetishism has played a particularly potent role in the construal and regulation of racial and gender difference.[12] I propose in this chapter to develop these accounts by arguing that children, and their play, represent a particular kind of otherness that has occupied an insufficiently recognized role in the development and function of the fetish as a concept. The fetish contains, sedimented within it, a complex set of oscillations between religion and superstition, value and worthlessness, inanity and threat—precisely those instabilities that come to the fore in the scene of iconoclastic child's play itself. Childhood is a distinct form of otherness because it is (by definition and in theory) temporary, yet it is persistently aligned with, or serves as a figure for, otherness of various kinds—the woman, the savage, or the insane person as a perpetual child. The child is both a threat—the wild, untamed other in the heart of the household—and the form of otherness that seems (at least in theory) to be the easiest to tame, whether by proper education or by strategies of trivialization and sentimentalization. Nowhere is this instability clearer than in child's play—the most threateningly opaque and cheerily innocent form of activities—and it is also for this reason that the fetish, and the object of iconoclastic play, can be aligned in a process of mutually illuminating juxtaposition.

Rather than turning to the triangular sixteenth-century context in which fetishism emerged, I will take a more oblique approach, focusing first on some examples from twentieth-century anthropology that accentuate the difficulty in distinguishing religion and play as ways of relating to objects in non-Western contexts, especially among non-Western children. I then offer an account of the role of children and their play in the historical emergence of the category of the fetish, which both drew on—and sought to stabilize—the status of children as wild "misvaluers." Finally, I return from this excursion through the early modern to the modern and suggest how this historically informed account of children as both fetishists and fetishes can inflect the functioning of the concept today—especially as enabled by the writings of Theodor W. Adorno, in which, I argue, the toy and artwork emerge in parallel as objects that sustain their potential significance because of, and not despite, their tendency to be fetishized. It is the conspicuous combination of sensuous particularity and replaceability, of violence and care, of the replication of prevailing systems of value and their disruption that emerge for Adorno in both the art-thing and the plaything, and it is this commonality that the scene of iconoclastic child's play illuminates with unique clarity.

———————

Let me begin with Claude Lévi-Strauss, who was deeply interested, throughout his career, in the cultural significance of play. In the opening chapter of *La Pensée sauvage*, he ended his famous discussion of *bricolage* with a discussion of the relationship between rituals and games, concluding that although both are "played," rituals are conjunctive while games are disjunctive. Earlier in the same chapter, he discusses the formative role of playthings: "A child's doll is no longer an enemy, a rival or even an interlocutor. In it and through it a person is made into a subject."[13]

Elsewhere, he wrote of the ways in which iconoclastic action and social attitudes toward children come to be intertwined, especially in his dazzling discussion of an incident in Dijon in 1951, in which an effigy of Father Christmas was publically hanged and then burned before several hundred Sunday school pupils: Lévi-Strauss ingeniously argued that "beyond the conflict between children and adults lies a deeper dispute between the living and the dead," and he linked this conflict to the numerous festivals revolving around "those who, in one way or another, are incompletely incorporated into the group, who, that is, share the *otherness* which symbolizes the supreme dualism: that of the dead and the living . . . foreigners, slaves, and children." We will return to these interrelated forms of otherness in a later chapter. For now I would note that the story of Father Christmas, in this virtuosic account, exemplifies the dynamics of what I have called, following Michael Taussig, "the adult's imagination of the child's imagination": Lévi-Strauss explores the function *for adults* of what he calls "the muddled prayer we increasingly offer each year to little children—traditional incarnations of the dead—in order that they consent, by believing in Father Christmas, to believe in life."[14] Though he does not use these specific examples, it is notable that Boris Wiseman begins his recent discussion of Lévi-Strauss's aesthetics with an account of the anthropologist as a boy building a miniature Japanese house in a box. Wiseman reads this anecdote by way of Baudelaire's essay on the toy, which "presents the child's relationship to his toys as the prototype of the adult's relationship to the work of art," and suggests that Lévi-Strauss's lifelong determination "to understand the nature of his 'intimate relation' to the objects that so fascinated him" was an extension of these early toy-relations.[15]

Whether or not this biographical claim is accurate, these discussions of play, particularly because of the seemingly clear distinction that he draws between play and ritual in *La Pensée sauvage*, have tended to be read in terms of what Rosalind Morris calls Lévi-Strauss's "infinite binarisms"—the dyadic splitting of complex phenomena in order to understand them—that came to be synonymous with high structuralism.[16] When we turn to Lévi-Strauss's ethnographic writings, however, this drive toward the binary is far less clear-cut. The moment on which I want to focus occurs only fleetingly, in the context of his fieldwork in Brazil. In the mid-1930s Lévi-Strauss visited and studied the Kadiwéu, or Caduveo, an indigenous people in central Brazil, and wrote at length about their customs and practices in *Tristes Tropiques*, published nearly two decades later in 1955. While he was principally fascinated by their complex systems of body painting, and by the violent processes through which they killed their children and adopted "replacement" children from neighboring tribes, he also observed their children at play:[17]

As playthings for the children, the women made figures representing characters or animals with anything that came to hand—clay or wax, or dried husks, which they simply adapted to the required shape by the addition of modelling.

We also saw the children playing with little, carved wooden statues, usually dressed in cheap finery, which served them as dolls [*qui leur servaient de poupées*], while other statuettes of similar type were carefully preserved by a few old women at the bottom of their baskets. Were these toys [*jouets*]? Divine statues? Or figures representing ancestors? One cannot say since they served contradictory purposes, and especially since the same statuette might have first one function, then the other. Some, which are now in the Musée de l'Homme in Paris, have an undeniably religious significance, since one can be recognized as the Mother of the Twins, and another as the Little Old Man, a god who came down from heaven and was ill-treated by mankind. . . . On the other hand, it would be too facile to interpret the handing over of the *santos* to the children as a symptom of the collapse of a religion; this situation, which seems so unstable to us, had been described in exactly the same terms by Boggiani forty years before, and by Frič ten years after him; it is also mentioned in observations made ten years after mine. Circumstances which remain unchanged for fifty years must, in some sense, be normal.[18]

This is a remarkable moment in Lévi-Strauss's description, in which he dwells on the ethnographic confusion between sacred object and plaything. Arguing that the two categories are not identical and that distinctions can be made, he nonetheless acknowledges not only that the categories of cult object and toy overlap in practice but that a society can function perfectly well in the midst of this confusion. I argued in Chapter 2 that the confusion of dolls and other kinds of figurines is inescapable rather than incidental, and here we see the same potential for indistinguishability in action, played out in the context of the alien society that the anthropologist observes. Crucially—and I will return to this point in the next chapter—Lévi-Strauss identifies the status of these objects as something that shifts and changes through time ("the same statuette might have first one function, then the other"), such that the problem of categorizing can never be solved once and for all. There is not one use that is proper and primary, from which the other derives. Lévi-Strauss's sincere interest in these objects is suggested by the fact that he acquired the items "in the Musée de l'Homme in

Paris," initially for his private collection, before he was required to sell them in
1951 (along with a set of Kachina dolls that he sold to Jacques Lacan).[19] These objects are anthropomorphic but lacking in ornamental detail—some have carved
limbs, one has arms but no facial features, another is effectively a block of wood
with eyes, nose, mouth, and a neck—and their very simplicity seems paradoxically to make them more amenable to the forms of ambiguity that Lévi-Strauss
describes, as if it is their relative blankness that allows them to move fluidly between piety and play.[20]

What distinguishes Lévi-Strauss's analysis is his willingness to acknowledge
this ambiguity as irreducible rather than seeking to resolve it with a piece of
virtuosic ethnographic interpretation. The other accounts of the Kadiwéu to
which he refers are by ethnographers who have now mostly fallen into obscurity,
but, if one takes the trouble to track down their accounts, Lévi-Strauss's claim
is accurate: Guido Boggiani identifies some "*ídolos*" with which children play
"*a modo de bonecas*" (the same Portuguese term for a doll used by the Jesuits in
sixteenth-century Malacca) but links this growing indifference to a form of religion "*em declínio*"; A. V. Frič's account contains pictures of two sets of objects,
which are often indistinguishable from one another, but he nonetheless identifies
one set as "*Holz-Idole*" (wooden idols) and another as "*Puppen*" without justifying the basis on which such a distinction is made.[21] The "observations made ten
years after mine" to which Lévi-Strauss refers are probably, as his editors suggest, those of Kalervo Oberg—who adds some more local color, claiming that
the "small wooden figures . . . that look like dolls" are carved by shamans and
put into children's beds to guard against evil spirits—and Darcy Ribeiro, who
quotes these earlier accounts while adding little analysis but, notably, does so
in a section of his book titled "*Fetiches*," the first of the ethnographers whom
I have considered to use this specific and loaded term.[22] Before I return to the
concept of the fetish, however, I want to insist again on the feature that distinguishes Lévi-Strauss's analysis from these other accounts. When he considers
Boggiani's claim that children playing with sacred objects is a sign of religious
decline, Lévi-Strauss continues: "There has certainly been a decline in religious
values, but the explanation is to be sought not so much in this as in a way of
dealing with the relationship between the sacred and the profane which is com-
moner than we are inclined to think. The opposition between the two terms is
neither as absolute nor as continuous as has sometimes been asserted."[23] Like
Natalie Zemon Davis considering the "Indian Babies" of Margrieta van Varick,

he allows play, piety, and impiety provocatively to overlap rather than partition-ing them too neatly; these modes of relating to this array of figurines can neither be elided entirely nor be neatly distinguished. It is a constitutive fact about the categories of object and action that they overlap with and periodically come to resemble one another. The actions of the Kadiwéu in blurring these boundaries are a sign neither of straightforward decline nor confusion on their part; rather, for Lévi-Strauss their actions demonstrate that sacred things and playthings are, structurally and necessarily, *confusable*.

Where does this brief ethnographical excursion leave us? One specific outcome is that it might lead us to rethink the use of Lévi-Strauss made by some theorists of play.[24] As I noted in my first chapter, it was as a critique of Lévi-Strauss that Jacques Derrida first advanced his enormously influential account of the "move-ment of play, permitted by the lack or absence of a centre or origin": he associates Lévi-Strauss with *"sure* play . . . limited to the *substitution* of *given* and *existing, present,* pieces," and with a form of interpretation that "dreams of deciphering a truth or an origin which escapes play," and he opposes to this his mode: "Nietzs-chean *affirmation*, that is the joyous affirmation of the play of the world."[25] It may be, however, that this moment in *Tristes Tropiques* anticipates and preemptively complicates Derrida's critique, for what Lévi-Strauss insists on is precisely that the scene of child's play in this Brazilian village *cannot* be definitively deciphered; he is, and consents to remain, unsure of both the meaning and the parameters of this play and of its objects.[26] His ethnographic encounter with these children precisely undoes the clearer conceptual distinction between ritual and play that he postu-lates in *La Pensée sauvage* and pushes him to rethink "the relationship between the sacred and the profane" in general as potentially inextricable. This occurs not through affirming the highly abstract "play of the world" that Derrida envisages but through attention to the concrete actions of the children.

If Levi-Strauss's ethnographic tact can complicate the role he played in de-constructive play, it also provides me with an opportunity to say something about psychoanalytic approaches to play—a relevant consideration for this chapter, given the psychoanalytic use of the concept of the fetish. Thus far I have re-ferred to psychoanalysis only intermittently, although it has deeply informed my thinking about iconoclasm as child's play. In fact, Freud himself wrote very seldom of child's play, beyond the account of the Fort-Da game in *Beyond the*

Pleasure Principle and his rich but short account of the child at play as akin to the creative writer, in that each "creates a world of his own, or, rather, re-arranges the things of his world in a new way which pleases him."[27] It was thanks to the influence of Melanie Klein, and the rise of the British Object Relations school of psychoanalysis, that child's play came to the fore in psychoanalytic practice, and I have already cited thinkers broadly in this tradition such as D. W. Winnicott and Christopher Bollas.[28] What interests me in this context, however, is not so much any specific psychoanalytic interpretation *of* child's play but the way in which psychoanalysts were divided on the question of whether child's play should be interpreted at all; this question encapsulated the broader uncertainty, inherited from Freud's richly self-divided oeuvre, of whether psychoanalysis should strive for definitive interpretations of psychic phenomena, or whether these were secondary (and sometimes directly opposed) to the patient's ability to live well.[29] There was, for any psychoanalyst, a question as to whether the roots of an individual fetish *should* be subjected to scrutiny if the patient was getting along just fine. The same question arose in relation to the playing child, and the differing stances assumed by Klein and Winnicott are particularly instructive. Klein's preoccupations resemble my own in certain respects. She insists on the meaningfulness of moments of aggression toward toys, insisting that "the child's attitude towards a toy he has damaged is very revealing" and can involve "fluctuations between love and hatred." Yet what is particularly notable is her insistence on "the importance of interpretations for play technique" and her belief that the analyst both *can* and *should* offer to the child interpretations of the ways in which he or she plays: "constant interpretations," she advocates at one point.[30] Klein believes that these interpretations can be accommodated to the child's mode of understanding and that "the effect of such knowledge, gradually elaborated, is simply to relieve the child" of paralyzing anxiety.[31]

It is on this point that Klein differs most significantly from Winnicott, whose influential account of the child's "transitional object" insisted that the child should not be quizzed as to its nature, asked to interpret or subjected to interpretation: "we agree never to make the challenge to the baby: did you create this object, or did you find it conveniently lying around?"[32] The child's relationship to these charged objects should be allowed to *remain* mysterious, both to the child and to watching adults, including the analyst. As Barbara Johnson puts it: "the transitional object is part of a contract of nonformulation."[33] For Winnicott the aim of analysis is not to give the child helpful interpretations but to allow the child to recapture an ability to play that has been blocked or arrested, and there are many occasions on which the analyst's interpretations are entirely superfluous, would only impede further play. Analysis is in large part for him an exercise in tact and requires the ability to hold one's own ingenuity (or desire to feel or appear ingenious) in check: "the significant moment is that at which the child surprises himself or herself. It is not the moment of my clever interpretation that is significant."[34] Elsewhere, describing an insight at which one of his patients arrived in the course of analysis, Winnicott notes: "Here was an example of an interpretation made by the patient that could have been stolen from her if I had made it earlier in the session."[35]

I am not suggesting that child's play should never be interpreted, but I would suggest that Winnicott's psychoanalytic reticence resonates with Lévi-Strauss's ethnography in that both can help us to attend to the particularities of iconoclastic child's play, as a form of action that itself illuminates the conflicting kinds of attention that child's play in general can attract, the challenging sense in which it seems both to exclude and to draw in the adult observer. Yet for all of these illuminating similarities, their settings are significantly different insofar as Lévi-Strauss attends to the play of non-Western children. As I discussed in my preface, so-called savages were construed, in and before the early modern period, as children by nature, and children and savages were groups to whom extremes of depravity and naive innocence could be imputed at different moments. Within these broader dynamics the savage child has always been a complex category: such a creature, uncivilized by virtue of both race and age, is doubly Other; but the sentimental temptation to see the child as innocent, closer to nature, not yet tainted fully by the savage environs in which he or she exists, makes the savage child a testing ground for the competing forces of natural and cultural influence. The non-Western child might be doubly savage or only half a savage.

There is often a particular temptation to minimize cultural difference when it comes to children at play, as if this most spontaneous and natural activity were one place in which difference could be circumnavigated. Brian Upton, for example, insists that "everywhere we look, *how we play* is the same."[36] This assumption was profoundly challenged by pioneering anthropologists like Bronislaw Malinowski and Margaret Mead, whose work focused at various points on such playing as a crucial node of cultural analysis.[37] While these studies, like Lévi-Strauss in *Tristes Tropiques*, suggest that the role and nature of child's play differ among cultures, they also confirm that child's play is a challenging mixture of the readily familiar and the resolutely opaque, regardless of the context in which it is encountered. The nature of this mixture may change, but the difficulty of interpreting such activity, of fixing and confirming its meaning, does not. The value of these modern analyses for my own attempts to explore iconoclastic child's play lies in the fact that anthropologists often have reasons, via their ethnographic work, to bring the opacity of child's play to the fore when they describe cultures like the Kadiwéu, in which the boundaries of such play seem unclear or in which play takes startling, unexpected, and sometimes horrifying forms. In the eminent play-theorist Gregory Bateson's early ethnographic work in Papua New Guinea, for example, Bateson described the ceremonies of the Iatmul tribe known as "Naven," undertaken to mark notable accomplishments. Bateson showed that these enormously significant ceremonies often had a histrionic and exaggerated quality that seemed to resemble play, and they seemed to generate parodic forms: as well as the more sober ceremonial house, for example, "there is a small junior ceremonial house for the boys. Here they carry out in miniature the ceremonial of the senior house and here they imitate their elders in mixing pride with buffoonery."[38] I will return to scenes of this sort, in which it becomes difficult to distinguish educative preparation for ritual from its parodic deflation, in the next chapter; what interests me here is that Bateson also describes a more brutal side to this ambiguity between ritual and play. When a group of children playing in the river, "shooting the straight stalks of elephant grass with toy spear-throwers," accidentally fired one into a canoe and pierced the string bag containing croton leaves used to ornament representations of the demonic figure known as *wagan*, the boy responsible was killed for his sacrilegious act.[39] Play is allowed to shadow and mock ritual in this tribal context, but, if it disrupts it in the wrong fashion, it is violently excised. In his later work Bateson produced a subtle and influential account of how animals and humans distinguish playful and nonplayful acts—how playful acts communicate the implicit message "this is play"—but he continued to stress "the labile nature of the frame 'This is play,' or 'This is ritual,' " and insisted that "the ritual blows of peacemaking are always liable to be mistaken for the real blows of combat."[40] Bateson first recognized this potential for the confusion of the playful and the deeply serious through the forms of child's play encountered in his ethnographic fieldwork.[41]

More recently, Stephen Lee Rubenstein has discussed a practice among the Shuar in Latin America that seems, on the surface, to closely resemble iconoclastic child's play. The Shuar would traditionally collect shrunken heads known as "tsantas" as the ultimate sign of victory in battle; when they returned victorious, a set of ceremonies would take place in which these objects were invested with enormous power. "Accounts of what happened to the tsantas after the feasts are contradictory," Rubenstein notes.[42] Some Western observers claim that they were kept as souvenirs or endorsements, but Philippe Descola insists that "the tsanta is not a relic commemorating some exploit. At the end of the ritual it is simply discarded, without fuss. Nor is it a kind of amulet, a source of energy and power. . . . Far removed from the robust vitality of the fetish, this object without substance or content functions, rather, as a logical operator, an abstract mark of identity which . . . can be used to construct new identities."[43] Rubenstein mentions in a footnote an account by an American engineer at the very end of the nineteenth century that seems to support Descola's argument. The engineer, de Graff, observed the feats of a culturally similar tribe called the Aguaruna, after which "the heads themselves have now lost their value. . . . It is curious that the fanatical jealousy with which they are guarded up to the time of the festival should give place to that complete indifference which allows them to be thrown to the children as playthings and finally lost in river or swamp."[44] Rubenstein observes that this account may reflect European beliefs about such practices rather than their reality, but this is precisely my point: in describing such play as "indifference," this observer is imagining the Aguaruna, imagining their children, and imagining them imagining their children, all at once. The nineteenth-century account assumes that giving these objects to children can only connote "complete indifference," and Descola's account, in which the heads are "simply discarded," seems to support this. But his insistence that the object thus liberated from its ceremonial setting "can be used to construct new identities" opens up the possibility, as with iconoclastic child's play, that what might seem to Western eyes like trivialization or indifference could also include an openness to novelty, to future possibilities, created in play. Once again the encounter with the alien religious object as a toy seems to fix its meaning but serves ultimately to destabilize it—as if child's play captures in miniature the challenges of ethnographic as well as analytic observation, revealing the possibility that those actions that seem most natural and quotidian, the sorts of thing that we frequently see Western children undertaking, could in fact be utterly alien and opaque in their meanings. Interpretation of such activity can neither be abandoned nor assured; the possibility of absolute difference can neither be asserted nor disavowed. This is always the potential and profound challenge of the child at play.

The concept of the fetish has surfaced once or twice in the preceding discussion, used by Darcy Ribeiro and Philippe Descola. I now want to return to where I began and suggest that we can see this theoretically ubiquitous concept in a new way if we relate it to these ethnographic and psychoanalytic problems of interpreting children, their play, and their playthings. In fact, I want to argue, the concept of the fetish emerged in part from the prehistory of the anthropological problems that I have been discussing. Throughout the historical vicissitudes of the term, the child's presence has been a near-constant, with the child either seen as uncivilized fetishist or the fetishist as uncivilized child. This is true of Rousseau, who uses "the fetishes of Negroes" to argue that "every child who believes in God is, therefore, necessarily an idolater"; it is true of Auguste Comte, for whom, as Sarah Kofman observes, fetishism is "a kind of childhood period in which the human spirit was least developed"; it is of course true of Freud, whose appropriation and reinvention of fetishism involves a specific narrative of childhood development, in which the fetish is a surrogate penis created by the child's unconscious as compensation for "the woman's (the mother's) penis the little boy once believed in and—for reasons familiar to us—does not want to give up"; and it is true in a different way of Adorno, who calls musical fetishism "childish" and its regressive quality "the reversion to a childhood."[45] In fact, this set of connections between the fetishist and the child emerges in the work that coined the term *fétichisme*, with specific reference to the behavior of children at play. In *Du Culte des dieux fétiches*, Charles de Brosses writes:

When we see that men in such different centuries and climates, who had nothing in common apart from their ignorance and their barbarism, have had similar practices, it is even more natural to conclude that man is made in such a way that if he is left in his raw and savage natural state, not yet formed by any reflective idea or imitation, primitive mores are the same as practices in Egypt as well as in the Antilles, in Persia as well as in Wales. . . . Since no-one is astonished to see children who do not raise their minds above their dolls, believing them to be animated [*l'on ne s'étonne pas de voir les enfans ne pas élever leur esprit plus haut que leurs poupées, les croire animées*] and interacting with them in keeping with that belief, why would we be surprised to see peoples, who constantly spend their lives in perpetual childhood and who are never more than four years old, reason without any sense and act how they reason?[46]

If this strain in the history of the fetish has not been adequately recognized, it is precisely because it seems so obvious, so ready-to-hand: of course savages are compared to children, and of course their ritual is demeaned as mere play. I hope that we are now better placed, in the light of the arguments of the preceding chapters, to step back from the obviousness of de Brosses's analogy, and turn it on its head. One form of activity—barbaric religious practice—is demeaned via comparison with another piece of supposedly obvious shallow nonsense—children's play with their dolls—and the comparison takes the place of explanation by implying that in neither case is there anything to explain. There is no *there* there: the shared emptiness of such practices is supposedly clear for all to see.

Reinserting de Brosses's account into a longer history of fetishism, I would argue that the apparently offhanded confidence of this comparison is a poker-faced but ultimately anxious and defensive instance of the strategies of trivialization that we have repeatedly encountered in relation to iconoclastic discourses of child's play. One set of practices that is opaque and difficult to understand, that seems to operate according to a troublingly alien set of norms and values, is being tamed and nullified by comparison with another. Here, again, Bruno Latour's analysis is helpful. Returning to the early modern context in which the fetish as a concept first emerged as a way of stabilizing alien beliefs about the nature of subjects and objects and the limits of agency, Latour observes that Europeans persistently imputed to the Africans whom they met the belief that their idols and fetishes were potent, godlike, alive; but, he insists, in fact such religious practice "has nothing to do with belief, it is all about behavior." In fact, he goes on to claim provocatively, "No one in practice has ever displayed naive belief in any being whatsoever."[47] Or rather, to put it in necessarily tortuous terms, when Europeans imputed naive belief to Africans, the only naive belief truly present was their belief in this belief: only they practiced the error that they professed to condemn. Elsewhere, Latour describes iconoclasm as this form of misconstrual put into violent practice: "It is only when the statue is hit by the violent blow of the iconoclast's hammer that it becomes a potential idol, naively and falsely endowed with powers that it does not possess. . . . Before it was smashed to bits, the idol was something else, not a stone mistaken for a spirit or any such thing."[48] There is a parallel of sorts here with Baudelaire's account of the child who breaks the toy not to deny that it possesses a soul but precisely in order to find it: violence toward the object is *predicated upon* belief, reinscribing rather than abolishing it.

Identifying the recurrent presence of children and their playing in discussions of the fetish, I am suggesting, opens up new vantage points on the history and the utility of this overdetermined concept, which both illuminates and is illuminated by the practices of iconoclastic child's play. As Pietz has shown, the fetish emerged in a context that placed enormous pressure on European conceptions of value, both religious and economic, that circled yet again the idea of the trifle: "Just as blacks seemed to overestimate the economic value of trifles, so they were perceived to attribute religious value to trifling objects."[49] Fetishes were preeminently *misvalued* objects, imbued with a degree of value that was both extravagant (that is to say, entirely arbitrary or disproportionate according to Western standards) and unstable: any object could become a fetish, and the fetish might be revered one minute and disregarded the next. It was this combination of arbitrariness and instability, I have argued, that made the comparison with child's play appealing; indeed, it emerged in the very earliest identifications of fetishism in West Africa, a century and a half before de Brosses. In his account of Guinea from 1602, translated into English as part of Samuel Purchas's vast compendium of travel accounts, the Dutchman Pieter de Marees claims that the Guineans "play many apish and childrens sports, thinking that they doe excellent well," and that they use "many foolish toyes and vaine shewes" in their prayer.[50] In his Dutch original, as Pietz points out, Marees deployed a variety of terms for this childish play—*Apenspel, Guychelspel,* and especially *Kinderspel.*[51]

When Protestants like Marees deployed language of this sort, the mockery that they aimed at African fetishists blended seamlessly with the language of anti-Catholic polemic: the Guineans, he wrote, "hang divers Wispes of straw about their Girdles, which they tie full of Beanes, and other *Venice* Beades, esteeming them to be their *Fetissos,* or Saints."[52] The apparent offhandedness of this postulated equivalence—"*Fetissos,* or Saints"—is a fine piece of polemical nonchalance. In a slightly later period the Dutch trader Willem Bosman wrote that "if it was possible to convert the Negroes to the Christian religion, the Roman-Catholics would succeed better than we should, because they already agree in several particulars."[53] Yet the breeziness of these trifold dismissals on the part of Protestants—of native Guineans, children, and Roman Catholics as equally inane players—sought to gloss over the multiple challenges that fetishes presented. European Protestant responses to local fetishisms were necessarily equivocal. On the one hand, mocking Africans for their inane behavior was supposed to have a salutary and edifying effect. The women who "play many apish and childrens sports," Marees writes, "desire not to be seene by strangers, because they laugh and jest at them, and then they are ashamed." The Dutch tried to use this shame for their own ends. Some Guineans "have as firme an opinion of their *Fetissos* as possible may be. But when the *Netherlanders* saw them use such vaine toyes, which were so foolish, and laught and jested at them, they were ashamed, and durst make no more *Fetissos* in our presence, but were ashamed of their owne apishnesse." Ultimately he hopes that they might "beginne to leave those foolish toyes, and to have some understanding of Gods Word, which they do by reason that wee mocke and jest at their foolish ceremonies."[54] This was in keeping with the widespread insistence that, in the words of Sir George Peckham, "the use of trade and traficke, (bee it neever so profitable) ought not to bee preferred before the planting of Christian fayth."[55]

These lofty words were largely hollow, however; the same Peckham advocated that to establish "trade and traficke with Infidels or Savages . . . there must be presented unto them gratis, some kindes of our prittie merchaundizes and trifles: As looking Glasses, Bells, Beads, Bracelets, Chains. . . . For such be the things, though to us of small value, yet accounted by them of high price and estimation."[56] Similar accounts were rife in European writings, but, as Jeffrey Knapp suggests, there was more than a little bluster about these English claims, since "the savage love of trifles speaks directly to England's fears . . . about its own extravagant trading habits."[57] There was a long-standing concern that English patterns of trade and consumption were disadvantageous, with the country's wealth being squandered on luxuries and trivialities, often decried using the language of child's play—from as early as the 1436 poem *The Libelle of Englyshe Polycye*, which lamented the import of "thynges of complacence" from Venice and Lombardy, mere "Apes and japes and marmusettes taylede, / Nifles, trifles, that litell have availed," to Thomas Smith bemoaning the import of "glasses, puppets, rattles and such things" in the sixteenth century.[58]

Once we recognize that the European accounts of native fetishism were partly defensive—that they mocked the Guineans and other non-Western peoples as the naive, misvaluing children that they feared they themselves might be—the intersection between fetish and plaything takes on a different tenor, coming to function as an index not of obvious and glaring difference but of forms of potential similarity that can only awkwardly be acknowledged. If we read further into Marees's account, we find that, for all its derision of mere *Apenspel*, *Guychelspel*, and *Kinderspel*, Marees was fascinated by Guinean children and the prominent role that fetishes played in their lives:

The children being a moneth or two old, then they hang a Net about the bodie thereof, like a little shirt, which is made of the barke of a tree, which they hang full of their *Fetissos*, as golden Crosses, strings with Corall about their hands, feet, and neckes, and their haire is filled full of shels, whereof they make great account, for they say, that as long as the young childe hath that Net about him, the Devill cannot take nor beare the child away. . . . The Corals which they hang about the child, which they call a *Fetisso*, they esteeme much, for that hanging such a *Fetisso* about the childes necke, they say, it is good against vomiting; the second *Fetisso*, which they hang about his necke, they say, it is good against falling[;] the third, they say, is good against bleeding; the fourth, is very good to procure sleepe, which they hang about the necke thereof, in the night-time, that it may sleepe well; the fift, is good against wild beasts, and the unwholsomenesse of the Aire, with diuers other such like *Fetissos*, each having a name a-part, to shew what vertue it hath, and what they are good for.[59]

It becomes clear in this extraordinarily detailed passage that the fetish is not simply a trivial trinket that can easily be mocked and shamed by Western observers, with pedagogical effect. Marees is well aware that such objects provide ways of carefully ordering, structuring, and safeguarding the child's existence. The fetishes with which the child is adorned proliferate, but they do so as part of a carefully managed system in which each has its role and function.[60] It is notable that Marees does not subject this practice to mockery. In fact, he is grudgingly admiring of the way that the Guineans raise their children, admitting that "they teach their children to goe [i.e., walk] very young . . . and teach them to speake very soone, whereby you find many children there among them that can both goe and speake ere they bee a yeare old, and some of them speake so plainly, that you may understand what they say in their Language, for they speake and goe farre sooner then our children doe, which we wondred at, besides this, they are strong, fat and well disposed."[61] Being festooned with fetishes clearly does these children no harm. Quite the opposite. In this moment the Guineans seem not so much like an entirely inferior and childish people as like a strange inversion of European generational norms, with their infantile, superstitious adults and their precocious, even superior children.

Little has been written about European attitudes to non-Western children, but the fleeting discussions of them in early modern texts tend to capture *in nuce* their strange status, seen at once as transparently knowable and as threateningly other and opaque—the same tension, as I have suggested, that is integral to the instabilities of iconoclastic child's play. This is true, too, of colonial contexts, even when the language of fetishism was not invoked, such as in North America. The mathematician Thomas Hariot's widely read work *A Briefe and True Report of the New Found Land of Virginia* (1588) seems to reproduce the tropes of colonial bafflement and contempt inspired by the chronic misvaluations of the Virginians: "In respect of us they are a people poore, and for want of skill and judgement in the knowledge and use of our things, do esteeme our trifles before thinges of greater value." Their childish naivety was confirmed by their initial response to the English: they "began to make a great an horrible crye. . . . But beenge gentlye called backe, we offred them of our wares, as glasses, knives, babies, and other trifles, which we thought they delighted in." Hariot also described the "yonge daugters of 7. or 8. yeares old" in the town of Pomeioock who "are greatlye Diligted with puppets, and babes which wear brought oute of England," and also depicted one at her play.[62]

While the adults won over by mere trifles suggest the ease with which advantageous trade might be conducted, and therefore confirm the difference between traveler and native and the superiority of colonizer over colonized, the description of the children suggests a point of cultural similarity. The English may cast themselves as adults and the native Virginians as children, but English children play with the very same objects and are prone to the same misvaluations. The natural propensity of the Virginian girls to play with the same dolls and rattles as their English counterparts might confirm that the Virginians are *intrinsically* infantile: the image, like the descriptions of all the people and then the children in particular as delighted by "babies, and other trifles, . . . puppets, and babes," might be designed to conflate adult and child, to suggest that this is a people whose childhood is perpetual, whose putatively adult religious and cultural practices are just so much play. Alternatively, it might be that these children, once given Western playthings, comfortingly resemble English infants. This might be the first step toward culture and away from savagery. While Hariot does not use the language of fetishism, his text captures the equivocal manner in which, in the early modern period, the plaything in the hands of the Other became a potential locus of wildly oscillating misvaluation—whether this Other was located on the Guinean or Virginian coast, or was one's own child, the Other at home.

Iconoclasm as child's play can usefully illuminate and be illuminated by the history of the fetish as a concept, then, because it alerts us to the role that children and their playing have assumed in this history. I would like to end this chapter by turning from anthropological and psychoanalytic to broadly Marxist accounts of the fetish and suggest why the object of iconoclastic child's play might be a meaningful forebear for the modern fetish. Andrew Cole has recently argued that Marx's account of commodity fetishism should be read as an engagement with, and development of, "a fundamentally medieval eucharist drawn from Hegel."[63] There can be no doubt that Hegel was perpetuating the polemical strategies begun by Protestants like Marees and Bosman when he implicitly juxtaposed "Negro" fetishists, who revere "the first thing that comes in their way" such that the object of reverence is in fact "the fancy of the individual projecting itself into space," with Roman Catholics who idolized "the Host, this *Thing* . . . set up to be adored as God," but whose conception of the highest holiness is, like the rampant but ultimately meaningless object world of the African fetishist, fragmented into "isolated and detached phenomena, in which the rational form of existence is utterly perverted."[64] I would add to Cole's account that Hegel may have had the medieval cult of relics equally in mind—another form in which the holy was subject to potentially endless fragmentation, as we have seen, and even more akin to fetishism in that whereas only bread and wine can be transubstantiated, any object, no matter how lowly or incidental, can become a relic and hence a receptacle for sacred power. One particular feature of fetishism as it was described by Westerners that had its counterpart in the medieval cult of relics was the infliction of violence and punishment on objects that failed to fulfill their apotropaic role: "If any mischance occurs which the Fetich [*sic*] has not averted," Hegel wrote, "if rain is suspended, if there is a failure in the crops, they bind and beat or destroy the Fetich and so get rid of it, making another immediately."[65] As I mentioned in the last chapter, this sort of coercive or outraged violence was sometimes aimed at saints' relics in medieval Europe, part of an oscillating dynamic between tentative care and indignant rejection that created the potential resemblance between the cult and child's play.

Though he includes a single formulaic dismissal of Catholics' "absurd and childish" credulity, however, Hegel makes nothing of the polemical dismissal of such practices as mere child's play that was such a pronounced feature of Protestant polemic. This is despite the fact that Hegel was responding in part to Kant's more scattered account of fetishism, and, as Rosalind Morris acutely notes, "the fetish and play are linked for Kant," with the fetish operating as a corrupted form of the sublimity that is one goal of aesthetic play.[66] There is no sign of such play in Hegel's reading, but if we follow Cole's reading of Marx's engagement with these earlier traditions and reconsider Marx's careful reading of de Brosses in

1842 (including, as we saw, de Brosses's comparison of barbarians to children "believing that their dolls are animate and acting with them accordingly"), then the famous account of the "transubstantiated" materiality of the commodity in *Das Kapital* appears in a different light.[67] "A commodity," Marx writes in a famous passage, "appears at first sight an extremely obvious, trivial thing." Once wood, "an ordinary sensuous thing," enters into a commodified form as a table with a specific value, however, "it changes into a thing which transcends sensuousness. It not only stands with its feet on the ground, but, in relation to all other commodities, it stands on its head, and evolves out of its wooden brain grotesque ideas, far more wonderful than if it were to begin dancing of its own free will."[68] Though *Kapital* antedates *Pinocchio* by two decades, this description seems irresistibly to resemble a cavorting marionette; and, as we have seen, plenty of stories about the awkward and uncanny liveliness of puppets—their ability to incarnate in their seemingly flimsy and ludicrous forms kinds of unreflective vigor unobtainable to humans—existed when Marx wrote. Marx's seriocomic account of the grotesque ideas that teem in the wooden brain of the table elide it with a chain of polemical targets from earlier periods: the Eucharist as jack-in-the-box, leaping with inane exuberance; the savage fetish, arbitrarily and whimsically revered; and the child's toy, an object that also invariably "appears at first sight an extremely obvious, trivial thing" but that can be, for the children in question, animate and lively.[69] Behind Marx's account hover the overlapping worlds of medieval Roman Catholicism, "barbarian" fetishism, and child's play, in each of which thing and person blur and blend, and trivial objects teem with thoughts and spill over with value.

This has been recognized in part by Giorgio Agamben, who seeks to incorporate the Marxist and Freudian accounts of fetishism into a general claim that "the entrance of an object into the sphere of the fetish is always the sign of a transgression of the rule that assigns an appropriate use to each thing." Agamben then suggests a form of violation of proper use, which frequently manages to escape the charge of transgression leveled at fetishes of all kinds, economic and sexual: "In our culture, even if not apparently sanctioned, this system of rules [for proper use] is so rigid that, as ready-made products demonstrate, the simple transfer of one object to the sphere of another is sufficient to render it unrecognizable and disquieting. But objects exist that have always been destined to such a particular function that they can be said to be withdrawn from all rules of use. I am speaking of toys."[70]

Agamben has written more penetratingly about the nature of toys than any other contemporary thinker, and I will return to his account of play and temporality in the following chapters; but here, in fully eliding the toy and the fetish—"children maintain a fetishistic relation to their toys," he bluntly states—he overstates the extent to which toys are "withdrawn from all rules of use."[71] As is often the case with Agamben's work, Walter Benjamin's thought hovers in the background here, and the placement of toys beyond rules of use might be read as a gloss on Benjamin's claim that if we "glance at the child playing, we may speak of an antinomian relationship. It looks like this: On the one hand, nothing is more suitable for children than playhouses built of harmonious combinations of the most heterogeneous materials—stone, plasticine, wood, and paper. . . . On the other hand . . . however unified and unambiguous the material is, the more it seems to embrace the possibility of a multitude of figures of the most varied sort."[72] As I argued earlier, however, what distinguishes Benjamin's analysis of child's play is precisely his awareness that the toy is a site of conflict between adult and child—that is, the meanings that the child generates and those that the adult will allow. It is this sense of the toy as a site of convergence, of potential tension and conflict, that is lost in Agamben's insistence that it straightforwardly exists beyond "all rules of use." I would argue, instead, that it is precisely the suspension of the object *between conflicting modes* of use and valuation that usefully aligns the toy and the fetish. As W. J. T. Mitchell acutely observes, while fetishes are "*special* things," "things that *want* things," "animated, vital objects," "they are not simply manifestations of coherent world pictures or cosmologies whose myths and sacred geographies might be securely mapped and narrated, but sites of struggle over stories and territories."[73] It is as "sites of struggle," as objects suspended between competing and mutually exclusive forms of understanding—as objects that are misvalued both charmingly and dangerously; objects whose misvaluation the observers both fear and tell themselves that they can control—that the toy and the fetish resemble one another.

It is also on this basis that—just as the fetish first emerged as a term within a triangular relationship of interpretation and misinterpretation in the early modern period—it can usefully be reinserted into a triangle of overdetermined and unstably valued categories of modern object: *fetish—plaything—art-thing:* the same contested and overlapping categories that are also, I have suggested, ambiguously foregrounded by the practice of iconoclastic child's play. As Jean-Luc Nancy observes, in a tantalizing analysis of the fetish that links it both to puppets and to dolls with shells for eyes, "here everything revolves discreetly around art, around its artifices and its false gods."[74] While Benjamin made relatively scant use of the concept of the fetish, the work of his friend Theodor Adorno points toward the implications of this triangulation. Adorno—notorious for the grimness of his sweeping pronouncements—might seem like an unlikely theorist of the ludic, but as Jane Bennett has cautioned, we should not underestimate the necessarily "playful element" in his style of thought, the "clowning" that emerges as one response to the impossibility of knowing nonidentity directly.[75] If Adorno, as I noted in my introduction, rejects the idealization of aesthetic experience as play that he identifies in the work of Schiller and Huizinga, this is because he is skeptical of the valorization of play for its own sake, which easily becomes the ratification of vacuous experience—in the aesthetic realm, this "degrades art to *fun*," and in the social realm it leads to the forced and hollow pseudo-enjoyment of compulsory leisure activities, in which "free time is nothing more than a shadowy continuation of labour."[76] For Adorno, however, the aesthetic object does facilitate a form of responsive play, but it is play that is understood in very different terms from the sentimental idealizations that he denounces. "Playful forms," he writes, "are without exception forms of repetition"—the unfolding, discontinuous rhythms of play that I have already discussed—and, he continues, "art that is totally without play is no more thinkable than if it were totally without repetition." Art is necessarily playful, then, but in acknowledging this, Adorno is urging that we rethink the very basis on which the claim is made, for art and play are not alike in their shared freedom and spontaneity: "Only when play becomes aware of its own terror . . . does it in any way share in art's power of reconciliation."[77]

Play and art as alike in their terrifying repetitions? What could he mean by this striking inversion of the standard alignment that has played such an important role in the history of modern aesthetics? Adorno follows this claim—coming close to clowning, as he often does, through forms of baroque hyperbole—with an uncommonly interesting reading of *Homo Ludens*. Though he criticizes large parts of this book, he observes that Huizinga

recognized that from the perspective of the subject, modes of aesthetic comportment that he comprehends under the name of play are at once true and untrue. This helps him to reach a remarkably compelling idea of humour: "One would like . . . to ask whether the primitive's belief in his holiest myths is not, even from the beginning, tinged with a certain element of humour." . . . The religious festivals of primitive peoples are not those "of a complete ecstasy and illusion." . . . There is no lack of an underlying consciousness of things "not being authentic." . . . It is in this consciousness of the untruth of the true that all art participates in humour. . . . In Huizinga's formulation, "The unity and indivisibility of belief and disbelief, the indissoluble connection between sacred seriousness and pretense and 'fun,' are best understood in the concept of play." What is here predicated of play holds true for all art as well.[78]

If Adorno's acceptance of an aesthetic of play relies on an erosion of the distinction between play and terror, it also abolishes the opposition between primitive credulity and civilized knowingness on which the history of the concept of the fetish is largely predicated. This striking moment, in which he embraces Huizinga's account of the so-called primitive attitude to the object as in fact a complex amalgam of belief and disbelief, retrospectively illuminates the similarly transformative account of the artwork as fetish that Adorno advances in *Aesthetic Theory* as a whole. Commodification, Adorno claims, has reached the point where exchange value has practically obliterated use value, and the production of exchange value has become an end in itself: "The more inexorably the principle of exchange value destroys use value for human beings, the more deeply does exchange value disguise itself as the object of enjoyment."[79] But this situation of ubiquitous fetishism is not to be nostalgically lamented but understood as the condition of possibility for certain newly emergent kinds of aesthetic creation and experience. Adorno does not exempt the artwork from the realm of the reified—"Nothing remains of the autonomy of art," he writes, "other than the fetish character of the commodity"—but the fetishization of the artwork is double-edged.[80] The artwork cannot escape commodification, and for the artist to pretend that it can would be to sink into deluded irrelevance. But art that refuses to delude itself and is instead willing to appear as the "alien and rudimentary fetish" that it is always at risk of becoming manages to offer a glimpse of something other than the world fully defined by exchange value.[81] As Adorno puts it: "Artworks are plenipotentiaries of things that are no longer distorted by exchange, profit, and the false needs of a degraded humanity." But they cannot intimate these distant possibilities by evading their double character as fetishes—both as objects with monetary value that are integrally part of an economy of exchange and as objects that are delusory insofar as the undistorted world that they impossibly promise does not and cannot exist. Rather, "the truth content of artworks, which is indeed their social truth, is predicated on their fetish character." In the bluntest of these formulations, Adorno claims: "Although the magic fetishes are one of the historical roots of art, a fetishistic element remains admixed in artworks, an element that *goes beyond* commodity fetishism."[82]

There is, I am suggesting, a link between Adorno's attempt to break down distinctions between "primitive" and aesthetic play, and his erosion of the boundary between the regressive, commodified fetish and the artwork. If, for Adorno, the artwork is a fetishized object that nonetheless has the potential to go (or at least to point) beyond fetishism, and if aesthetic experience offers a negative image of impossible freedom, this is also true for him of the objects and actions of child's play. He does not consider these in *Aesthetic Theory*, where the discussion remains within the boundaries of aesthetic play determined by Schiller, but there is, I want to argue, a close parallel between Adorno's discussion in that text of the artwork as a fetishized but still valuable plaything and the scattered discussions of children and their toys in *Minima Moralia*. In that remarkable text Adorno (probably recalling Baudelaire's account of the child searching for the soul of its toy) recognizes the pseudo-iconoclastic violence that, I have argued, we should understand as a moment of play rather than its opposition. "Talent," he claims, "is perhaps nothing other than successfully sublimated rage, the capacity to convert energies once intensified beyond measure to destroy recalcitrant objects, into the concentration of patient observation, so keeping a tight hold on the secret of things, as one had earlier when finding no peace until the quavering voice had been wrenched from the mutilated toy."[83]

Like the "terror" of repetitive play on which he insists in *Aesthetic Theory*, here Adorno contends that even the violent moment of play in which the toy is ripped apart is itself a form of the ability to transform recalcitrant objects that creativity requires (like the violence of the act of making itself that is foregrounded in the divine puppet). For Adorno, this very violence safeguards the secret of the object through its ability to remake. Just as his *Aesthetic Theory* is devoted to arguing that certain artworks are able both to inhabit the impoverished world that he describes and to offer glimpses of that world transfigured through specific human techniques, in *Minima Moralia*, by stressing its (potentially violent) creativity, Adorno suggests that child's play might serve a similar function. Children, Adorno claims, are "still aware, in their spontaneous perception, of the contradiction between phenomenon and fungibility, and they shun it. Play is their defence." Play can assume this defensive role by protecting the object from its dissolution into the ceaseless flow of commodified exchange and by making use of it in new ways that accord it alternative forms of value: "In his purposeless activity the child, by a subterfuge, sides with use-value against exchange-value. Just because he deprives the things with which he plays of their mediated usefulness, he seeks to rescue in them what is benign towards men and not what subserves the exchange relation that equally deforms men and things."[84] The child *seeks*, even if the search cannot fully or finally succeed. In stressing the spontaneity and purposelessness of play, Adorno might seem to offer an uncharacteristically sentimental glimpse of a route out of the world of near-ossified exchange relations that he describes with such morbid rigor. Play, I have suggested, turns out in practice to be remarkably fragile, subject to the interrupting, shaping presence of others, particularly adults, and this is one way in which the possibility that Adorno glimpses might be snuffed out. But the very need to continuously shape and guide play in this fashion should encourage us to take Adorno's claim seriously: the anger or contempt that adults often feel for the incorrect systems of value that the playing of children produces can be seen as testimony to its potential significance, as a realm in which genuinely new possibilities and novel ways of relating to objects ceaselessly surface and are then submerged. This means that play retains, for Adorno, a utopian core: "The unreality of games gives notice that reality is not yet real. Unconsciously they rehearse the right life."[85]

Considering the historical origins and later vicissitudes of the concept of the fetish has led me back to Adorno's work as offering the best resource for thinking through the dimensions and the rich contradictions of iconoclasm as child's play as I have come to understand them. The objects given to children by the Dutch in East Asia; the "Indian Babies" collected by Margrieta van Varick and taken to New England; the sacred playthings seen by Claude Lévi-Strauss and other ethnographers in Brazil—these are all objects that slide between geographical worlds and analytical categories, that unsettle observers, whether contemporary or historical, with the opacity of their meanings. This is the kind of challenge and disturbance that the fetish, yet another category of trivialization and dismissal, emerged in to exorcise; its use was supposed to stabilize instability. It was a way of reasserting a system of order and of value that was at risk of appearing arbitrary. Iconoclastic child's play was a closely related attempt to banish other modes of valuation (those of Roman Catholics and children) by dismissing them as intrinsically empty and inane, but Adorno's account helps us to understand both the great attraction of play as a form of iconoclasm and its necessary limitations. Child's play is an effective way of revaluing or devaluing an object, wrenching it from a context in which its holiness is taken for granted and bringing it into a childish world of mucky trinkets. But, as encounters with such play anxiously recognized, this also meant introducing holy things into a world of new values from which adults were periodically shut out, a world separate, at least in part, from "the mighty and mysterious league of the grown-ups, the magic circle of the people of sense," as Adorno puts it—no matter how hard these people of sense tried to enter this world and to shape its values on the model of their own.[86] If giving an object to a child to play with was akin to dismissing it as a fetish, this was, as the later vicissitudes of the concept would reveal, only to confirm it not as an object that did not matter but as a trivial object perennially prone to matter too much.

5 PLAY

ABOVE THE MAIN STAIRCASE of Audley End House, near Saffron Walden in Essex, hang imposing portraits of its former owners, projecting the image of smooth and glorious ancestral continuity that is *de rigueur* in English stately homes. Toward the back of the house, however, a humbler staircase contains a much less straightforward history. Not currently open to the public, and seemingly trodden fairly seldom by the staff or current occupants, its whitewashed walls are punctuated by a series of wooden figures around eighteen inches high (see, e.g., fig. 7), whose details are hard to discern in the dim light. There is nothing in situ to identify what these figures are or how they ended up in their unprepossessing location. The 1836 *History of Audley End*, written by its then occupant, Richard Lord Braybrooke, explains that one Dr. Gretton, vicar of Saffron Walden and nearby Littlebury at the end of the eighteenth century, placed a cedar altarpiece in the parish church in the latter village: "He also placed there several figures of apostles and saints, rudely carved in oak, which had belonged to Walden church; but the archdeacon of the diocese objecting to them, as savouring of idolatry, they were again removed, and converted into dolls by the children at Littlebury. Shortly after, Mr. Samuel Fiske obtaining possession of some of them, they were given by him to the author of these pages, and placed on the staircase at Audley End."[1]

These actions took place some two centuries after the instances of iconoclasm as child's play that I have previously discussed, suggesting a *longue durée* for this practice, even if the other instances that I have found were clustered in the sixteenth century. In the last chapter I cited parallels from different cultural contexts, including South American headhunting, but other later instances can be found: Anthony Ossa-Richardson observes that, following the debates that raged

FIGURE 7. Medieval wooden statue, Audley End House, Essex. Photograph by the author.

in the eighteenth century around the Holy Tear of Vendôme, once one of the most sacred relics in France, it was "shorn of its accoutrements . . . taken to the district office and kept by a bureaucrat named Morin, where his children had it for a plaything."[2] As with the shrunken heads given to children once the victory ritual was complete in South America, it is possible that this vignette suggests the genuine loss of the Holy Tear's power, though of course we cannot know what Morin and his children made of this once-great relic lying about the place or whether it added a sense of transgressive thrill to their play. With the statues at Audley End the case is still less clear. The reason for the statues' removal—"savouring of idolatry"—suggests that this dispute self-consciously continued the debates around the status of images that had flared up during the Reformation, though it is interesting to note Lord Braybrooke's claim that they were "converted into dolls *by the children* at Littlebury." The agency here is displaced onto the children themselves, which is quite different from the compulsion to play, and to play in a specific way, under which the children in Roger Edgeworth's sermon operated. Braybrooke dismisses the aesthetic quality of these objects, "rudely carved in oak," but nonetheless has them installed on his back staircase, deeming them unworthy either of destruction or of prominent public display. They were neither hidden away beneath floorboards nor flaunted but tucked away like a mildly embarrassing yet open secret. He ushered into his house, albeit by the back door, objects that he knew had passed through several stages of significance and use: they had originally been in the church at Saffron Walden; removed, presumably during the Reformation, but survived for reasons and by means unknown; emerged and were reinstated in a different church;

removed again and made into dolls (perhaps given to children for this express purpose, perhaps claimed by them for their games from some rubbish heap on which they had been dumped); and finally restored to display, in characteristic nineteenth-century fashion, as rude but worthy remnants of a lost medieval past—museum pieces, or something akin to primitive artworks.

When I viewed these statues at Audley End, what struck me most was the extreme contrast between their extraordinary trajectory—the locations through which they had passed, the actions and activities that had converged on them across the centuries—and their mute simplicity and immobility. These are objects, calmly at one with themselves, that have nonetheless undergone jagged and repeated movements through several categories—holy image, idol, plaything, and now (perhaps) art-thing. My final two chapters take their lead from two different features of this set of objects. In this chapter I begin with their temporal variegation as they have existed through time—and the way in which an awareness of this temporal variegation informs my encounter with them in the present—in order to foreground the questions of temporality and historicity that have recurred throughout my discussion of iconoclastic child's play; in the next chapter I turn to their blank, static faces that seem at odds with this sense of temporal dynamism. While I maintain the skepticism, stated in my introduction, that an adequate and comprehensive definition of *play* is possible, here I bring the word itself to the fore and suggest that play itself must be understood, both historically and theoretically, as a way of organizing, occupying, and being occupied by time.

———————————

The deep connection between child's play and temporality was stated, at once most bluntly and most inscrutably, in one of the fragments of Heraclitus, which Charles H. Kahn translates as follows: "Lifetime [*aiōn*] is a child at play [*pais paizōn*], moving pieces in a game [*pessoi*]. Kingship belongs to the child." Kahn calls this the "most enigmatic of Heraclitean riddles," which is saying something. Nothing about it is clear, from the nature of the play itself—which, Kahn writes, could suggest "childlike and random movements" or, given that a specific ancient board game (*pessoi*) is mentioned, might emphasize "the fact that these moves follow a definite rule." Likewise, *aiōn* can mean human life or vitality, but Kahn notes that it comes to be both "a synonym for 'time' (*chronos*)" as it is lived and a technical term for eternity.[3] Time itself is akin to play, the fragment suggests, and child's play to time, but both sides of the equation are unstable—wavering between human and cosmic temporality, between ordered and disordered action.

Heraclitus's fragment was not widely known during the early modern period and remains obscure. I introduce it here not in order to offer an interpretation but as a first step toward understanding what is at stake in attempts to bring the playing child alongside and into time. It is as a series of such attempts that I propose to understand the (generally unspoken) ambitions of most schemes for child-rearing and education. "Play," writes Bruno Bettelheim, "is anchored in the present, but it also takes up and tries to solve problems of the past, and is often future-directed as well."[4] This claim—seemingly unobjectionable, even bland—can be brought into new focus via the scene of iconoclastic child's play; we must return yet again to Roger Edgeworth's sermon and read it as, among other things, a contest over the meaning of time itself, the way it must be experienced and organized. According to Edgeworth, let us remind ourselves, "when the children haue theym [the images] in theyr handes, dauncynge them after their childyshe maner, commeth the father or the mother and saythe: What nasse, what haste thou there?" I have already discussed this encroachment on the child's play as a symptomatic attempt to control and reassure the adults of various sorts of *meaning* (of the play, of the image, of the children), and I am now suggesting that we specifically think of this attempt as, among other things, a way of situating and regulating both the object and the child *in time*. Here, I again recall Elizabeth Freeman's description, quoted in my introduction, of the modes of "chrononormativity," by which "manipulations of time convert historically specific regimes of asymmetrical power into seemingly ordinary bodily tempos and routines, which in turn organize the value and meaning of time."[5] The way in which particular activities are designated as "play" or "work," the acceptable rhythms between these activities, the forms of acceptable and unacceptable trajectory that play itself is permitted to follow—these are among the powerful ways in which children's sense and experience of time is thus manipulated and formed. I will have more to say about these processes below, but what makes their presence in the scene of iconoclastic child's play so uniquely and illuminatingly loaded is that, in this particular context, the mundane ordering of the child's time coincides with—is supposed to instantiate—the large-scale ordering of epochal, historical time. The change in status that the putatively holy object undergoes when it becomes a plaything is intended both to educate the child in the worthlessness of the object with which he or she plays and to encapsulate in miniature the decisive historical transformation under way in the Reformation, in which centuries of childish error will be swept away and replaced with newly pristine truth. Iconoclasm, as I argued in my introduction, is always implicitly both an argument about and an intervention in historical time; with iconoclastic child's play the unfolding temporality of play is supposed to coincide with, to recapitulate, the movement of history itself. In this scene, no less than in Heraclitus's riddling pronouncement, the movement of time itself is encapsulated in the playing child: what the child plays with is time.

To approach the scene of iconoclastic child's play through this temporal lens is to recognize it as a *pedagogical* scene that is entirely typical in some respects and deeply unusual in others. It is typical, I have suggested, insofar as it involves the careful regulation of play and its emergent meanings; it is atypical insofar as the play that is to be encouraged is the sort that demeans and damages its object and would therefore be discouraged and punished in most other contexts. In order further to unfold the peculiar temporal dynamics of iconoclastic child's play as an educative process of a sort—an education in the meaninglessness and emptiness of its object—it is helpful to relate it to some important strands in the history of attitudes to children and their learning. This is obviously a vast field, but it is fair to say that the question of what to do with a child's basic impulse to play is recurrent within it. One does occasionally encounter examples of children who are said to lack this impulse altogether, but these tend to be exceptional instances; some have insisted that the young Christ's difference from other children was manifest from an early age in his natural aversion to play. Milton's Jesus, for example, proclaims:

> When I was yet a child, no childish play
> To me was pleasing, all my mind was set
> Serious to learn and know, and thence to do
> What might be public good.[6]

Some saints' preternatural holiness was manifest in their unremitting seriousness: in the *Vita* of the twelfth-century bishop Hugh of Lincoln the saint proclaims, "I never knew or learnt how to play."[7]

Such disinclination to play was by definition unusual, even exceptional. It was far more common to acknowledge the play impulse as natural to the young child's stage in its life, and this acknowledgment entangled play within a complicated set of temporal dynamics. In the Middle Ages, as J. A. Burrow notes, there was a widespread tendency to "represent *pueritia* as the age of play," a tendency encapsulated by the stained-glass window installed in Canterbury Cathedral in the twelfth century showing the Ages of Man that depicted a boy with a curved stick and ball for the second stage.[8] In similar fashion the Pilgrim in John Lydgate's fifteenth-century *Pilgrimage of the Life of Man* meets a feathered girl named Youth who desires

> to spende my yonge age
> In merthe only, & in solace
> ffolwe my lustys in ech place.

And the early sections of Jean Froissart's "L'Espinette Amoureuse," from the preceding century, provide some of the most vivid extant depictions of medieval "children's games / Of the kind they take up under the age of twelve," ranging from damming brooks, playing "with little piles of mud," making pies from dirt, riding a stick like a horse (which he named "Grisiel"), and toying with spinning tops and soap bubbles.[9] Narratives of this sort made the urge to play acceptable so long as it was seen as transitory, a stage to be moved beyond as part of the Pauline setting aside of childish things. To see play as ideally a temporary stage within a human life necessarily raised questions about its temporal and developmental role: if one was to make, as Ptolemy wrote in his *Tetrabiblos*, "a change from playful, ingenuous error to seriousness, decorum, and ambition," was one to do it by limiting and gradually suppressing the impulse to play or by fulfilling it in carefully structured ways?[10] If child's play could not be fully suppressed, was it to be permitted only begrudgingly and sparingly, as a refreshing interlude from more serious pursuits, or could children develop past the play stage by means of playing? Could play be made, in this fashion, to undo and supersede itself?

The answer to these questions advanced in the humanist classroom as it emerged in England during the sixteenth century was a cautious yes, though the proper temporality of play remained an issue. As Rebecca Bushnell observes, "The humanists idealized the schoolroom, in Roger Ascham's words, as the 'house of play and pleasure, and not of fear and bondage,'" although this was, in fact, just one side of a perennially vexed balancing act in which "an insistence on play, pleasure and kindness, a respect for the child's nature, and an admiration of variety and range in reading struggle[d] against a will to control, a love of purity, and a belief in hierarchy and exclusivity."[11] The playful side of this dynamic had ample and important precedent: Quintilian had proclaimed of a child's course of study, "*Lusus hic sit*" (let it be play); Jerome endorsed this advice in his famous letter on the education of Paula, writing, "Have a set of letters made for her, of boxwood or of ivory, and tell her their names. Let her play with them, making play a road to learning [*Ludat in eius, ut et lusus eius erudition sit*]"; and Erasmus helped canonize the views of these predecessors for sixteenth-century educators when, in his colloquy *De lusu*, two boys complained that their master is too strict and somber, quoting to him Quintilian's claim "that wits are stimulated by moderate play" and enumerating the stimulating and orderly games that they will undertake.[12] Play may notionally have been welcome in the humanist classroom, but the question remained as to what sort of play was to be allowed and how it was to be understood, especially in its temporal role. As Bushnell notes, "Education was driven by time. Just as the early modern teachers fluctuated between their call for play and their drive to work, they also tried to combine their respect for the child's development with their anxiety about time's passing."[13]

There were, I will argue, two recurrent ways to assuage these doubts about the proper forms that play could take and the proper forms in which time could be passed, two ways in which one might strive to create an ideal intertwinement of play and time. The first, whose implications I will discuss for the remainder of this chapter, was more commonly articulated and explicitly justified: this view saw play not as free, noninstrumental, and goalless (attributes that many modern theories would see as definitive of true play) but as a teleological process, one that could be given a clear direction and goal and could be organized to facilitate a smooth onward progression. On this model, play is seen not necessarily as a dangerous way of spending time but precisely as a way for the child to be placed in and to occupy time, and it is a form of play that, if all goes well, will evolve seamlessly, even imperceptibly, into adult forms of piety or productivity. Instrumentalized models of this sort see play fundamentally as a form of *habituation*—a way of inculcating proper modes of thought or action behind the child's back as she or he gets on with her or his childish business. This is a model of play with deep roots in Western culture, and an important—because both particularly influential and explicit—formulation of it can be found in Plato's *Laws*, a text in which, as we have seen, a theology of play is presented in which mortals function joyfully as divine puppets. Elsewhere in this text, the Athenian states that "he who is to be good at anything as a man must practice that thing from early childhood, in play as well as in earnest [*paizonta te kai spoudazonta*], with all the attendant circumstances of the action. Thus, if a boy is to be a good farmer, or again, a good builder, he should play, in the one case at building toy houses, in the other at farming, and both should be provided by their tutors with miniature tools on the pattern of real ones."[14]

Such play can be specifically tailored to suit the inclinations or destined vocations of individual children, and this, for the Athenian, makes play the foundation of education: "the sum and substance of education is the right training which effectually leads the soul of the child at play on to the calling in which he will have to be perfect, after its kind, when he is a man."[15] The connection of play with the cultivation of the child is not only asserted in the *Laws* but woven into its verbal texture. Just as Heraclitus's riddling fragment brought to the fore the connection in Greek between childhood and play via "the triple occurrence of the stem 'child' (*pais, paizōn, paidos*)," as Kahn notes, Plato frequently draws attention to the link between the words *paideia*, meaning education or formation, and *paidia*, meaning play, a term derived from the word for child (*pais*).[16] The connection between the words suggested to Plato that child's play, far from being contemptible or trivial, lay at the foundation of the norms and processes of *paideia* that ensure the perpetuation of the *polis*.

The verbal resonance between *paideia* and *paidia* in the *Laws* captures in miniature the developmental temporal scheme in which Plato sees play as ideally functioning. Like a smoothly running stream, play of this sort carries a child seamlessly forward toward his or her adult vocation: play is valid insofar as it is an imperceptibly incremental preparation for productive adulthood. While Aristotle was to disagree with Plato as to the eventual role that *paidia* should play in adult life, he basically agreed as to its role in *paideia* for young children, arguing in book 7 of his *Politics* that, until the age of five,

no demand should be made on the child for study or labour, lest its growth be impeded; and there should be sufficient motions to prevent the limbs from being inactive. This can be secured, among other ways, by play, but the play [*tas paidias*] should not be vulgar or tiring or effeminate [*mēte aneleutherous mēte epiponous mēte aneimenas*]. The "Directors of Education," as they are termed, should be careful what tales or stories the children hear, for all such things are designed to prepare the way for the business of later life and should be for the most part imitations of the occupations that they will hereafter pursue in earnest.[17]

Play, by all means—but not all play; only play in ways that are carefully selected, guided, and shaped by adult directors and that imitate and prefigure adult roles. Play on this model, especially thanks to Aristotle's emphasis on *physical* training, is a way of cultivating what Marcel Mauss called "techniques of the body"; it is an induction into the forms of action and behavior that a given culture often takes to be natural and performs unthinkingly.[18] This is play that is easy to fold into the model of habit and habituation, most commonly linked to Aristotle but also owing a great deal to Plato, that had such a wide influence in medieval and early modern thought.[19] It might seem strange to describe play as a form of habit, which tends to be associated in modern discussions with deadening and unthinking repetition, not joyous spontaneity, but it becomes less strange if we accept Paul Ricoeur's reading of the Aristotelian tradition, according to which habituation is the means by which the consistent but still varied rhythms of experience are formed: "Custom fixates our needs . . . in their rhythm. . . . All needs run through a cycle from the phase of lack and tension to repose, passing through quest and satisfaction. The initial function of habit is in fixing these periods."[20] The way in which a child played was likewise seen in the early modern period as crucial to the establishing and fixing of these rhythms early in life, regardless of exactly how the child was viewed. Steven Ozment, in his brisk overview, argues for two views of childhood in this period: the first claimed that "the key to a child's development lay in its imitative nature: children, like monkeys, adapted to the environment in which they were placed and realized their adult selves by internalizing the behaviour, skills and virtues they saw around them in others"; the second "stressed the individuality of the child over a malleable generic nature, portraying every child as having its own inborn talent, which interaction with others elicited."[21] Whichever view was adopted, however, the implications for child's play were similar: it was supposed to lead, shape, and form children through time and lead them into their adult future, whether this meant *creating* or *revealing* the habitual rhythms of experience that would constitute their true selves.

The importance of child's play to the formation of virtuous habit, and the continued importance of Plato to this way of thinking, is confirmed by Michel de Montaigne's essay "Of Custom." Montaigne stresses the hold that habits have over us once inculcated—habit as fixed and immutable destination rather than habituation as dynamic process.[22] "*Custome*," he claims (in John Florio's English translation), "*is a violent and deceiving schoole-mistris. She by little and little, and* as it were by stealth, establisheth the foot of her authoritie in us; by which mild and gentle beginning, if once by the ayde of time it have setled and planted the same in us, it will soone discover a furious and tyrannicall countenance unto us, against which we have no more the libertie to lift so much as our eyes."[23] Habits, Montaigne observes, solidify into unshakeable dictates of action rather than modulating its rhythms and orientating its spontaneous unfolding. He then presents childhood as the crucial stage in which proper habits are inculcated and play as the action responsible for their inculcation:

> *Plato* did once chide a child for playing with nuts, who answered him. *Thou chidest me for a small matter. Custome*[,] replied Plato, *is no small matter.* I finde that our greatest vices, make their first habit in us, from our infancie, and that our chiefe government and education, lieth in our nurses hands. Some mothers thinke it good sport to see a childe wring off a chickins necke, and strive to beat a dog or cat. And some fathers are so fond-foolish, that they will conster as a good Augur or fore-boding of a martiall minde to see their sonnes misuse a poore peasant, or tug a lackey, that doth not defend himselfe; and impute it to a ready wit, when by some wily disloyaltie, or crafty deceit, they see them cosine and over-reach their fellowes: yet are they the true seeds or roots of cruelty, of tyrannie, and of treason. In youth they bud, and afterward grow to strength, and come to perfection by the meanes of custome.[24]

Montaigne's account is the inverse of Plato's in the *Laws*, since he focuses over-whelmingly on the formation of habit as the inculcation of vice—infantile play as the origin of *bad* habits—with less to say about whether virtue is similarly the product of habits playfully begun in childhood. The terms in which he criticizes the parents who encourage the cruel play of their children merit consideration. The point is not that parents tend to see such play as innocently frivolous or to pay it no heed; in fact, they do read habits of play for clues as to what their children will become, but they utterly misread them, mistaking "the true seeds or roots of cruelty, of tyrannie, and of treason" as evidence for incipient wit and martial prowess. It is only the child whom Plato meets who sees play as "a small matter" and is chided for his belief—adults subject the playing of their children to interpretation, but they do it ineptly. The close connection between play and habituation raises markedly the significance of the interpretative activity in which these parents fall short, and it leads Montaigne to conclude with a warning against the sort of trivialization of play that we have repeatedly encountered: "truely it is to bee noted, that Childrens playes are not sportes, and should be deemed as their most serious actions."[25] This is doubly true: true for the adults, who should take child's play seriously by attending closely to it; true for children, whose absorption in their play seems unwittingly to reflect the decisive role that it has in their formation.

While Montaigne's citation of Diogenes Laertius on Plato suggests the continued importance of classical views of child's play as habituation, these developmental accounts of child's play also, as Ozment notes, "accommodated the Judeo-Christian belief in the fall of Adam and Eve and its effect on human nature, which encouraged devout educators and parents to pursue a highly structured and religious upbringing for children at home and at school."[26] We have repeatedly seen in previous chapters the deep ambivalence woven into Christian thought toward playfulness in general and the playfulness of children in particular: if play could not be suppressed altogether, except in the most anomalous, saintly and Christlike of children, the habituating narrative of play allowed it to be seen ideally as a smoothly linear route to a pious Christian adulthood rather than as a sign of the child's inanity or sinfulness. Versions of this view can be identified in numerous contexts prior to the early modern period. John Duffy has identified a fascinating genre of Byzantine tales, organized around "the theme of young people playing at ritual," that focus in various ways on children exactly recapitulating the rites of the church in their games—but to tellingly varied effect.[27] In one such tale, recorded in the collection of John Moschus (compiled in the early seventh century and first printed in the seventeenth), a group of boys near Apamea in Syria decided to play at celebrating the Eucharist with bread and a jar of wine; they appointed a priest and deacon from their ranks, who happened to know the words of consecration exactly. As soon as they finished, fire flashed from heaven, destroying their play-altar completely and leaving them cataleptic. When the local bishop heard their tale and saw evidence of the fire, "he sent the boys away to become monks, made the place into a monastery and built a spot over the church where the fire had descended."[28] The message that this story conveys about the status of the boys' play is equivocal: insofar as it merits a heavenly inferno, it appears transgressive, but having their play scorched in this fashion seems to mark the boys as suitable for a holy life. They seem to have chosen the right game, even if they chose to play it in the wrong way; their game must be aggressively interrupted only to be resumed, by other means, in a monastery, and continued for the remainder of their days.

There are other, later versions of this story—including one with a predictable anti-Semitic twist in which a Rabbi's son is converted by playing at the Eucharist with his Christian friends and repeatedly survives the murderous retribution of his furious father; but the most interesting contrast is with an earlier story in Moschus's collection, translated into Greek from Rufinus's Latin, that concerns the fourth-century bishop of Alexandria, Athanasius.[29] Bishop Alexander of Alexandria was looking at the sea one day and "saw a group of boys amusing themselves on the seashore, playing bishop and imitating church services. Paying closer attention he realized that they were performing secret parts of the divine mysteries and it disturbed him." Interrogating the boys, Alexander discovered "that they had picked the boy Athanasius as their bishop, had chosen clergy among themselves, and were baptizing some catechumens." In fact, it transpired that these children "had been baptized fully in accordance with church custom." Alexander "decreed that those who had been given holy baptism had no need to receive the sacrament a second time," and he commanded that the subsequent education of Athanasius and his pious companions be entrusted to the church.[30]

These extraordinary tales are clearly intended in part as interventions in the arguments, recurrent in the history of Christianity, surrounding the intrinsic power of the sacraments and the rituals surrounding them: so immense is the holy force of the Eucharist and of baptism that it survives even in the playful versions of ritual enacted by children. The power of these stories suggests that—in certain contexts and when properly holy children are involved—child's play and liturgical ritual can not only resemble one another but converge. The impulse among these children to play at piety both helps to prepare them for a holy life and is already efficacious: in Athanasius's case play points toward a pious future that it already instantiates. If we look toward the early modern period, we can find other contexts in which children were categorized according to the play in which they chose to indulge and in which the role of that play in habituating them into a life of adult piety was emphasized. A notably vivid account of this process is provided by the Dominican Giovanni Dominici in his *Regola del governo di cura familiare*, written at the start of the fifteenth century, and is worth quoting at length:

The first regulation is to have pictures of saintly children or young virgins in the home, in which your child, still in swaddling clothes, may take delight and thereby may be gladdened by acts and signs pleasing to childhood. . . . Make of such pictures a sort of temple in the house. . . .

But make a little altar or two in the house, dedicated to the Saviour whose feast is every Sunday. You may have three or four different coloured little vestments, and he and the other children may be sacristans, showing them how on all feasts they should variously endorse this chapel. . . . They may . . . have in place the little bell and run to ring it at all hours as is done in the church. They may be dressed in surplices as acolytes, sing as well as they know how, play at saying Mass, and be brought to the church sometimes and shown how real priests do it, that they may imitate them. Teach them to preach after they have heard preaching several times in the church . . . you and the family remaining seated while they speak from above, not laughing but commending and rewarding them when they have imitated the spiritual office.[31]

Dominici emphasizes the imitative capacity of these young children and, in this instance, makes clear that this process must begin when they are very young, indeed, "still in swaddling clothes." It is a process designed to make the gradual entry of the child into a life of piety not painful and limiting but "pleasing" and full of "delight"; as with Athanasius, devotion is to be continuous with their natural playfulness, not an attempt to repress or restrain it. Dominici's passing reference to the rest of the family, who must refrain from laughter, is both wonderfully vivid—one can imagine these Florentine parents stifling their giggles as the children play with exaggerated importance at the saying of Mass—and telling: pious play can be gladdening, but it must not be allowed to lapse into a mocking or overly ebullient laughter that, although perhaps prompted by the cavorting of the children, could all too easily remove some of the sheen from the rites themselves, as iconoclasts sought later to do. Like the Byzantine tales, in which adults were initially alarmed because children had spontaneously chosen among themselves to play at piety when no adults were present, here adults must not only be in attendance at all times but regulate their own behavior, as the playful inculcation of piety constantly veers toward the possibility of impious mockery. The temporality of children playing at piety while the adults look on is, like the scene of iconoclastic child's play, complex and potentially unstable; it teeters between the pious and the impious, while the adults aspire to shape it into a guided playfulness that unconsciously inculcates piety in the children, while remaining aware that this might lapse into a more dangerous and chaotic form of play in which the rites themselves would be demeaned by the childish actions supposed to transform them into pious habit. Similar accounts of pious habituation through play emerged in England in the very decade in which Roger Edgeworth preached. In his *Boke Named the*

Gouernour (1531), written to offer guidance for the education of young noble-
men, Thomas Elyot drew a distinction between children who "swere great othes
and speake lasciuious and unclene wordes, by the example of other whom they
heare, wherat the leude parentes do reioyce" (the same sort of parents criticized by Montaigne), and a more laudably pious sort of child: "Contrary wise
we beholde some chyldren, knelynge in theyr game before images, and hold-
yng up theyr lytell whyte handes, do moue theyr praty mouthes, as they were
prayeng: other goynge and syngynge as hit were in procession: wherby they
do expresse theyr disposition to the imitation of those thynges, be they good
or iuell, whiche they usually do se or here."[32]

   Elyot draws a clear distinction between good and bad forms of child's play,
and the good and bad adults who guide and shape it. For Elyot, who emphasizes the imitative proclivities that formed the basis of humanist pedagogy,
children are profoundly malleable and will necessarily assume the characteristics of the adults whom they imitate, by means of the games that they
are encouraged to play. Children are construed as creatures of habit, entirely
passive and absorptive, a causally determined product of the environment in
which they are formed. Elyot was a religious conservative, but an emphasis
on formative, pious play was by no means foreign to reformed thought, and
Luther himself approved of such activity—though he insisted that it must be
properly restricted to childhood and then abandoned. Discussing the gestures and objects of traditional religious practice, Luther wrote: "If these
things had been left as child's play for youth and young pupils, so that they
would have had a childlike image of Christian teaching and life, as one must
give children dolls, puppets, hobby-horses, and other kinds of children's toys
. . . then it would be possible to tolerate the palm-ass, Ascension, and many
similar things."[33] On this account, pious play is permissible so long as it remains among children; what is reprehensible is the papists' refusal to grow up
and their determination to continue playing like children when going about
the serious business of adult worship. There is, then, a temporal difference
between Luther's account of child's play and Dominici's: for the former it is
permissible, but it does not blur gradually into piety. There is a caesura in this
developmental account, even if it is not specified—a moment when childish
things must be set aside.

———————

The felt need among these writers to manage and curate child's play through time is a reminder that, as I have argued, such play prompted alarm and attempts at control not just because children were often seen as valuing the wrong objects in the wrong ways—the basis of their affinity with the fetishist—but specifically because these values seemed temporally protean, prone to shift from one moment to the next. Children, claimed John Chrysostom, "when they see a robber entering and taking away the furniture, far from resisting, even smile on him in his mischievous craft; but shouldest thou take away the little basket or the jingles or any one of their play-things, they take it to heart and fret, tear themselves, and stamp on the floor."[34] Descriptions of this sort were enshrined as conventional wisdom in the entry "Of a childe" in Bartholomeus Anglicus's thirteenth-century encyclopedia, *De Proprietatibus rerum*, which appeared in a new English translation in the sixteenth century. "Sith all children be teached with evill manners," this entry claimed, "and think onely on things that be, and regard not of things that shall be, they love playes, game, and vanitie, and forsake winning and profite." The playing child on this account lives in a perpetual, frozen present, lacking the sense of futurity on which proper desires—for "winning and profite"—are founded. This presentism is disrupted when they are brought into the flow of educative time. The childish life lived in such a timeless present is construed as an inversion of value: "things most worthye they repute least worthy," claims the encyclopedist, "and least worthy most worthye." The impassive account of the encyclopedia threatens to give way to disgust at the child's willful disregard for the values of the adult world, as well as for the child's own incessant feculence: "They desire things that be to them contrary and grievous, and set more of the image of a child, than the image of a man, and make more sorrow and woe, and weepe more for the losse of an apple, than for the losse of their heritage. . . . Sodainly they laugh, and sodainly they weepe. Alway they crye, iangle, scorne, & disdaine, that unneth [unless] they be still while they sleep. When they are washed of filthe, anone they defile themselves againe."[35]

A similar account, of children as bafflingly impermanent and changeable, can be found in poetic accounts from the Middle Ages like *Stans Puer ad Mensam*, which included the following lines:

> In children werre is now mirþe & now debate,
> In her quarel is no violence,
> now pleie, now wepinge, & selde in oon state.[36]

This last phrase, "selde in oon state," renders the child a protean force. On the one hand these examples suggest those qualities that enabled children and their games to be easily dismissed; but on the other hand they reveal precisely those qualities that made the playing of children such a temptingly deflationary but necessarily unstable form of iconoclasm. In giving the holy thing to a child as a plaything, the adult allows for the object to be integrated into this new and unfolding temporality that resists full comprehension and control, a rhythmic but uneven time in which new modes of response can emerge and proliferate, rather than providing for the meaning of the object to undergo a single, seismic, and irreversible change.

By suggesting that this assumption—that children learn in and from their play—is an attempt to integrate them and their playthings into a specifically ordered temporal scheme, I hope to provide a degree of critical distance from what is a quite widespread modern assumption. The idea that one can learn by playing is likely to garner assent from most modern readers. From the origins of the Kindergarten movement in Germany to more recent philosophies of education, the emphasis on learning with and through play (as opposed to, say, harsh discipline and rote repetition) has come to seem the hallmark of progressive, child-centered educational models. While I do not dispute these claims, I do think it is worth asking what is at stake in making the claim that a child's play and learning can and should seamlessly converge—what we as adults mean when we make it, what version of the child's imagination we are imagining, and into what kind of specific temporal scheme we place children in so doing. Writing of Plato's discussion of formative child's play in the *Laws*, Mihai Spariosu notes that such play "must constantly be surveyed and guided by adults," and this is true of most of the texts that I have cited—from the "Directors of Education" who control the children's playful experiences in Aristotle's account to the onlooking bishop of Alexandria who sees Athanasius's pious play to Dominici's watching adults.[37] Conversely Mark Golden, describing Plato's Athens, writes that while "children's play was of surprising interest to the Athenians . . . the interplay of child's play and adult life is less tidy than these [Greek] theorists of play would prefer." Some games "give children a chance to manipulate and to deny social categories that structure their world and the world of adults too."[38] Purely developmental models of play are designed to limit these possibilities.

I now turn to some more recent accounts of children's play and its developmental role in order to ask how this historical sojourn—as well as its emphasis on the watching, shaping, interpreting adults in the scene of iconoclastic child's play—might affect some widespread current assumptions about learning and playing. Quite properly, there has been a great deal of recent commentary on the role of play in the formation of gender roles and, crucially, in the formation of racial and sexual identity as well. The principal contours of these processes are easy to recognize: boys are permitted and encouraged to play rambunctiously and roughly, girls kindly and caringly, with both sexes engaging in activity that is typically held *both* to reflect their intrinsic nature *and* to bring it to fruition; countless dolls and action figures, toy kitchens and toy guns, reinforce these narratives, along with the beliefs that, for example, light skin is both the default and the general aspiration. Much discussed though these phenomena are, they remain depressingly prevalent in mass-marketing and in a wide set of cultural discourses about what childhood is and should be. My aim here is to supplement and assist the important and ongoing critique of such phenomena by drawing attention to the fact that scarcely less potent, but less frequently recognized, assumptions are often at work in the very act of designating specific activities as play and determining which may and may not be permitted. Underlying these various ideological assumptions regarding what a particular child is or is supposed to be is a potent set of *temporal* assumptions, concerning the nature of the time in and through which the child is held to exist. We may be less comfortable than Plato in openly asserting that a child should be prepared for his or her specific vocation via forms of guided play, or in distinguishing in the manner of the early modern writers cited above between good and wicked children or parents, but, I would suggest, similar forms of judgment have survived in subtly different forms. As Ian Hacking observes: "We no longer ask, in all seriousness, what is human nature? Instead we talk about normal people. We ask, is this behaviour normal? Is it normal for an eight year old girl to . . ."[39] Hacking's choice of a child for his example is no accident: the narratives of play that I have been describing are among the most potent ways that Western cultures have sought to determine, and continue to determine, the normal course that childhood is allowed to follow.

Brian Sutton-Smith, a prominent modern play-theorist, surveys many of these narratives under the rubric of what he calls "rhetorics of progress," which see play as helping a child, in one way or another, to develop and learn—and he comes to the startling conclusion that, in fact, play invariably exceeds, or cannot be adequately accounted for in terms of, this purely functional interpretation. He writes, "the progress rhetoric appears to serve adult needs rather than the needs of children," and he concludes that "the hegemony of adults over children [is] revealed in the way in which the theories provide rationalization for the adult control of children's play: they stimulate it, negate it, exclude it, or encourage limited forms of it."[40] These are chastening words for anyone practicing what Adam Phillips calls "the religion of contemporary middle-class child-rearing" and who might be tempted to equate permission to play with an enlightened attitude.[41] While I do not dispute that a general shift of emphasis from an educational philosophy of discipline and punishment to one of play is a positive development, I caution against a smug assumption that encouraging play is a straightforward decision undertaken for the child's sake as the creation and safeguarding of a space for innocent freedom and creativity. After all, at least in Anglo-American culture, the child's freedom to play is invariably punctuated by the ceaseless directive to *play nicely*. Sutton-Smith's skepticism can help us see that an apparently benevolent narrative in which the child learns and grows in and through play might be of more use to the adults who have a stake in the child than it is to the child herself. To quote Phillips again: "Ideas about progress or development may be the ways we have bribed ourselves to believe and have confidence in change."[42] Elsewhere in his work, Hacking has proffered a stimulating account of what a "historical ontology" of childhood might look like—an account of the historical conditions under which an understanding of the child as a particular kind of being emerged and continues to emerge. "Our idea of what a child *is*," Hacking writes, "has been formed by a scientific theory of development. It forms our whole body of practices of child-rearing today, and, in turn, forms our concept of the child. Those ideas and practices form children themselves, and they also form parents. The child, its playmates and its family are constituted within a world of knowledge about child development. . . . The celebrated Dr. Spock tried to undo the regimen of normal development with his maxim that children should develop at their own rate—but *develop* they must, and at a *rate*, if only their own."[43]

To illustrate the pervasiveness of these assumptions, Hacking turns to anecdote. Narratives of child development, he says, "produce a feeling of inevitability. How could we not think in terms of child development if we interact with children at all? Well, I noticed recently when playing with two of my grandchildren, aged two and four, that I really did not think of them that way. They are changing daily. Since I see them less frequently than I would like, I notice change more than their parents. But the changes are totally idiosyncratic, personal, and do not strike me as matters of development."[44] Hacking goes on to note both the concrete *material* and institutional *conditions* under which the seemingly neutral narratives of child development emerge and by which they are reinforced. Playing "store-bought games," he observes that they "had been designed in order to promote and incorporate certain skills. They were not innocent children's games, but games manufactured in the world of child development." Likewise at school, "the first lesson learned . . . —a lesson so pervasive that the carers and teachers do not even notice that they are inculcating it—is that each child is a developing entity, so that the child cannot conceive of itself otherwise."[45] Hacking's remarks bring to the surface, with unusual clarity, the surprising common ground between the modern assumptions that he mentions and the historical phenomena that I have sketched above. I agree with him that we should seek to understand the conditions under which particular narratives of childhood, its nature and its temporal course, emerge and the interests that they serve; and, while I am somewhat skeptical of his seeming distinction between "store-bought games" and "innocent children's games" (are there such things?), toys should indeed be approached and understood in terms of the roles that they perform, not just for children but for the adults who construct these narratives of who and what children are.

It is therefore crucial to ask—as the analysis of iconoclastic child's play has repeatedly led me to ask, and in the spirit of Hacking's historical ontology—which forms of activity are categorized as play in a given historical moment and which as nonplay, whether that means seriousness or work? Within the activities categorized as play, which are encouraged or permitted? Which are discouraged or impeded? And what function do these decisions serve for the adults involved in the rearing or education of children? What is at stake for them in the way that play is organized through time, and time through play? What version of the child's imagination are they imagining when they do so? Here, once again, Walter Benjamin's observations on child's play and its fluctuations are particularly apposite. In certain respects Benjamin's discussions seem to reinforce the developmental narratives of play proffered since Plato, especially when he stresses the *imitative* proclivities of the child: "Child's play," he writes, "is everywhere permeated by mimetic modes of behaviour." Elsewhere he stresses the way in which the repetition of these mimetic acts shapes the child's behavior in later life, "for play and nothing else is the mother of every habit. . . . Habit enters life as a game, and in habit, even in its most sclerotic forms, an element of play survives to the end." Habits are formed through "the law of repetition," which is, for Benjamin, "the great law that presides over the rules and rhythms of the entire world of play."[46]

What distinguishes Benjamin's analysis, however, is its combination of clear-sighted awareness of the ways in which these characteristics make child's play particularly suitable for adoption by smoothly developmental narratives and his countervailing insistence that the mimetic repetitions and habituations of play have a propensity to escape from or exceed the narratives to which they are assigned. The child's mimetic games are "by no means limited to what one person can imitate in another," and they are therefore not easy to restrict to the sort of vocational training that Plato envisages: "The child plays at being not only a shopkeeper or teacher but also a windmill and a train," ambitions that are, one might say, harder to fulfill in later life.[47]

As we saw earlier, Benjamin sees the scene of play—in a manner that becomes unusually explicit in case of iconoclastic child's play—as a form of *agon* between adult and child. He insists that "the most enduring modifications in toys are never the work of adults, whether they be educators, manufacturers, or writers, but are the result of children at play."[48] To put this another way: if play, as Benjamin insists, is governed by mimetic and habituating repetition, then the co-option of play for temporally smooth narratives of development tries to ensure that only repetition of a certain appropriate sort, leading in a certain direction, can transpire. But, as Deleuze and Guattari note in their study of Kafka, playful childish repetition can take the form of *estrangement* and *differentiation* (what they call *deterritorialization*) of what is repeated rather than ensuring the perpetuation of the same: "Children are well skilled in the exercise of repeating a word, the sense of which is only vaguely felt, in order to make it vibrate around itself. . . . Kafka tells how, as a child, he repeated one of his father's expressions in order to make it take flight on a line of nonsense: 'end of the month, end of the month.' "[49] Repetition, rather than ensuring the homogenization and internalization of a word or an object's meaning, can engender a new and separate form of strangeness. As humans, Benjamin insists, "we experiment early on with the basic rhythms that proclaim themselves in their simplest form in . . . games with inanimate objects. Or rather, these are the rhythms in which we first gain possession of ourselves."[50]

———————————

Let me return, via Benjamin and Deleuze's accounts of play's rhythm as the perpetual discovery of the unexpected, to the statues lining the staircase at Audley End House. I began this chapter with them because they seem to offer one model for thinking about the remarkable transformations that objects can undergo, as they have moved from holy thing to plaything to some kind of art-thing, or at least a numinous remnant of a past era. My discussion of the temporality of play, however, has led me to be cautious of linear narratives of this sort, which risk reinforcing accounts of iconoclasm as the progressive liberation of the aesthetic such as those discussed in my introduction. I do not adduce the varied histories of these objects to suggest that they are *really* children's toys still—that this is somehow their essence—or that they have achieved their destiny as autonomous modern objects, liberated from the church and the children's hands. Instead, the point of opening up their history is to question the security of linear narratives of this sort. If there is one lesson that the history of iconoclasm teaches repeatedly, it is that the disappearance or destruction of an object is often less decisive than it appears. One thinks of the village of Morebath, where, as Eamon Duffy has shown, altar stones and holy waterpots that had been hidden in a dunghill were brought triumphantly back into the church at Queen Mary's accession.[51] Objects disappear only to reemerge, capable of generating new practices and meanings; they are restored to uses from which they had been removed, and sometimes then removed again, in recursive and decidedly nonlinear processes incorporating regression and relapse, as well as decisive change. This is both a more challenging and more persuasive way of construing the temporality of the object of iconoclasm as child's play and, I would suggest, of construing the time of the child. A partial parallel can be drawn with the practice, vividly described by Stephen Greenblatt, whereby "when the Reformation in England dismantled the histrionic apparatus of Catholicism, they sold some of its gorgeous properties to professional players."[52] While I would want to distinguish the displaying of these properties on the public stage from the remarkable welcoming of the object into the reformed household that takes place in iconoclasm as child's play, it is worth remembering that the lists from Lincolnshire included "three banner clothes . . . geven awaie to childerne to make plaiers cotes of." It is unclear whether the children were performing themselves or, somehow, making coats for other players; in any case, the process seems to have involved the construction of something akin to dramatic costume. That such objects were open to repeated rather than decisive transformation becomes clear from the example of King's College, Cambridge, in the sixteenth century, as Alan Nelson observes: "In Edward VI's Protestant reign the college transformed liturgical garments into playing gear, but in 1552-3 and 1554-5, in the Catholic reign of Mary, the college changed the

garments back to their original use"—and they may once again have become players' clothes at the start of Elizabeth's reign.[53] The very possibility of such multiple
and reversible changes was a refutation of the total iconoclastic transformation
that had supposedly occurred when vestments took to the stage. So long as the
object remains in play—and so long as the child remains, playing—subsequent
and unanticipated transformation is a real possibility.

This possibility is, however, precisely what the developmental narrative of play
seeks to tame and to regulate, and I must not overstate the ease with which such
narratives, powerful through their general acceptance, can be evaded. The most
penetrating account that I have encountered of the abuses and excesses to which
such narratives are prone is developed by the psychoanalyst Christopher Bollas,
in his description of a tendency in human interaction to which he gives the somewhat cumbersome name "extractive introjection." This occurs, Bollas states, "when
one person steals for a certain period of time (from a few seconds or minutes, to
a lifetime) an element of another individual's psychic life." As an example of what
this curious notion might involve, Bollas describes the following scene:

B is a four-year-old at play. He is moving small figures about and engaged in a private
drama that is nonetheless realized through actual objects. The space is entered by A,
who creates such distraction that B loses his playfulness. This is a common enough occurrence, particularly if we say that A is also four. But let's imagine that A is the mother
or father, and that each time B sets up a small group of objects to play with, the parent
enters the scene and appropriates the playing by telling the child what the play is about
and then prematurely engages in playfulness. B might continue to play, but a sense of
spontaneity would diminish and be replaced by expectant gamefulness. If every time
B is spontaneously playful the mother or father takes over the play and embellishes it
with their own "play," the child will come to experience an extraction of that element of
himself: his capacity to play.[54]

What is immediately remarkable about this imagined scene for our purposes
is how closely it echoes the scene of iconoclastic child's play as Edgeworth describes it. The child is playing spontaneously, but the adult enters and abolishes
this spontaneity, replacing it with the single correct significance that the play is
allowed to have. Bollas's fine phrase "expectant gamefulness" captures the anxious mood of the child who can no longer lose him- or herself in play because of
the didactic interruption that he or she learns to anticipate. "Extractive introjection" in the play scene that Bollas describes is, I would suggest, not an aberrant

event to be opposed to "normal" or "real" play (interruption of or distraction from play is, as Bollas notes, a routine aspect of interaction between children); rather, it is a version of a norm pushed to damaging extremes. Not all children experience their ability to play being expropriated in this way; thankfully, not every little boy or girl is "emptied by the active violation of the other, his internal life having been extracted from him," like the four-year-old whom Bollas describes.[55] Child's play has, however, throughout its history often been subjected to a degree of scrutiny, surveillance, and control by adults and by other children with the overarching end of organizing it developmentally in time; and children begin to play in anticipation of and response to interventions of this sort, even if not pushed to this damaging extreme.

Let me end this chapter with a final and somewhat less bleak example of the way that child's play can serve a crucial cultural function while simultaneously retaining an integrity of its own. In his discussion of the "vicissitudes of objects" in Indonesian society, Webb Keane notes one of the ways in which families dispose of a child's umbilical cord—a fraught prospect, since this liminal object is potentially loaded with significance, such that it cannot straightforwardly be kept nor easily discarded. Keane describes one way out of this bind: "The parents should not intentionally throw it away. They store it until the child is old enough to play, then wrap it in cloth and give it to the child to use as a ball. In this way, it just becomes lost."[56] This extraordinary process both differs from and resembles iconoclasm as child's play in that it captures the way in which a seemingly straightforward act of playing can function as a convergence between distinct adult and child modes of understanding and nonunderstanding. The children fulfill a function for the adults: a culturally fraught problem, how to dispose of an object that both is and is not part of a body, flesh that belongs to no individual, is outsourced to them. It is assumed that objects of play will be lost, will flow into and out of the child's object-world, so its losing *just happens* without the decision to discard it. Like sixteenth-century iconoclastic play, this Indonesian scene confirms the value of children and their play as a way of handling an impossibly potent object through time.

6   MASK

WHEN THE Shakespeare Birthplace Trust compiled its list of "Shakespeare in 100 Objects," the forty-fifth was "a wooden doll, possibly from the seventeenth century, of German, Dutch, or French origins," that might shed light on what Grumio has in mind in *The Taming of the Shrew* when he mentions "a puppet or an aglet-baby" (fig. 8). Elizabeth Sharrett, writing about this object, acknowledges that "it is uncertain whether the doll . . . is definitely a child's toy." Ellen Mackay proposes that this uncertainty springs in part from the fact that this walnut figure and its "adamantine constitution" differ so strikingly from the "squished-in vinyl heads and fabric bodies," the "manipulability and manipulativeness," of mass-produced modern toys.[1] I start with this object because its wooden recalcitrance reminds me of the figures from Audley End with which I began the previous chapter, and putting them side by side returns me to the *latent confusion* of doll and religious figurine that I discussed in Chapter 2. It is the meager expressivity of the doll, combined with its material recalcitrance, that makes it hard for the modern interpreter to imagine it serving the function of modern dolls: while these latter are often equipped with eerily verisimilar eyes, these earlier figures have in common a blank and unseeing visage. They seem not just mute and in-expressive in the way that every block of carved wood must be but almost to be representations *of* impassivity and inexpression.

This doll brings to the fore the sense in which, in my encounter with the Audley End figures, a tension emerged between the temporal dynamism of their historical trajectories and their inscrutability as objects; but the tension is generative, not inhibiting. I suggested at the close of the previous chapter that these statues' movement through different categories of object helped me to conceive of the child at play in less coercively neat developmental terms, and I

FIGURE 8. Wooden doll, early seventeenth century. Shakespeare Birthplace Trust. Reproduced with permission.

would like now to suggest that the affinity between these works and the children who once played with them is in fact further accentuated, in a curious way, by the inexpressive blankness of the carved faces. I want to approach this affinity via a category of object that I have not yet considered but that for much of its complicated cross-cultural history has, like the object of iconoclastic child's play itself, hovered among the worlds of ritual, antiritual, and play: the mask. As will become clear, although I am interested in a particular masked child in early modern art, I propose to give masking a broader significance suggested by these objects: the blank face that seems both to demand and to thwart interpretative effort.

The immediate reason that I turn to the mask, however, is that it has frequently been discussed in ethnographic contexts amid complex instances of what Michael Taussig calls "the adult's imagination of the child's imagination."[2] A notable example appears in the writing of the French psychoanalyst Octave Mannoni, discussing the structure of fetishism. Mannoni wonderfully suggests that the phrase "*Je sais bien, mais quand même*" (I know well, but all the same) encapsulates the way in which the fetishist retains certain commitments while acknowledging that they cannot be empirically sustained, such that "a belief can be abandoned and preserved at the same time."[3] To explore this dynamic, Mannoni develops a lengthy discussion of the memoir of the Hopi chief Don Talayesva, which he summarizes as follows: "Hopi masked dancers are known as Katcinas. At a certain season in the year, the Katcinas appear in the Pueblos, much as Santa Claus appears in our culture; and, again like Santa, they take a strong interest in children. They also resemble Santa Claus in that they conspire with parents to deceive them. The imposture is very strictly maintained, and no one would dare to expose it. Unlike the ambiguous but easygoing Santa Claus, however, the Katcinas are terrifying figures, for, if they are interested in children, it is because they want to eat them."[4]

When Talayesva finally reached maturity and was initiated into the adult cult, it was revealed to him that the spirits behind the masks were in fact his fathers and uncles, and he was furious and bitterly disappointed at having been deceived for so long. But, as Mannoni notes:

> What is truly puzzling here is the fact that this ceremony of demystification and the blow it deals to the children's belief in the Katcinas provide the institutional foundation for the new belief in them that forms the heart of the Hopi religion. . . . "Now you know," the children are told, "that the *real* Katcinas do not come to dance in the pueblos *the way they did in the old days*. Now they only come invisibly, and, on the days of the dance, they dwell in their masks in mystical fashion." . . . The Hopi distinguish and contrast the way the children are deceived and the mystical truth into which they are initiated. . . . A crucial feature of every initiation is that the initiated make a solemn vow to keep the secret. They will take part in perpetuating the imposture in their turn; one might say that the children are a kind of prop for the adult belief.[5]

Christian Metz, summarizing Mannoni's account, observes that "these societies have always 'believed' in the masks, but have always relegated this belief to a 'long ago.' . . . This long ago is childhood, when one really was duped by masks; among adults, the beliefs of 'long ago' irrigate the unbelief of today, but irrigate it by denigration (one could also say: *by delegation*, by attributing credulity to the child and to former times)."[6] Just as I ended the previous chapter with an instance in which a complex cultural act—the disposal of an umbilical cord—is *delegated* to the child at play, it is on the basis of this delegation of childish credulity that I want to introduce the mask into my discussion—not so much (or not yet) in its literal sense but as a figure for this sort of powerfully significant object, the naive belief in which is "delegated" to the child, who functions as "a kind of prop for the adult belief." Taussig has explored similar operations in the masking and unmasking ceremonies of Isla Grande, in which the true identity of the men behind the masks is what he calls a "public secret," something that those external to the cult and its mysteries *know not to know*; but children, he observes, with their frequent failure to keep secrets and play reliably by the rules of the game, endanger "the cunning with which the public secret plays with revelation and concealment . . . and thus do children, in the particulars of their blend of innocence and astuteness, slide either side of the public secret, graceful for all of that, but unable as yet to achieve the performative maturity required to modulate the claims reality makes upon illusion."[7]

I would like, however, to suggest an important corollary of these accounts of the roles that children and their imaginations are asked to assume amid the unstable dynamics of adult masking and unmasking. Mannoni suggests that masks feature prominently in these scenes wherein adults seek to reassure themselves of the credulity and naivety of children because they allow a fetishistic logic to be sustained—the establishment, as Metz puts it, of "the lasting matrix, the affective prototype of all the splittings of belief which man will henceforth be capable of in the most varied domains, of all the infinitely complex unconscious and occasionally conscious interactions which he will allow himself between 'believing' and 'not believing.'"[8] That is to say: the child is enlisted as a prop to allow irreconcilable beliefs on the part of the adult to be maintained. But it may be the case that, as I have argued in relation to iconoclastic child's play, there is a double fixing or taming of unruly multiple possibilities at work here: the child is used to stabilize the fraught structures of adult belief, as Mannoni and Metz suggest, but I would add that *these beliefs are also used to stabilize the child*, who in this sense is not simply a prop for the practice but its object. By attributing naive belief to children, as we saw in my earlier discussion of fetishism, the adult can claim certainty regarding exactly what the child knows and believes. And this is a pressing concern, I would suggest, because the face of the child *itself* can often appear to the adult as a blank, inscrutable surface, imperfectly revealing a set of qualities or proclivities that do not cohere into the right kind of organized self that adult society demands. Children are confronted with threatening masks, that is, precisely because they often appear to adults *as a form of threateningly masked creature*; the fear with which they are ritually confronted is also that which, by virtue of their place at the unavoidable limits of adult comprehension, they provoke.

―――――――――――

This is the possibility whose implications I now propose to explore as the basis of a partially connected but ultimately very different model of the temporality of play to the smoothly developmental models that I explored in the previous chapter. I will return now to these questions of temporality, before finding my way back to the child and its masks, understood in more literal terms. As a way into this second, alternative understanding of the temporality of child's play, I would like to return to Plato's account of its role in the formation of adult vocations in the *Laws*. Commenting on this passage, Jacques Derrida observes that Plato "praises play 'in the best sense of the word,' if this can be said without eliminating play beneath the reassuring silliness of such a precaution. The best sense of play is that which is supervised and contained within the safeguards of ethics and politics." This containment involves, Derrida claims, "the progressive neutralization of the *singularity* of play," a neutralization to which play seems doomed as soon as it is discussed: "*Either* play is *nothing* (and that is its only *chance*); either it can give place to no activity, to no discourse worthy of the name—that is, one charged with truth or at least with meaning—and then it is *alogos* or *atopos*. *Or else* play begins to *be* something and its very presence lays it open to some sort of dialectical confiscation. It takes on meaning and works in the service of seriousness, truth, and ontology. . . . As soon as it comes into being and into language play *erases itself as such*."[9]

Derrida suggests that even to talk about play, never mind to define it, is to ruin and inhibit it as surely as the laborious explaining of a joke removes its humor. Plato, he claims, *confiscates* play by absorbing it into a developmental narrative, in which it forms and reveals the nature of the child. "Play is always lost when it seeks salvation in games," Derrida writes.[10] It becomes something other when a single nature; order and direction are assigned to it. What, though, would it mean to affirm the alternative model of play toward which Derrida gestures and avoid erasing play in this fashion? If the only alternative is play as *nothing*, as Derrida says, then can we say anything of it at all? Is this the gleefully playful affirmation of nothingness that saw Derrida attacked as a pointlessly playful nihilist by his many detractors?

I would suggest, instead, that Derrida's reading points toward a much more mundane and everyday understanding of child's play as, in a sense, a particular and peculiar presence of the null or the neutral, about which we can talk without seeking to fold it back into a confiscatory narrative of linear and incremental significance. It is this possibility that I find inspired by the other aspect of the Audley End statues and the walnut-wood doll—their mute and impassive blankness, the simplicity that belies their complex historical trajectory. One everyday way into this alternative mode is to consider a common synonym for play activities, in the early modern period as now: *pastimes*. To view play as a form of pastime is a version of the defensive trivialization that we have repeatedly encountered in previous chapters; but rather than seeing play as wicked or inane because trivial, this viewpoint sees play as neither good nor bad in itself but harmless, and therefore useful not so much for what it is as for what it is not: onerous and serious action, whether piety or productivity of some sort. According to this cluster of accounts, children and others can be permitted periods of play that punctuate the pursuit of these more laudable goals; they do not contribute to such pursuits, but neither do they detract from them. This justification of play, as a limited period of time with seriousness on either side, has deep roots in Christian practice: some monastic orders, for example, would permit novices and child-monks strictly limited times allocated for play, often as seldom as an hour per week or per month, and they would subject them to particularly close scrutiny after these carefully delimited periods in order to check that they had not compromised their pious selves.[11] Just as there is both continuity and difference between the medieval and early modern narratives of progressive play as learning that I discussed above, there was space for similarly structured intervals of play in humanist pedagogy. Jeff Dolven has developed a subtle account of the temporal complications of the humanist classroom in practice: he quotes John Brinsley's *Ludus Literarius* to the effect that " 'honest recreations' improve the boys' concentration at their proper tasks; they 'gaine so much time every day, as is lost in those intermissions.' Such breaks are worthless or 'lost' in themselves, but they are a necessary condition for the success of the lessons they interrupt, a kind of pastime or meantime." This has the curious effect of accepting play only on the condition that it is evacuated of any content—of any effect, positive or negative. It takes up time but only as what Dolven calls a "blank interval"—one of the various "indeterminate middles" that humanist pedagogues were prone to create but could seldom justify.[12] It is this notion of play as a "blank interval," akin to the "nothing" described by Derrida, that I wish to bring to the fore as an alternative model of its temporality. Again this conception can be identified in the writings of Erasmus: in the colloquy *Confabulatio pia*, the preternaturally pious and somber Gaspar explains his serious commitment to piety, allowing only intermittent play as a refreshing interlude from more serious matters: "After grace is said I relax, if I have nothing else to do, by playing some wholesome games with companions until it's time to return from play to school."[13] *If I have nothing else to do*: play can fill empty time if it is itself empty, "wholesome" but vacuous, neither improving nor corrupting the child who plays.

There is a connection here, I would suggest, with the ambitions of adults who placed holy things in the hands of playing children, including the impassive Audley End statues. One way for iconoclasts to achieve their paradoxical aim of nullifying the object without running the risk of its fragmentary survival or total obliteration was to make it the object of an action understood as a form of enacted emptiness; playtime as a "blank interval" confirms the equal blankness of the object on which it is enacted. The ways in which the managed temporality of play in the classroom, with time for learning punctuated by intervals of mysteriously restorative vacuity, might resonate with the religious contexts against which iconoclasm was played out becomes clearer still if we turn to one of the most extraordinary but surprisingly overlooked discussions of play produced in the sixteenth century: "A Treatise on Playe," by the courtier, godson of Elizabeth I, and translator of Ariosto John Harington. The treatise explores play in general and not the playing of children in particular, but it is certainly informed by the humanist-inflected pedagogy that Harington experienced at Eton, where he and his schoolmates translated portions of Foxe's *Book of Martyrs* into Latin.[14] The explicit motive for Harington's treatise—which was never published but circulated in manuscript copies—was the abuse of gambling in Elizabeth's court, but rather than limiting the "Playe" of his title to this specific meaning, he revels in a wide-ranging exploration of its many senses. At the start of his work Harington quotes a patristic definition of play: "*LUDUS, id est, locutus vel operatio in quo nihil quaeritur nisi delectatio animalis.*" His own translation, however, brings out a temporal dimension that is only implicit in the original: "A spending of the tyme eyther in speeche or action, whose only end is a delyght of the mynd or speryt."[15] Harington emphasizes the noninstrumental quality of play stressed by theorists before and since—true play must be an end in itself—but also stresses the time spent in such activity. Having offered this general definition, he quickly—and, again, traditionally—splits play into its component parts, distinguishing between its best and worst, or acceptable and unacceptable, forms. This, too, was a widespread conception, as we saw above with Thomas Elyot and Montaigne, and it was one that Erasmus helped to canonize: in his influential treatise *De civilitate morum puerilium* he took it for granted "that boys' characters are nowhere more readily apparent than in a game," with good children playing well and bad children wickedly.[16] Strikingly, however, Harington does not initially identify good play with the blank spaces between pious and productive times; instead, he straightforwardly begins with devotion, "which kynde of recreation," he claims, is "absolutely the best." Play, on this account, does not punctuate piety: it *is* piety, in a manner that we have seen more ambiguously asserted elsewhere. It must be said, however, that when he comes to substantiate this claim and enumerate the forms of pious playfulness, or what he calls "Holy virtuous pastymes," Harington expands the definition of play beyond what many readers might accept: " 'Singing salmes, and himms, and spiritual songs,' as St. James counselleth those that are mery; walking abrod and meditating, as Isake did, like a dove; recording some of the elloquent and excellent soliloquyas of St. Awgustin; or, if they be unlearned, singinge one of David's dyvine salmes well translated into meeter."[17] Surely the definition of play is becoming more than a little stretched if it can include meditating like a dove or reciting St. Augustine, recalling Huizinga's wearied admission that "play is a category that devours everything."[18]

Harington proceeds to contrast "Holy virtuous pastymes" with "unseemly pleasures, provoking to wantonnesse." Were he to limit himself to this binarism, Harington's account would be quite unremarkable, but it takes a striking and original turn when he introduces a third category, those "games designed for pastyme" (including games of chance and organized sport), which, he claims, "the moste of which being *adiaphora*, things indifferent, and both to good and bad uses in all the ages of man, are consequently the principall grownd and project of this my discowrse."[19] In making this claim, Harington both offered an unusually direct account of play as a way of filling vacant time—a vacancy or blankness *within* time—and imported an enormously loaded theological term into his ludic discourse. The category of *adiaphora*—typically translated into English, as it is here, as "things indifferent"—first came to prominence in the writings of the Greek Stoics and Cynics (who used it to designate worldly matters toward which the philosopher was to adopt an apathetic attitude) before the term was appropriated and adapted by several of the church fathers, for whom it took on a more narrowly theological significance, referring to those activities that were neither explicitly approved nor proscribed by the scriptures. Determining the nature and limits of the category of *adiaphora* became a matter of urgency during the Reformation, especially in iconoclastic contexts: according to Stephen Gardiner, the conservative bishop of Winchester, the wave of iconoclasm in 1547 was undertaken by those who rejected the doctrine of *adiaphora* and who insisted rigidly that only that which is specifically mandated by scripture is to be permitted.[20]

When particular actions are described as *adiaphora*, as Bernard Verkamp notes, "the overall net result of such a designation was to 'free' or 'neutralize' the matters so designated."[21] This category—although it seemed tailor-made for self-professed moderates like Harington, who wanted neither to endorse nor to interdict a wide range of liturgical practices—also opened up complex philosophical and risky theological questions.[22] What did it mean to designate any human action, never mind play, as entirely neutral and indifferent? To accept that *some* human activity was indifferent was to risk reducing *all* activity—and especially pious activity—to neutrality relative to the majesty of the divine, which was precisely what the Spiritualist Sebastian Franck claimed in a letter to the radical Lutheran John Campanus in 1538, which circulated widely in manuscript. Franck ridiculed the notion that God somehow depends on the human performance of ceremonies, stating that "everybody imagines that God has need of our work and service and takes a special pleasure in these things like children with their playthings." But, rather than being the true playthings of God, such external rites are in fact merely the infantile pastimes of his church: "God permitted, indeed gave the outward signs to the church in its infancy, just like a doll to a child, not that they were necessary for the Kingdom of God nor that God would require them of our hands. Instead, the church in its childhood did not want to dispense with such things as a staff; and God therefore favored the infant church as a father gives something to a child so that it won't cry."[23]

According to this view God is not a playing infant but an overindulgent parent, and the refusal of the church to relinquish its ceremonies is the stubbornness of a child who refuses to set aside its toys and move beyond them to more mature pastimes. Franck's letter reveals the potential danger that the category of things indifferent ushered into theological discourse: the possibility that it could swell to the point that it threatens to devalue all forms of religious practice. To accept that some activity is entirely blank and neutral is to open up the potential of the indifference of all human action, to reduce it all, as Franck would have it, to mere child's play relative to the distant magnificence of the divine. This helps to explain the tortuous difficulties that Harington has in maintaining the category of indifferent play that he introduces: he argues that "the trew use of play" is "to recreat the speryts for a short tyme, to enable them better to seryows and wayghty matters," which echoes the Erasmus of the *Confabulatio pia*, seeing play as a blank interlude amid seriousness.[24] But the nature of play seems to fluctuate for Harington: it is, on the one hand, an innocent interlude, a valid form of nothingness that allows a refreshed return to the serious matters of life; but, on the other hand, he also wonders "how we may allay the covetouse humor of play, for satisfye it we never can, being the verry dropsye of the minde, whose thirst encreaseth with drinking; a wolfe whose famine abates not with raveing; a sea that augmenteth not his waters with fillinge."[25] How can play be all of these things: the basis of recreative piety; a pleasing interlude from the seriousness of life; and a raging, rabid desire, unable to be fully satisfied? Play, in Harington's account, his seemingly neat taxonomy notwithstanding, fluctuates between seriousness and inanity, simple innocence and raging necessity. His conception of play as neutral or indifferent fades from sight, and such activity continues to oscillate between the irreconcilable poles of pious distraction and manic disorder. The best he can finally do is utter an exclamation that is at once defiant and rather belated: "But now, for God's law, I must confess I finde no commandement that says, 'Thow shalt not play.'"[26] Play survives only in the form of a double-negative, as a nonproscribed action. In the absence of explicit divine condemnation or approbation, perhaps play as a period of blank and ultimately unjustifiable neutrality is the most that we can acceptably allow ourselves.

———————————

Harington's difficulties are not incidental to him but symptomatic of the various ways in which play comes to be ordered and the difficulties into which these attempts tend to run. The two approaches to the temporality of child's play that I have identified—one that folds it into a developmental narrative and *identifies* it with the progression of time understood as teleological habituation; and one that sees it as a minimally acceptable period of blank neutrality *within* the progression of time—are by no means mutually exclusive: they often appear in the same writer's work, as we have seen with Erasmus. They can be understood as responses to the same underlying conception of the child—two different forms of the adult's imagination of the child's imagination. "The child seen from the point of view of adult aspiration," as Adam Phillips aptly summarizes this view, possesses "too much desire; too little organization."[27] Early in the twentieth century, with a mixture of affection and grumpiness, George Herbert Mead gave unusually explicit voice to this view, writing that children "are not organized. . . . [The child] does not organize his life as we would like to have him do, namely, as a whole." Mead goes on to observe that in "the situation of play . . . the child is one thing at one time and another at another, and what he is at one moment does not determine what he is at another. That is both the charm of childhood and its inadequacy. You cannot count on the child. . . . He is not organized into a whole."[28] Mead recognizes the determining force of adult desires—"as *we* would like to have him do"—but he sees the temporal organization of the consistent self as a necessary goal. One might say that the developmental and teleological model of play sees the child, ideally, as organizable, or as in the process of growing incrementally more organized. There is little room for the momentary changeability of play described by Mead in the accounts by Plato, Dominici, or Elyot. Conversely, the model of play as blank interlude seeks to organize play within time in a different but complementary fashion, precisely by maintaining a clear separation from the pious or productive activity for which it refreshes the child.

The interrelation between the organization of play and that of time can once again be approached via an account developed by Adorno, who, in the section of *Minima Moralia* titled "Timetable," describes the absolute separation between labor and leisure as one of the definitive features of late capitalist modernity: "Work while you work, play while you play—this is a basic rule of repressive self-discipline."[29] For Adorno, this total distinction deforms both work and play by expunging the possibility that one might take any kind of pleasure from the former or benefit in any substantive way from the latter. The split is enforced by the compulsory regularity of working hours, which imposes a rhythm onto human life, in which periods for productivity and idleness are rigidly mandated. Enjoying oneself when freed from the imperative to work becomes merely another imperative, to be pursued with a joyless determination to pack as much pleasure as possible into the limited time available. As Adorno writes: "Free time remains the reflex-action to a production rhythm imposed heteronomously on the subject, compulsively maintained even in the weary pauses."[30] The division between work and play becomes internalized as a division within the individual:

Atomization is advancing not only between men, but within each individual, between the spheres of his life. No fulfilment may be attached to work, which would otherwise lose its functional modesty in the totality of purposes, no spark of reflection is allowed to fall into leisure time, since it might otherwise leap across to the workaday world and set it on fire. While in their structure work and amusement are becoming increasingly alike, they are at the same time being divided ever more rigorously by invisible demarcation lines. Joy and mind have been expelled equally from both. In each, blank-faced seriousness and pseudo-activity hold sway.[31]

Thus the supposedly strict line that the structure of the workday and the rhythms of weekends and holidays draw between work and play ensures the asymptotic convergence of the two. The two narratives that I have described—one of which effectively identifies work with play for children, one of which maintains a separation between them—collapse into one another in the historically later situation that Adorno analyzes. His unflinchingly grim appraisal of this situation is, however, interrupted by a carefully and tentatively intimated glimmer of alternative possibility: "Only a cunning intertwining of pleasure and work," he writes, "leaves real experience still open, under the pressure of society."[32] It is clear that Adorno has primarily in mind "the mode of life befitting an intellectual" who "acknowledges no alternative between work and recreation."[33] But, given Adorno's claim elsewhere in this work (as we saw in the previous chapter) that the "purposeless activity" of the child "sides with use-value against exchange-value" and "seeks to rescue in [things] what is benign towards men and not what subserves the exchange relation that equally deforms men and things," it seems plausible that such playing can also offer new possibilities for meaningfulness. This is so not because its gaiety is a riposte to the seriousness of the adult world (an idealizing view of childish frivolity that neutralizes it by other means) but because such play also refuses "the alternative between work and recreation": partly by oscillating, in its own right, between moments of the utmost seriousness and uncontrollable levity but also, perhaps, precisely via the kind of blank interval recognized by the second strategy for organizing play that I have been discussing. These blank intervals, I have suggested, have been made to serve an organizing function of their own: designating them as neutral, and therefore neither salutary nor harmful, is what allows them to be permitted, but I would suggest that the refusal to attribute positive content to spaces of this sort leaves them as a blank terrain that the child has the capacity to occupy, under certain circumstances and in certain moments, as he or she sees fit. Strangely enough, acknowledging the capacity of play to form a seemingly blank or neutral period of time might be a first step toward achieving a different understanding of its role in the life of adult and child alike. In an unusually sensitive analysis, Tzachi Zamir casts doubt not only on the possibility of defining play but on the damage that certain overly confident uses of the term itself can do: it is an "adult category that all too conveniently lumps together any disorganized, indefinable childhood state." For Zamir, the behaviors that we too quickly designate as play, in fact, allow the child "to linger in and enjoy a nonstructured experience," able to be both "the subject that he or she is called to become and the disorganized entity that he or she is, one that is aware of experiencing the world but also of the gaps in such experience, moments of nonexperience."[34] Erasmus, Harington, and the humanist schoolteacher offer a largely instrumentalized account of these gaps as periods that refresh for renewed productivity or piety or that allow the lesson fully to be learned. But these attempts at temporal organization also leave room, however unwittingly, for the disorganization to which they inadvertently testify. They try to create a narrative in which the pieces of the child all fit together, but they necessarily leave disorganizing spaces within this temporal narrative for the child to occupy. Allowing the child to be and to remain disorganized in the fashion that Zamir describes—permitting these moments of nonexperience—ensures the child's capacity to remain, in the seemingly blank moments of his or her play, a profound challenge to adult conceptions of what a person is or should be.

I have moved in the latter part of this discussion from the temporal organization of play in writings from and before the early modern period to more recent accounts of play and time with which these accounts resonate. For the remainder of this chapter I will return once more to the sixteenth century to focus my attention on an artwork in which, I will argue, the dimensions of play as challengingly blank interval are majestically and perplexingly foregrounded. The painting in question is Pieter Bruegel the Elder's *Children's Games*, painted in 1560 (fig. 9).

Bruegel's painting is among the most well-known representations of children at play, in the early modern or any other period, but it merits renewed consideration in light of both iconoclasm as child's play and the wider issues surrounding play and temporality that I have sought to elucidate in this chapter. *Children's Games* belongs to a series of a dozen works painted in the last decade of the artist's life that, as Joseph Leo Koerner notes in a powerful recent study, "seem to belong together as a coherent suite or cycle": mostly large (more than five feet wide) and horizontally orientated, "these paintings display human activity itself from a higher vantage point, almost—though never quite—from the point of view of the eternal," and from this vantage point we gaze down not at "landscapes but proper 'worldscapes,'" populated by teeming figures who evoke "the ceaseless mobility of creatures too incomplete to call this place a home."[35] While *Children's Games* certainly shares much with these other works, however,

FIGURE 9. Pieter Bruegel, *Children's Games*. Kunsthistorisches Museum, Vienna. Reproduced with permission.

we can appreciate its particular characteristics and achievement differently once we recognize that the nature and content of children's playing was a crucial issue both in and before the sixteenth century and that child's play raised important cultural and interpretative questions that were often deflected or suppressed by widespread strategies of trivialization. We see in this painting a unique and spectacular convergence between sixteenth-century anxieties about (and hopes for) the power of painted images, and sixteenth-century anxieties about (and hopes for) the power of children's play—and each set of anxieties and hopes both figures and reflects on the other. To put this more simply: I have argued throughout this book for a complex *longue durée* of postulated connections between play and the experience of artworks, and Bruegel's painting represents resoundingly the collision of these two activities. The painting suggests that the threat and the allure of observing children at play is isometric with the threat and allure of viewing an artwork.

Beholding this painting presents the viewer with a practical and immediate temporal question: where to begin? *Children's Games* has no obvious center or focal point; indeed, it seems rampantly and insistently decentered, requiring the viewer's eyes to dart across the canvas. The initial search for a center becomes, for the viewer, an unfolding awareness of the impossibility of finding one, by which time the process of trying to apprehend the work—or deciding what it would even mean adequately to apprehend it—has already begun. Koerner notes that "the activities depicted in *The Children's Games* . . . make visual sense only at very close range" but that this conflicts with the sense of the painting as a "worldscape" that demands appreciation as a whole; hence, "Bruegel made such pictures to be viewed from two distances, each morally as well as physically distinct."[36] Simply by virtue of the incompatibility of these vantage points, the viewer's experience of the work is required to unfold and mutate through time, as she or he boards what Harry Berger Jr. ingeniously calls "a perpendicular shuttle, moving forward and backward before the painting."[37] What I wish to stress is the way in which this fundamental feature of Bruegel's painting—the two incompatible distances from which it demands to be viewed—intersect and reflect on the two temporal models of child's play itself that I have identified: packed, fully productive time and eerily blank or vacant time. The difficulty for adults of deciding what to do with child's play—the ways in which it means or fails to mean, how to respond to its seeming fullness or emptiness—is the very difficulty that this painting meticulously stages, the difficulty with which it confronts its viewers.

What, then, does the viewer see? Most obviously, a seemingly endless swarm of children at play. Viewed or approached from afar, they remain a sprawling and undifferentiated crowd of players, to be viewed and perhaps enjoyed precisely *qua* undifferentiated mass; from closer quarters, however, they seem to invite the patient labor that is required to scrutinize each figure and the sort of action that each undertakes, to *read* the painting with meticulous care. A first question arises, regarding not the painting itself but the viewer's experience: is one of these responses akin to play and the other to work? Or might the laborious inspection of each child itself be a sort of responsive playing, which involves wondering whether each child will give pleasure by yielding up the secret of his or her activity, or a different sort of pleasure by withholding it? Might this be the sort of covert mingling of work and play that Adorno had in mind? Quite quickly, the subject matter of the painting raises the question of the kinds of thoughts or responses it might provoke and whether these might be further forms of the play that it represents. This response is entirely in keeping with—an extension of—the painting's subject matter, which, through the sheer diversity of activities that it depicts, illuminates the dizzying range of pursuits that can be grouped under the categories "play" or "game," and asks, in proto-Wittgensteinian fashion, what on earth they could all have in common.[38] To take a small selection, of the sort that we might compile once we approach the painting and begin to particularize its disparate surface: we have a child blowing bubbles; one that plays with a bird, another with a hoop; a group of children wrestle, while several hold one by his arms and legs and bounce him painfully off a perpendicular board. One child urinates on the ground—is this, in and of itself, a game, or only if it involves, say, drawing Pollock-esque patterns in the dirt?—while another stirs a pile of excrement with a stick. There are games that children play with other children, games that they play with external objects, games that they play only with their own bodies or bodily excretions. There are games that involve quiet concentration, games that involve exuberant role-play, games that involve danger and violence.

The proliferating variety of games was a topic of interest to ludic humanists, as Rabelais's wonderful and lengthy list of "the Games of Gargantua," containing everything from "trudgepig" to "Bumdockdousse" to "prickle me tickle me" confirms; but insofar as the status of such activities has attracted scholarly attention, they have tended to be subsumed into a wider discussion of the carnivalesque.[39] The central question that this series of Bruegel's works poses for modern interpreters is whether or not the works are to be *deciphered*—that is to say, whether Bruegel's peasants, his representations of pleasure or exuberance or rusticity, are to be seen as encoding a higher form of moral significance that it is the discerning viewer's duty to extract, or whether these are works whose meanings are, in whatever sense, overt, there for all to see, and whose surfaces can therefore be enjoyed and appreciated in their own right.[40] This question is, of course, not particular to Bruegel but was one of the central issues throughout twentieth-century art history—most obviously in Erwin Panofsky's often erudite and supple iconographic readings—and these were, in turn, only the latest stage in the longer history of debates about what images should be and do and the relationship between their surface and their ultimate significance. The assumptions of the iconographic approach are laid bare in its most ingenious application to Bruegel's painting, by Sandra Hindman: "The very subject of children's games suggests at the outset that Bruegel may have wished to illustrate folly. Late medieval texts used childhood to connote a state devoid of thought, lacking in understanding, and synonymous with folly, a view which continued through the seventeenth century. Children's games were similarly equated with an easy, thoughtless, and sometimes foolish activity."[41] Hindman expends considerable erudition in confirming this account, but she has effectively determined in advance the horizon of significance within which Bruegel's painting must operate. It is a form of powerfully circular reasoning: play, from the later Middle Ages through the seventeenth century, is equated with thoughtless and foolish activity; therefore, the activities taking place in Bruegel's painting, as instances of the children's games of its title, must be subspecies of this foolishness. Hindman's learned iconographic scrutiny paradoxically obviates the need to consider any specific act of play in detail: play is predetermined as foolish; ergo, any act of play is ipso facto an act of foolishness. My aim is not, however, simply to dispute Hindman's analysis or the iconographic approach that it exemplifies. Rather, I see it as a perspective that the painting actively solicits but as only one aspect of the dynamically irreconcilable forms of response that it provokes.

The principal weakness of the iconographic approach to this painting is its indifference to the specifics of painterly technique, since each playing figure is held to point beyond itself to a higher significance. Each figure is reduced to functional transparency; furthermore, each is separated from the other by being assigned a self-contained, monadic meaning: as Edward Snow observes, this overlooks the relationship between the kinds of playing depicted, the "elaborately structured syntax [which] is the medium in which the painting's ideas take form," and he claims that "the differential 'thinking' of the painting counteracts the impulse to isolate individual images with moral content."[42] Snow himself, however, is too quick to dismiss the iconographic impulse, which is of interest to me precisely as a form of the recurrent desire to fix and determine the meaning of children's play—just as his eventual insistence that the painted children "are lived images" whose experiences we share "with an utter visceral particularity" seems to enter too swiftly and easily into the world of the painting, sentimentalizing the children's play and assuming that we can easily share in its kinetic exuberance.[43] Both of these approaches *make something* of children's play in a manner partially encouraged in the painting, but we would do well to heed Koerner's observation elsewhere that, insofar as it engaged with iconoclastic debates about the status of images, "Northern art of the sixteenth century is riddled with conflicting directives for its viewing, incompatible enactments, as it were, of its rhetorical status."[44] Bruegel's painting, I believe, is *about* the incompatible ways in which we find ourselves viewing both paintings and children at play, and his specific technique offers up his work and the playing children whom he depicts to be both clinically deciphered and joyously celebrated, while suggesting the inadequacy of either response.

The finest and most unsettling account of the techniques by which these responses are solicited by this painting remains Hans Sedlmayr's 1934 essay "Bruegel's *Macchia*," a work that is impossible to read in isolation from the fact that Sedlmayr joined the Nazi Party in 1932–33 and that his contempt for decadent modernity seamlessly coincided with the Nazis' infamous *Degenerate Art* exhibition of 1937.[45] Sedlmayr is in no doubt as to which possibility for apprehending Bruegel's paintings—distantly, as a whole, or in proximity to its proliferating parts—is ultimately dominant: "Without any activity on our part," he writes, "simply through steady, passive viewing and extended attention (and for some viewers immediately), the human figures of typical pictures by Bruegel begin to disintegrate, to fall into pieces and thus to lose their meaning in the usual sense."[46] For Sedlmayr this experience of incipient disintegration is dominant for the viewer, and he sees it as the product of a disparity intrinsic to Bruegel's paintings between calculatedly awkward and unnatural human figures, created from nonfigurative splashes and patches of color, and the meticulously naturalistic rendering of the world into which they are placed; hence, Bruegel's figures "are connected to their environment in an oddly unsteady, precarious way."[47] The inhabitants of Bruegel's landscapes, Sedlmayr claims, are present in the form of mere scraps and fragments, or they are caught in the act of fragmentation: "the motifs in which forms are broken, shattered, fragmented or torn from are countless. . . . Figures are completely closed off from each other and from the space that surrounds and connects them." He discusses several works in this regard but returns to the manic scene of play with particular frequency, arguing that the painting conveys this strong effect of seeming collectivity falling apart into fragmented isolation: "In the bustle of *Children's Games*, each child plays alone."[48]

These citations give some sense of the tremendous power of Sedlmayr's reading, as well as the chilling, clinical fashion in which he extricates from the scene of child's play a vision of a decadent modern world in the process of collapse, bereft of meaning and cohesion: his "dehumanizing and aestheticizing gaze," as Koerner aptly calls it, "is that of the subtle, but cruel elite."[49] What I would like to add to Koerner's description is the possibility that Sedlmayr's focus on *Children's Games* is no accident—that we can read his essay not only as an expression of a retrograde contempt for the modern tinged by his Nazism but also as a revealing instance of the peculiar mixture of fascination, rage, and contempt that child's play itself can provoke. He writes that the beings toward which Bruegel is drawn "are all manifestations of life in which the purely human borders on other, 'lower' states that threaten, dull, distort or ape its substance. Primitives—a hollow form of human; the mass—more raw and primitive than the individual man; the deformed—only half human; children—not yet completely human; the insane—no longer human. These are liminal states of humanity in which and through which the nature of man is cast into doubt."[50] The cool alacrity with which Sedlmayr accepts this array of judgments on the subhumanity of "primitives," the deformed, and the insane is stomach-churning, yet there is something odd about the presence in this list of the phrase "children—not yet completely human," which, taken out of context, sounds comparatively harmless and is perhaps the only entry in the list to which we might, in certain circumstances, assent. There is nothing novel about this aspect of Sedlmayr's account: Plato and Aristotle, as Mark Golden notes, grouped children not only with "women, slaves and animals" but with "the sick, the drunk, the insane and the wicked."[51] We have repeatedly seen the way in which children, especially when they play, appear like an ambiguous sort of Other, the Other at home—akin to savages, artists, lunatics, but different in that their condition is seen (especially in the case of male children) as temporary. It is both horrible and deeply revealing that Sedlmayr groups children (or rather sees Bruegel as grouping children) along with collectives toward which he feels such patent fear and contempt, and this becomes clearer still when he turns back to *Children's Games* and describes its scene not only as barely human but as actively monstrous, demonic: this painting, he claims, is the "first and classic product of [Bruegel's] estranged turned on to the everyday":

If one disregards what children's games are, and what they mean for us and for children, then what children do when engaged in these games is as absurd, uncanny and suspicious as the behaviour of a band of lunatics or other beings incomprehensible to us. There are monsters with ten legs and three heads. The blindfolded boy looking for a pot with a staff is reminiscent of an executioner, the stilt walker of a cripple, the contortions produced by the games of epileptic seizures, the strange toys of magical apparatuses— the whole scene is one of "indescribable mania."[52]

This account is, in its way, as chilling as Sedlmayr's litany of subhumans. Who, one might ask, could find such horror in a scene of childish exuberance? In fact, I find this passage both shocking and powerful in its bleak honesty; child's play, I have suggested, very often seems monstrously other to adults, incomprehensible in its refusals of cohesion and its lurching illogic, but it is rare to find an expression of this attitude in such a pure and unapologetic form. More commonly, the regulation or the sentimentalization of play serves, among other things, as a way of fending off the fear that it can inspire of the child as absolute other, resident of a play-world from which the adult is radically excluded. Sedlmayr is, I think, *right* that Bruegel's vision of child's play is estranging and unsettling: the painting emphasizes what Jean-François Lyotard calls "the obscure savageness of childhood," a description glossed by Avital Ronell as the "irrevocable creepiness of childhood" that "enters a breach into the very concept of the human and makes us ask what it means to be human."[53] Sedlmayr captures the discomfort prompted by the painting in its provoking of this question, a provocation created in part by the viewer's difficulty in deciding on the best vantage point from which to view the work: both iconographic ingenuity and joyous celebration before the painting may be ways of evading the alien, demonic challenge of the playing children that it contains. Bruegel's painting courts both of these mutually exclusive ways of apprehending child's play, with their long and intertwined histories, simultaneously, tempting us at once to give such play a fixed and elevated moral meaning, to affirm it in its joyful superabundance, and to recoil in horror before it.

––––––––––––––––

Let me, then, loop back to the emphasis on implacable masking with which I began this chapter and move toward one or two of the details that the work contains in order to suggest how the dynamic that I am describing permeates its individual elements and is not merely a function of the teeming whole. When I eventually disembark from Berger's "perpendicular shuttle," it is the left of the canvas, as I gaze at it, to which I find my eyes drawn, especially the window and doorway of the building there. The stone structure at the rear of the scene has a few children visible in its windows—one waving a long ribbon, one dangling a basket—but the interior spaces that can be glimpsed within the building at the left foreground are very different kinds of interior space, teeming with activity that seems to take up the entire room, as if these are self-contained worlds within the "worldscape" of the painting. At the upper window two faces peer over the sill—or, rather, we realize as we move closer, one face and a mask held over a second face (fig. 10).

A great deal of attention has quite rightly been paid to this mask, for, once noticed, it stands out as both unique within this painting and emblematic of Bruegel's painterly practice: as Koerner points out, the mask is "out of place not

FIGURE 10. Pieter Bruegel, *Children's Games* (detail). Kunsthistorisches Museum, Vienna. Reproduced with permission.

just because it shows an adult [but] because, alone among the toys in the picture, it is of sophisticated manufacture."[54] This object has been thrust into the child's hand, not rescued from the world of scrap materials; this child has not only been given a toy but literally been given a face by an adult. Sedlmayr sees the mask as "the essence of [Bruegel's] process of estrangement concretized as a device," and he observes that, rather than contrasting with the "real" faces by which it is surrounded, the difference between them shrinks by virtue of their juxtaposition. His terms betray yet again his horror at the inscrutability of the playing children, whose expressions are "indeterminate and indifferent . . . impossible to differentiate and seemingly empty. Everything that can bear expression is minimized, above all the eyes. The faces betray nothing of what goes on behind them; they are mute."[55] If we peer at the second face that appears next to the mask in the upper window, we can see what he means: oddly round and plain, its dark eyes and nostrils and blandly upturned smile begin to seem, as one gazes at it, like eerie parodies of simple friendliness. While Koerner develops a scintillating account of masking in Bruegel's works, I would modify his claim that "we know it is a mask . . . yet we respond to it as a face."[56] I would suggest, instead, that the juxtaposition of face-like mask and mask-like face uncomfortably erodes the distinction between the two, insisting that the "real" face, insofar as it exists in this painting, is just another blank screen onto which the viewer projects his or her idea of what a child is. Viewed from close quarters, the facial features of the smiling child who stands next to the masked child start to look like currants pushed into a cake or lumps of coal into the face of a snowman—the child's visage is an object that, like the mask, has been ostentatiously *made* by the adult artist, in deliberately rudimentary fashion. In a sense it is a representation, not of a child but of what adults see when they look at children playing: this face, adjacent to the mask, *is* the blank, disorganized, neutral, vacant interval of the child at play; it *is* the fear of the child's otherness and inscrutability that Sedlmayr articulates so piercingly.

We find a similar interplay of levels of unreality in the adult view of child's play, expressed in less ostentatious but no less consequential fashion, in the lower chamber of the same building. In this space, which disappears indeterminately beyond the edge of the canvas, we see two girls playing with what appear to be dolls, as well as a small altar on which several objects have been placed (fig. 11).

The ways in which this corner of the painting has been interpreted are again indicative of the various responses that adults have to children at play.

FIGURE 11. Pieter Bruegel, *Children's Games* (detail). Kunsthistorisches Museum, Vienna. Reproduced with permission.

For Hindman, the girls "mimic the actions of their mothers" in playing with their "babies," and "the mock altar and the girls playing with dolls are clearly coded as games."[57] That is to say, she assumes that this scene depicts a proper process of smooth habituation for the girls who play—that their dolls prepare them for their roles as adult wives like the play implements and altars described in the previous chapter, toys subtending a smooth narrative of teleological development. Snow, in contrast, relates this part of the scene to the persistent association of reviled religious practices with mere puppetry or play in the sixteenth century: "the conjunction of the mock altar at the lower left of the painting and the two adult-looking children playing with dolls beneath it," he writes, "seems to construct a visual equivalent of the language of contemporary iconoclasm." But "a modern viewer unaware of how insistently that language linked Catholic ritual and image worship with doll playing, black magic, and childish superstition would scarcely think to see the two images in relation."[58] I am less sure: while Snow is no doubt right about the specific historical reference of this portion of the painting, we can still read the doll-play in this corner as part of a wider vision of child's play as troublingly inscrutable that can be derived from the painting itself. Just as, in the upper window, the presence of the mask accentuates the already mask-like blankness of the accompanying face, there is here a similarly disquieting echo between the dolls whose almost entirely vacant, featureless faces can be seen—the one that stands next to the small cradle in fact has three minute grey dots that mark its features in the barest fashion, visible only from close proximity to the canvas—and the blankness of the girls themselves. One girl is viewed only from the side, with the slightest curve of a nose discernible but no facial features; the doll that she holds functions almost like a hand-mirror, echoing the blankness that we are led to impute in turn to her. Only the side of the other girl's face, similarly featureless, can be seen. Here, even more so than in the upper window, Bruegel gives us a concentrated image of the child at play *as* an embodiment of troubling vacancy, the sheer unrecuperable neutrality of a disorganized experience. This blankness actively invites the projection of adult hopes—like Hindman's comforting claim that the girls play in imitation of their mothers—and fears—like Sedlmayr's demonic vision of "indescribable mania" in which "strange toys" become "magical apparatuses."

As I noted in Chapter 2, early modern English was just one of numerous languages in which the standard word for a doll—*baby*—blurred the distinction with the child who possessed it: the same is true of the Greek *kore*, the Latin *pupa*, and, in Bruegel's Dutch, *pop*. This corner of *Children's Games* ruminates brilliantly on this blurring of the two, since the girl playing with her doll appears as one blank-faced figure playing with another, with each figure at once imbued with, and denied, an unsettling and inaccessible kind of liveliness. A contemporary critic of Bruegel derided him for ornamenting his paintings "like carnival dolls," and this barb cuts to the heart of his technique in this part of *Children's Games*, in which the painter lays bare the processes by which adults are tempted to construct versions of what children and their playing might mean.[59] It is no accident that this play takes place in the canvas's gloomiest corner, which urges us both to peer into the children's playworld and to recognize our exclusion from its logic. The girls could be playing with holy dolls of some sort; the cradle could be akin to the cradles of the Christ child that were quite common in the medieval period and were at once holy thing and plaything; the altar could be like the miniature play-version that Giovanni Dominici recommended to parents for the proper habituating of their children, as we saw in the previous chapter.[60] If so, the scene would involve the most reassuring, temporally smooth version of child's play that adults can imagine. It could even be that this corner shows iconoclastic child's play in action; but, if so, it only confirms how difficult it is to distinguish it from other modes of play or pin down its meaning once children actually start playing. Even if the iconoclastic reference is primary, we must still ask, with Snow, "Does the image refer to iconoclastic judgements approvingly? Derisively? In some vaguer ironic or thematic sense?"[61] Alternatively, it could be that the blank-faced girls with their vacant dolls are indeed engaging in the sort of alien, demonic rite that Sedlmayr fears. We cannot know; we cannot choose; we cannot, as adult viewers, avoid lurching between these options as we seek to imagine these children's imaginations at work, at play.

Sedlmayr, I have suggested, is shockingly honest in his willingness to acknowledge that the playing of children can appear "bizarre, strange and demonic, ridiculous, and at the same time terrifying."[62] The mask, I suggested at the start of this chapter, is often a prominent component of cultural practices in which children are involved precisely as *depositories* for a naivety and credulity of which adults wish to absolve themselves; but, I suggested, this is in part because the child itself frequently appears in play as challengingly masked and inscrutably alien, exemplifying what Eugen Fink sees as an extreme possibility of play, the "withdrawal from the real world" that reaches "a point of total domination through the demonic power of the mask."[63] There is a connection between these forms of masked, demonic blankness and iconoclasm as child's play insofar as the latter purports to place an inane object (the holy thing) in the hands of an inane creature (the child) and subject it to an inane practice (play); it becomes necessarily unstable, however, because it is intrinsically prone to a very different reading, in which a demonically charged object (an idol) is placed into the hands of an equally demonic creature (a child) undertaking a potentially demonic activity (play).

The threatening, masked vision of the child as a demonic other has become a dreary and rather repulsive modern trope, beloved of horror film directors and tabloid editors, that can itself be seen as a form of reassuring repository for the much wider fear that children are, in and of themselves, demonic, absolutely other. This tends to come to the fore in moments at which children hurt, kill, or sexually abuse other children: such events allow for the conveniently Manichean view that underpins many attitudes to modern childhood to emerge into the open, with the perpetrators seen as unremittingly evil to the core, worthy only of punishment (and often treated, morally or judicially, as adults), while their victims are the embodiment of innocent purity.[64] A less obvious and emotionally fraught version of this comforting moral clarity is often at work in the way that children at play are routinely viewed. Such playing is ideally innocent, joyous, formative, free; but it is sometimes seen as an opaque world of meaning from which the adult is excluded, and the vision of playing children as demonic is only the most extreme manifestation of the challenge that such play frequently presents. Children are associated with spirits, demons, and the world of the dead in many cultures. We saw in an earlier chapter Claude Lévi-Strauss's account of children as one of the groups who "share the *otherness* which symbolizes the supreme dualism: that of the dead and the living" and who are therefore "traditional incarnations of the dead"; likewise in classical Athens, as Golden observes, children sometimes assumed an important role in religious practice precisely because, "not yet fully integrated into the social world of the *polis*, they are interested outsiders, a status they share with the gods with whom they intercede."[65] Mariane Ferme, in her fine study of the Mende in Sierra Leone, observes that "infants and children are thought to operate according to a modality of concealed power that triggers an aesthetic of wonder and repulsion and thus to generate contradictory practices. . . . Furthermore, a dynamic of the insignificant is at work in the cultural representation of childhood. . . . It is precisely when children are regarded as insignificant—as liminal beings between the world of animality and madness—that they are perceived as potentially most dangerous."[66]

Without wishing to minimize the differences from the Mende worldview, I have suggested throughout this book that "a dynamic of the insignificant is at work in the cultural representation of childhood," albeit different in its specifics, in European contexts as well. The educational and habituating strategies explored earlier in this and the previous chapter, which seek to situate and organize children and their play in time, are intended in part to fend off extreme and curiously twinned views of children and their play as at once utterly insignificant and charged with demonic danger to bring the children into line with adult time. The notion of children as implacably masked and of their play as a blank, disorganizing interlude, terrifyingly resistant to incorporation into a smoothly developmental narrative, is barely acknowledged in these reassuringly teleological contexts. The threateningly alien dimension of the children at play on Bruegel's canvas is useful in this respect, for it points us toward the demonic in early modern culture as a locus for encountering this far more unsettling image of the child at play.

As with the comfortingly developmental models, earlier instances can be found of this convergence between child's play and the demonic: John Duffy cites a Byzantine tale in which a domestic servant possessed by a demon is brought to the monk Peter of Antioch, who forces the spirit to account for why it has chosen this particular girl to possess. It explains that it heard the maidservants telling stories of the monks of Antioch and their great power over demons: "Then the girls turned to pretending that they were possessed and raving mad. The next thing was, that servant put on a goatskin cloak and began exorcising them like a monk would." The demon therefore decided to possess the girl for real and test the monks' power.[67] The story fascinatingly inverts the tales, discussed in the previous chapter, of pious children like Athanasius, whose play perfectly recapitulates ritual practice: the girls' playing at possession and exorcism renders them vulnerable to that which they mimic and trivialize, and it becomes all too horribly real. If we look ahead to the early modern period, we find parallel forms of overlap between child's play and demonic possession in witchcraft narratives. As with anti-Catholic iconoclasm, the language of play was commonly deployed in this context as a way of both vilifying and trivializing the accused, but here the aim was to underscore the overlap in appearance between mere child's play and the horribly efficacious, demonic practices of witchcraft. Accused witches' familiar spirits and their magical paraphernalia were often described as akin to toys: a suspect in a witchcraft trial in Essex in 1582 "denyeth, that she hath or euer had any Puppettes, Spyrites or Maumettes," while another confessed "that she had foure Impes or spirites . . . one of them was called *Robin*, an other *Iack*, the thirde *William*, the fourth *Puppet alias Mamet*"; conversely, Samuel Harsnett attacked scenes of supposed exorcism as "the 'Pope's Playhouse' in which religion became 'a pageant of puppittes.' "[68]

If the language of child's play swirled around and converged with these accounts of demonic agency, I suggest that we read these moments partly as testament to, and as other ways of coping with, the tendency for the child at play to be seen as a kind of living mask, demonically other in the inaccessibility of its operations. This is one way of reading the numerous and horrifying cases, some (in)famous, of children testifying as witnesses in witchcraft trials and being tried as witches themselves. These cases serve as the clearest and grimmest confirmation of the specific terror that child's play can provoke among adults as a form of horrifying and malevolent otherness.[69] As Diane Purkiss observes, the involvement of children in witchcraft "reveal[s] deep fears of children themselves and of the infant within: fear of children's uncontrolled animality, voracity, violence."[70] In numerous instances a child's propensity to play, or to play in a certain fashion, was cited as evidence of demonic possession or witchery. In the 1593 account of "the bewitching of the five daughters of Robert Throckmorton Esquire," the proof for the possession of Elizabeth Throckmorton includes the following behavior:

Above all things she delighteth in play; she will pick out some one body to play with her at cards, and but one only, not hearing, seeing or speaking to any other; but being awake she remembereth nothing that she did, heard or spake, affirming that she was not sick, but only spake. . . . At dinner time it [the demon] played with her, (for sometimes she hath merry fits) putting her hand beside her meat, and her meat besides her mouth, mocking her and making her miss her mouth, whereat she would sometimes smile and sometimes laugh exceedingly.[71]

The possessed Elizabeth Throckmorton both plays and is an object of play. As if combining into one the uncannily similar figures in the corner of Bruegel's painting, she is an anarchic, unruly child and forlorn plaything combined into a single body. In a somewhat later period, during the hysteria surrounding child witches in Augsburg in the early eighteenth century that has been brilliantly studied by Lyndal Roper, parents denounced their own children as witches and saw them imprisoned and interrogated in horribly cruel circumstances. As Roper stresses, it was often specifically the playing of the children that was taken as evidence of witchcraft. It was particularly when they aped or adapted religious rites that their playing seemed the most dangerous—especially when their play had a sexual dimension: "The children's supposedly diabolic games expressed their understandings of religious mysteries, their conception of adult sexuality and their attitudes to punishment."[72] The same behavior that might otherwise have been excused as natural youthful exuberance or criticized as a simple moral failing became, in this charged confessional context, a sign of demonic possession. The children of Augsburg cut their fingers and exchanged blood; "fought with one another and engaged in rough games," but did so on the stairs behind a church; and "engaged in what their accusers termed 'indecency.' Trousers were dropped, shirts raised, skirts lifted, and the children 'kissed the shameful parts.' "[73] The emphasis on sexual behavior is particularly notable, given that the interpretation of children's sexual play remains one of the most fraught issues in the modern safeguarding of children, and there is barely an acceptable form of public discourse through which the difficulties presented by such behaviors can be discussed. Ian Hacking, in his remarkable study of the historical emergence and transformation of child abuse as a category, observes that "sex play among children, especially when there is a significant difference in age, is increasingly regarded as sexual abuse."[74] Jacqueline Rose, thinking along similar lines, makes a difficult but important point: "Touch a child out of intimacy, play or abuse. We often do not know—children often do not know—the difference."[75] There may be instances in which abuse disguises itself as play, and this horrifying possibility seems to demand constant vigilance; but it is vigilance that, pushed to an extreme, requires the constant surveillance and regulation of play, a paranoid insistence that the child at play is always the potential victim or perpetrator of demonically evil acts against others or even against themselves. Perhaps not insignificantly, children exploring their own genitals are still sometimes told today to stop "playing with themselves"—as if it is treating one's body as a toy, not the pursuit of sexual pleasure, that is the problem. These difficult questions raised by children's sexual play are, I have suggested, only the most extreme instance of the many ways in which child's play can seem like a demonic mask for something far more sinister and inspire forms of suspicious interpretation that would tear away the mask to reveal the truth of the action—if there is such a truth, and even if this means destroying or limiting play in many of its forms. This is what the parents in Augsburg were horrifyingly willing to do, as Roper shows. The sexual behavior and solemn pacts sworn between children as part of their games became, in this context, evidence of the dark ceremonies through which fallen Christians made a blood-pact with Satan; rough-and-tumble play near a church, denounced by Tudor moralists as mere ribaldry, here became a much more insidious form of impiety. "Parents found their children's behaviour intolerable and were unable to dismiss it as childish play."[76]

Both child's play and demonic magic take place within a threateningly self-contained world, a world that needs only its own logic to continue and needs no validation or corroboration from without.[77] Both generate strikingly "new configurations" as if from nowhere, transforming rather than being subordinate to reality as they develop. This is one way of understanding the face of the child's game as a demonic mask, the sort of alien configuration that prompted the fear of the adults of Augsburg, by whom the sum total of their children's actions were read as catastrophic moral failure—not merely wasted time or ribald impiety but demonic malevolence. This response is horrifying but not aberrant; it reflects the particularly challenging otherness of the child's play world. These accusations help us understand, up to a point, why such play could serve as an iconoclastic practice in carefully staged circumstances, so charged was its potential for impiety; but it also confirms the lurking danger implicit in any willingness to encourage children at play, even when their ribaldry was harnessed for the purposes of reform. The toying of children at play that sixteenth-century iconoclasts sought to appropriate for their purposes was, like the holy things that they attacked, both the most trivial thing imaginable and horrifying evidence of a masked world of meaning and value lying beyond their control.

CONCLUSION: TOY

THE UNPUBLISHED PAPERS of Sir Francis Bacon contain a bifolium, in which only the first page contains writing—a set of notes and snatches of thought gathered under the heading "Play." The list begins in apparently moralizing fashion: "The syn against the holy ghost termed in zeal by one of the fathers," it starts; "Cause of Oths; Quarrells; expence & unthriftynes; ydlenes & indisposicion of the mind to labours." But something pivots at the third entry in the list: "Art of forgetting; cause of society acquaintance|familiarity in frends . . . recreation & putting off of melancholy." Like John Harington in his "Treatise of Playe," Bacon is initially preoccupied with the moral perils of gambling as a subspecies of play, but he soon spirals out in other directions. "Art of forgetting" sounds dangerous: it is the means by which one forgets oneself, but this forgetting is seemingly proposed as the basis of sociality, as if we need collectively to forget ourselves in order to play together as friends. Bacon emphasizes the tension between play's ramifying variety and its cohesive force: in filling time, play involves the whole body—"Games of Activity & passetyme . . . quick[ness] of ey [sic] hand; legg, the whole mocion." It encompasses several moods, modes, and speeds: "Frank play; wary play, ventrous not venturous|quick slow" (here his words seem suddenly to perform what they describe in the notes' lilting rhythm and changing of pace). Simply put, as one entry reads in its entirety, there are "severall playes or ideas of Play."[1]

James Spedding, who included these notes in his monumental edition of Bacon's works, believed that they were "the plan of an elaborate treatise on the subject"— possibly the prospective *Historia ludorum omnis generis* (History of every variety of game/play) mentioned in the *Novum organon*. John Pitcher made the convincing alternative suggestion that "it could just as well be the basis of an unwritten and much shorter essay, *Of Play*," which would also make the notes an important insight into Bacon's working methods.² Regardless of their purpose, it is from one point of view quite surprising to find Bacon so interested in the forms of play, and the lengths to which his editors have gone to explain away this interest are revealing: Alan Stewart writes that "since, as Spedding puts it, 'no man was less given to play than Bacon,' it must be concluded that this apparently playful page had a serious goal."³ Must it? This is a piece of interestingly circular reasoning: Bacon's supposedly unremitting seriousness is taken as a settled fact, in terms of which his detailed interest in play must be interpreted, rather than vice versa. I do not intend to debate Bacon's character or personal propensities; rather, I want to scrutinize the impulse to label not just Bacon but anyone or anything—a person, a culture, a period in history—as intrinsically opposed to play. Such judgments have historically proven irresistible, but I am less and less convinced that I understand their value or how they would be either falsified or productively put to use.

In Bacon's case the temptation to make this judgment—the fact that it feels instinctively right—is linked, I would suggest, to the prominent fashion in which he rewrites and incorporates iconoclastic rhetoric into his famous account of the "four idols of the mind"—idols of the tribe, the cave, the marketplace, and the theater—against which his intellectual program was aimed. I noted in my introduction the ways in which iconoclasm and play have often assumed entirely opposed roles in grand narratives of historical and cultural change—iconoclasm as the essence of disenchanted modernity, play as that which is lost or rendered impossible as a result. I would now like to revisit this opposition in light of my arguments in the interceding chapters and ask what difference has been made to our way of approaching narratives about, and objects from, the past by my sustained consideration of the questions raised by iconoclastic child's play. The view of Bacon himself as both dourly joyless and as raising iconoclasm to the level of theory has implications beyond his particular writings, since it helped him achieve his status as doyen of disenchantment in numerous narratives of modernity, most notably that of T. W. Adorno and Max Horkheimer. They began *Dialectic of Enlightenment* with Bacon, to whom they attributed the ideal that "the human mind, which overcomes superstition, is to hold sway over a disenchanted nature. Knowledge, which is power, knows no obstacles. . . . Technology is the essence of this knowledge. . . . There is to be no mystery—which means, too, no wish to reveal mystery."⁴

The blurring of theological and natural philosophical discourse in Bacon's intellectualization of the language of idolatry and iconoclasm is part of what makes him useful for Adorno and Horkheimer, since it allows them to blend

Weber's parallel narratives of the reformation and the rise of modern science as quintessentially disenchanting modern processes. While this issue lies largely beyond the scope of my argument, Paula Findlen has shown in a series of remarkable studies that numerous figures prominent within the bundle of developments still usually termed the "Scientific Revolution," including Kepler and Galileo, stood "at the crossroads between playful and serious interpretations of nature."[5] Play might be a way of preparing oneself to pursue knowledge of the divinely formed world—following the same smooth trajectory envisaged by humanist educators—or it might be a way actually of knowing and engaging with that world, akin to playing with divine creation itself. Catherine Wilson has posed a related argument with particular force in relation to the practice of seventeenth-century English natural philosophers:

> The accusation that the ancients were childish in their sensory superficiality is balanced by the positive valuation, in the ancient literature from John Amos Comenius to Locke, of children's naive curiosity and delight in novel experience. Thomas Sprat in his *History of the Royal Society* argues that the formality and confinement of teaching by precepts and universal rules "suppresses the *Genius* of *Learners*," and asks whether "it were not profitable to apply the eyes, and the hands of Children, to see and to touch all the several kinds of *sensible things*?" . . . Even Plato, he says somewhat implausibly, encouraged the hands-on approach. The charm of what Hooke calls the "real, the mechanical, the experimental philosophy" lies in its similarity to child's play.[6]

In natural philosophical as in pious forms of activity, play keeps recurring, not as the opposite of valuable and worthwhile pursuits but as a version of them. If Adorno and Horkheimer saw technological domination as the epitome of disenchanting Baconian knowledge, it is worth at least considering Alfred Gell's claim that technology and magic are not opposed but alike, and alike precisely in their resemblance to child's play: "Technology develops through a process of innovation, usually one which involves the re-combination and re-deployment of a set of existing elements or procedures towards the attainment of new objectives. Play also demonstrates innovativeness—in fact, it does so continuously, whereas innovation in technology is a slower and more difficult process."[7] This claim disrupts a clear distinction between grim technological domination and winsome, playful forms of practice, or perhaps it brings out both the potential playfulness of the technical and the domineering capacity of the playful. The recurrent instability between disenchanting rationality and playful engagement must be borne in mind whenever we encounter one of the large-scale narratives that see play as depleted or disappearing under modernity. We should ask not whether these narratives are true (I am still not sure quite what it would mean for them to be true or how such "truth" would be measured) but what function they serve in the ways that we organize and interpret history and position ourselves in relation to it.

The only sustained attempt that I have encountered to discuss the general phenomenon of imputing play and seriousness as a way of thinking about the organization of history appears in Hans Blumenberg's *The Legitimacy of the Modern Age*. Blumenberg defends the reality and the value of the shift from the medieval into the modern period, but he focuses on liminal moments of transition between epochs and the figures that embody the complexities of such shifts (notably Nicholas of Cusa and Giordano Bruno) while nonetheless arguing that the change effected in the transition to modernity is real, decisive, and epochal. Andrew Cole and D. Vance Smith summarize his account: "for Blumenberg, a radical shift takes place between the Middle Ages, with its emphasis on sacred ontology and the divine presence infusing the intelligible world, and modernity, with its new modes of inquiry, self-reflection, and human agency via epistemology, hypothesis, new scientific cosmologies, and the processes of rationalization that render nature as inherently knowable in its laws."[8] What interests me here is not so much Blumenberg's account of modernity's *legitimacy* but the strategies of *legitimization* that agents of change employ to justify their actions as truly epochal. One of the important ways in which an epochal threshold is defined, Blumenberg claims, is through the emergence of a "consciousness of a new seriousness [which] puts the totality of the preceding attitudes, sympathies and actions under the suspicion of frivolity."[9] He develops this claim in a paragraph worth quoting at length:

And this same basic pattern of contrasting one's "new seriousness" with the past is repeated when the modern age, at its commencement, reproaches prior ages with the credulity of prejudice, with being oblivious of the world and neglectful of the experiences nearest at hand. To have relied on the world management of a hidden God looks like a sheer lack of prudence and care in an existence that is brief but correspondingly all the more in need of being secured. The nature that had been left uninvestigated emerges as not only a previously exposed flank of the art of living but also an inexhaustible source of material, subject to man's demiurgic power, to which no attention has been paid. The *laboriosa vigilia* (laborious wakefulness) that Descartes recommends in the last paragraph of the first of his *Meditations* is, once again, the tension of an extreme seriousness, which resolutely leaves behind it the past sleepiness and negligence in perceiving possibilities and in overcoming precipitateness of both judgment and action. To Bacon, the bygone interest in extraordinary phenomena in nature seems misguided to the extent that extraordinariness is supposed to be indicative of a transcendent violation of nature's regularity—misguided, then, as a form of the inquisitive industriousness (*curiosa industria*) that had amused itself with nature's unseriousness, with its supposed playfulness (*lusus naturae*) instead of showing itself to be capable of dealing with nature's serious usefulness (*seria utilitas*) by relying on the thoroughgoing lawfulness of its phenomena. . . . Now, just as it became intolerable to think that man should be a plaything, it became equally intolerable that he should be able to play.[10]

Blumenberg's account suggests the range of spheres in which perceptions of play, and an austerely determined refusal to play, might assume a decisive cultural role. He describes a unitary phenomenon—"the modern age, at its commencement"—but swiftly divides three spheres in which play was consequentially rejected: the Reformation (defined through its rejection of "the world management of a hidden God"); the birth of modern philosophical thought as "the tension of an extreme seriousness" through the figure of Descartes; and the rise of scientific investigation focused on "nature's serious usefulness," as practiced by Bacon. This triangulation of the central preoccupations of modernity produces three equally interrelated forms of increased care toward the world. The human individual becomes newly responsible for securing her own existence, for enacting her demiurgic power on material nature, and for revealing this nature's lawful regularity. Each of these responsibilities—crucial advances in the emergence of modern subjectivity—are achieved, he claims, through the suppression of play. While I have serious reservations about the overarching narrative of Blumenberg's book, this paragraph seems enormously valuable in reorientating energy from deciding which thinkers, schools, or periods really are or are not playful (a surprisingly frequent pursuit, as we have seen) toward a new attention to the actions that are and are not *deemed* playful, the forms of play that are and are not allowed, and the role that these decisions make both in the way that we understand our historical moment and the ways in which we organize and perceive history. If, as I have been arguing, iconoclasm as child's play encapsulates the way in which the adult's imagination of the child's imagination functions as a potent and unstable cultural force, then similar acts of imagination seem to be operative in the way that historical change itself is managed and interpreted.

The question with which I wish to close this book is, Does iconoclasm as child's play also provide us with a way of thinking about the historicity and temporality of human experience that avoids the sharp—and, in my view, untenable—divisions between modern and premodern on which these narratives tend to be founded? I believe it does, and in making this argument, I propose to turn my attention to a word that has haunted this book, an everyday word that I have frequently used while deliberately deferring attention to its precise status: *toy*. The resonance of this word during the early modern period is of particular interest since it was in the process of altering and expanding, in a fashion entirely germane to the practice of iconoclastic child's play itself. A glance at the *Oxford English Dictionary* entry for *toy* is highly instructive but renders it in some ways more mysterious; there is a single use of the word, meaning "amorous sport, dallying," in a text of 1303 and then no further instances whatsoever until the end of the fifteenth century, where its use as both noun and verb becomes widespread. Its etymological origins, however, remain opaque and a matter of conjecture. It seems to be of northern European origin but is entirely different from the German *spielzeug* and Dutch *speeltuig*. Whereas these and similar terms in Scandinavian languages designate such objects straightforwardly as things intended for play, the English term has a more gradual emergence that ties it tightly to the early modern discourses of triviality and trifling; we have already encountered some of the proliferating and alliterative phrases in which it appeared, such as "triflinge toyes and tromprie" or "toyes & tryfles." Indeed, sixteenth-century dictionaries saw *toy* as just another term for an inane and worthless object—Palsgrave gives "a tryfell, *truffe, friuolle*" as his synonyms, and Thomas Elyot chooses "trifles, thinges of smalle estimation, wanton toyes, thynges vnseemely for menne to vse."[11] Used throughout the sixteenth century to refer to the trifling, the pleasurable, the triflingly pleasurable, and the pleasurably trifling, the first citation that clearly means a "material object for children or others to play with" occurs in 1586, in Sir Philip Sidney's *Arcadia*: "There was never poore scholler, that having instede of his booke some playing toy about him, did more sodainly cast it from him."[12] The phrase "playing toy" sounds like a pleonasm to modern ears but indicates both that *toy* did not *necessarily* imply play for Sidney's readership and that it was beginning to do so. Sidney's use of the word in this form is particularly significant, since, as Katherine Duncan-Jones has observed, he referred to the *Arcadia* itself as an "ink-wasting toy" and a "toyfull book" in words addressed notionally to his siblings, rendering his literary and poetical works "splendid trifles."[13]

Literary works had been dubbed "toys" before Sidney, as a way of describing not just their emptiness but the dangerous and enervating pleasures that they could induce—"What toyes, that dayly readyng of such a booke . . . may worke in the will of a yong jentelman?" gasped Roger Ascham, exaggeratedly anxious about the effect of chivalric romances—but it was in no small part thanks to Sidney's influence that "vaine toyes" became, as Joseph Campana observes, "a signature phrase" in early modern discussions of poetry, especially when referring to what Thomas Campion termed "the childish titillation of rhyming."[14]

Even this brief detour through the vicissitudes of the term *toy* shows why its developing meanings resonate so suggestively with iconoclasm as child's play. *Toy* is, from the beginning, a paradoxical category of object—trifling but dangerous, self-evidently inane yet peculiarly, even overwhelmingly, alluring—and it is from this curious combination of qualities that the eventually dominant meaning, a child's plaything, emerges. Before they are playthings, toys are objects that seem empty and full at once—or, perhaps, brimming over with the emptiness that is imputed to them, an emptiness that is oddly rich and fecund. As I have suggested, this peculiar dynamic unites the varying and intertwined contexts in which, across the previous chapters, we have seen the term *toy* being used: it can refer to reviled objects worshipped by one's Christian enemies—"triflinge toyes and tromprie"; to the idols of pagan savages—the "many foolish toyes and vaine shewes" of the Guineans and their fetishes; to the "ink-wasting toy" that a poet or romancer might produce; and, increasingly, to a child's playthings. As the term emerges and its meanings change and expand, it circulates between the realms of religion and irreligion; the incipient domain of the aesthetic in which play had long assumed, and would go on to assume, a prominent role; and the realm of children. The spheres of potential significance through which, I have argued, objects of iconoclastic child's play have the potential to pass are precisely those between which the word *toy* itself flitted as it assumed its modern meaning in the course of the sixteenth century.

If, as I have argued, play itself can be understood, both historically and theoretically, as a way of organizing, occupying, and being occupied by time, then toys—as the objects that enable and structure certain forms of this play—can be understood as objects through which we initially and continually navigate the temporality of existence, akin to eddies in or intensified congealments of time as it is experienced. We saw in previous chapters the way in which adults seek to shape the playing of children into a sleekly linear developmental trajectory, but it is now important to stress that this occurred in no small part through the provision of particular objects. Plato claimed that boys destined to be builders or farmers "should be provided by their tutors with miniature tools on the pattern of real ones"; Dominici proposed that children playing at piety should be given "a little altar or two . . . different coloured little vestments . . . [a] little bell"; and we recall the dolls, masks, and other objects with which Bruegel's children play. These toys suggest a longer history, and a wider national diffusion, for what Roland Barthes once identified as the chief characteristics of "French toys":

All the toys one commonly sees are essentially a microcosm of the adult world; they are reduced copies of human objects, as if in the eyes of the public the child was, all told, nothing but a smaller man, a homunculus to whom must be supplied objects of his own size. . . . French toys *always mean something*, and this something is always entirely socialized, constituted by the myths and techniques of modern adult life: the Army, Broadcasting, the Post Office, Medicine . . . School, Hair-Styling. . . . The fact that the toys *literally* prefigure the world of adult functions obviously cannot but prepare the child to accept them all, by constituting for him, even before he can think about it, the alibi of a Nature which has at all times created soldiers, postmen and Vespas. Toys here reveal all the things the adult does not find unusual: war, bureaucracy, ugliness.[15]

Barthes gives an admirably lucid account of the role that toys provided by adults are implicitly supposed to assume: organizing children within time, limiting the range of meanings and horizons within which they are allowed to act and to signify, and naturalizing the historically contingent adult world for which they are destined. But, as I have suggested, this should essentially be read as a defensive maneuver, a process that needs careful managing precisely because of the tendency for children to spiral off into other temporal narratives and moods— destructive, joyous, troublingly blank.

We can begin to approach these alternative temporalities of play through the work of Giorgio Agamben, whose thought richly brings together play and iconoclasm as related temporal forms, without recognizing that they did periodically converge in the same activity. In his essay "In Playland: Reflections on History and Play," another discussion of play that begins with the work of Claude Lévi-Strauss, Agamben makes the striking claim that "everything pertaining to play once pertained to the realm of the sacred. . . . Everything which is old, independent of its sacred origins, is liable to become a toy."[16] This emphasis on the toy as the product of a process of *becoming*, as the outcome of extended temporal drift, is integral to the nature and status of such objects as Agamben describes them: "The essential character of the toy—the only one, on reflection, that can distinguish it from other objects—is something quite singular, which can be grasped only in the temporal dimension of a 'once upon a time' and a 'no more.' . . . The toy is what belonged—*once, no longer*—to the realm of the sacred or of the practical-economic. But if this is true, the essence of the toy . . . is, then, an eminently *historical* thing: indeed it is, so to speak, the Historical in its pure state."[17]

This is, perhaps, a surprisingly strong claim for a general connection between the toy and the nature of history in general, but it is at its most convincing as an interpretation of iconoclastic child's play. The adults who placed holy things in the hands of children sought to effect the sort of epochal change for which the iconoclast always in some sense aims, and in doing so, in Agamben's terms, they aimed to blend their epochal ambitions with the historical shift effected by the formation of the object into a toy. If Agamben's claim that the toy is a distillation of history seems grandiloquent, hyperbolic, then this is precisely the hyperbole of the iconoclast who seeks to enlist the help of the playing child in closing off one epoch and inaugurating another. Agamben loftily argues that "what children play with is history": this is, implicitly, the equally grand claim of the parent who placed holy things in a child's hands in order to help inaugurate a new era of religious truth.[18]

Ultimately, however, Agamben seems at odds with himself on the temporal nature of the toy and the mode of historical time that it embodies. In another essay he selects *profanation* as the term for what I have been calling iconoclasm, and there, too, he argues that "the passage from the sacred to the profane can, in fact, also come about by means of an entirely inappropriate use (or, rather, reuse) of the sacred: namely, play."[19] The ambiguity here—whether play recapitulates sacred use or departs from it—is deliberately delicate; but in this essay Agamben compromises careful analysis with the hoary claim that we, here, today, have forgotten how to play or to play properly: "Play as an organ of profanation is in decline everywhere. Modern man proves he no longer knows how to play precisely through the vertiginous proliferation of old and new games."[20] Agamben's version of this claim is quite original—we have forgotten how to play because we have forgotten how properly to profane—but the evacuation of play from the present is entirely traditional. The nostalgia for a mythical past time in which play was everywhere, and everywhere satisfying, is balanced in his work by another unusual but no more convincing dimension, which is his projection of play into a barely imaginable future. "To return to play its purely profane dimension is a political task," he writes, and elsewhere in his writing he offers a glimpse of what this task might involve, in relation to prevailing forms of law: "One day humanity will play with law just as children play with disused objects, not in order to restore them to their canonical use but to free them from it for good. What is found after the law is not a more proper and original use value that precedes the law, but a new use that is born only after it. And use, which has been contaminated by law, must also be freed from its own value. This liberation is the task of study, or of play."[21]

I am simply not convinced that we need this hazy future in order to think through the transformative potential of child's play. Although Agamben explicitly distances himself from a view of history as "the continuous progression of speaking humanity through linear time" in favor of "hiatus, discontinuity, epoché," there is underpinning his rich and valuable account of the temporality of play and playthings an oddly conventional vision of play unfolding in and through a continuous stream of time. A past in which it was integrally connected to the realm of the sacred through properly complex processes of transition and profanation gives way to an etiolated, impoverished present from which it was evacuated, while he gestures toward a utopian future in which it will somehow be rediscovered and reinstituted.[22] It is here, I think, that the object of iconoclastic child's play can usefully help us rethink what a toy is and what it does and provide alternative ways for thinking about the existence of subjects and objects through time. Let me return to Agamben's foundational claim—that "the toy is what belonged—*once, no longer*—to the realm of the sacred or of the practical-economic." While this account of the toy as outcome of a process of historical change is valuable, it is this sense of the transformation of the object as *decisive* and *irreversible* that I find less convincing. Agamben simplifies the temporal trajectories along which objects can pass; for all of its subtlety, his clearly delineated schema of play functioning differently in former, present, and possible future times reinforces what Bruno Latour calls "the very modern impression that we are living in a new time that breaks with the past."[23] Agamben usefully eschews the smooth, sleek linearity of temporal models underpinning the view of play as an entirely knowable form of development, but he remains wedded to linearity itself. By contrast Latour argues that

modern temporality is the result of a retraining imposed on entities which would pertain to all sorts of times and possess all sorts of ontological statuses. . . . Modernizing progress is thinkable only on condition that all the elements that are contemporary according to the calendar belong to the same time. . . . Then, and only then, time forms a continuous and progressive flow. . . .

The beautiful order is disturbed once the quasi-objects are seen as mixing up different periods, ontologies, and genres. Then a historical period will give the impression of a great hotchpotch.[24]

Latour's account builds on his earlier conversations with Michel Serres, in which Serres argued that "time does not always flow according to a line . . . but rather, according to an extraordinarily complex mixture, as though it reflected stopping points, ruptures, deep wells; chimneys of thunderous acceleration, rendings, gaps. . . . Every historical era is . . . multitemporal, simultaneously drawing from the obsolete, the contemporary and the futuristic. An object, a circumstance, is thus polychronic, multitemporal, and reveals a time that is gathered together, with multiple pleats."[25] Latour and Serres's account chimes with the earlier and rather less well-known claim by Siegfried Kracauer that "time not only conforms to the conventional image of a flow but must also be imagined as being not such a flow. We live in a cataract of times. And there are 'pockets' and voids among these temporal currents."[26] The object of iconoclasm as child's play—the holy thing that becomes a toy—is the polychronic object par excellence. Thanks to the fragmented evidence by which it reaches us, like the zigzagging trickle of a raindrop down a window rather than a gushing cataract, it constitutes just such a pocket or void in the flow of history.

The accounts by Kracauer, Latour, and Serres are only some of the various strands of thought from the past few decades that have stressed the uneven, tangled temporal trajectories of objects, their seeming capacity to collapse or telescope disconnected moments of time, to move in and out of different categories of being and meaning. I mentioned in my introduction the importance of feminist, queer, and postcolonial theorists in this regard, and I would add here the seminal work of Arjun Appadurai and Igor Kopytoff on the dynamic and reversible processes of commodification. Kopytoff observes that "the same thing may be treated as a commodity at one time and not at another . . . [and] the same thing may, at the same time, be seen as a commodity by one person and as something else by another. . . . Commoditization, then, is best looked upon as a process of becoming rather than as an all-or-none state of being."[27] Appadurai argues that since "things can move in *and* out of the commodity state," we should look "at *the commodity potential of all things* rather than searching fruit-lessly for the magic distinction between commodities and other sorts of thing."[28] I also observed in my introduction that many recent theoretical discussions of the nature of materiality and objecthood *tout court* have found themselves turn-ing to the toy as the paradigmatic or exemplary object, and my investigations have convinced me that this is no accident. I want to suggest in closing that we should rethink our everyday sense of a toy as an object that is *for* a child to play with and, adapting Appadurai's formulation, open up alternative possibilities for the temporality of play by considering *the toy potential of all things*. This might sound abstract, but it has eminently practical implications for the categories that we even consider deploying for new objects or ideas as we encounter them. I mentioned in Chapter 2 the difficulty that archaeologists have in distinguishing between children's toys and other kinds of figurine, but the problem becomes more challenging still once we appreciate that many kinds of object pass in and out of a child's play world for a period, without being obviously toylike. As Sally Crawford puts it, "*All* objects have and had the potential to be used by children as toys."[29] This practical possibility was demonstrated by a famous archaeologi-cal experiment conducted in the 1970s when a recently vacated Native Ameri-can camp was studied, and the fragments found there categorized and analyzed, with the findings then tested against the accounts of the former inhabitants. It was found that while some objects were immediately identified as "toy remains that are usually associated with juvenile behavioural patterns" such as "a plastic nut from a mechanical toy set . . . and a piece of plastic from an enigmatic toy," there were others that were misidentified altogether: "Dynamite wire recorded in area 1 and area 6 was used as a plaything rather than as snare wire. The stick with wire strung across it did not relate to hunting activities, but instead was used as a stick horse by the youngest member of the camp."[30]

I suggest that we try to approach the remnants of the early modern past as akin to these scraps of wire and wood, which might at different moments have eminently pragmatic or technological purposes (to explode, to hunt, to educate) but might also pass into being toys, permanently or for a time. We need to re-flect not only on the original intentions behind the designs of objects or texts but, as Webb Keane suggests, consider an object's "instigation . . . to certain sorts of action, and, thus, its futurity."[31] Let me consider the practical implications of this suggestion by returning a final time to my first and last examples of icono-clastic child's play—Roger Edgeworth's sermon and the statues at Audley End.

Iconoclasm as child's play, as I have extrapolated it from Edgeworth's scene, is a rich, fraught, and unstable phenomenon precisely because it involves a potential clash of temporalities and of statuses—on the part of the children, the object, and the play itself. The adults *require* the temporal unpredictability and disorganization of the children, their propensity to ruin the objects with which they play; offering the object up to the child's temporal world is a way of severing it from the carefully ordered forms of sacred time in which it had previously been embedded. But adults also *fear* the limits of the control that they can exert once the object enters into the unpredictable time of the child's play world, where new meanings proliferate; hence, they interrogate the children and stamp their approval on only one version of this play's meaning, turning it into an inverted form of the inculcation of pious habits through time. The object of iconoclastic child's play is thus potentially suspended between at least three temporalities: holy time, the unfolding playtime of the child, and the playtime mandated by adults. We might therefore say that if it is fair to designate the iconoclastic plaything as a toy, it is so in three senses, or in three time frames, simultaneously: a holy toy to a believer (in a manner undiminished, and perhaps even augmented, by its impious treatment, which is always potentially temporary and reversible); a child's plaything in one sense for the adults who watch and dictate the play (a trivial, worthless object); and, perhaps, an entirely different plaything for the children themselves, when the adults' vigilance slips, and they are no longer watching. Hence, the object of iconoclasm as child's play is emphatically polysemic and polychronic, and its possible meanings and timings resonate with a fourth bundle of temporalities, inhabited by those of us who might seek to apprehend this scene and the meanings with which it pulsates in the present.

If we turn back now to the Audley End figures, we might ask, Is it accurate to designate them as *toys*? We happen to know, thanks to a chance reference in an antiquarian work, that they spent part of their existence—their "biography," as Kopytoff would call it—as children's playthings, dolls; but we also know that they were not designed for this purpose. It is precisely this notion of an object as a *part-time toy*, however, that interests me. It might be argued that the survival of historical artifacts as toys is a marginal practice—the Audley End figures are, after all, the only objects to which I can point and say with absolute certainty that they endured for this reason—and some might say that I am overinterpreting the scant evidence in according them such significance. I would contend, conversely, that the question of what it means to interpret, underinterpret, or overinterpret material artifacts is precisely what these figures can help us to rethink: once we know that some objects survived, for however long, by being transformed into playthings, it must alter the way in which we view the material traces of the past and multiply the functions and meanings that they might have assumed at different points in their trajectories. This is a point with serious implications for museums and galleries (recall that the actual staircase at Audley End provides no information as to these objects' histories). The date and circumstances of a work's *creation* are typically seen as its only salient characteristics, but if we follow Keane's emphasis on the object's *futurity*, we might ask, with him, "What do material things make possible? . . . How might they change the person?"[32] An intensified awareness of the possible temporal trajectories and vicissitudes that an artifact can undergo is by no means a mere anachronism but part of what it means to encounter such objects *now*. Furthermore, as Alexander Nagel and Christopher Wood argue in their compelling account of the Renaissance visual arts, "no device more effectively generates the effect of a doubling or bending of time than the work of art, a strange kind of event whose relation to time is plural."[33] They analyze numerous works from the period that foreground or dramatize "the clash between temporalities," such as Botticelli's *Portrait of a Youth Holding an Icon*, which, by incorporating an actual icon of the Eastern church into its canvas, suggested both analogy and disjunction between two modes of making present, as well as *staging* holy things like icons as "portable objects with 'careers.' "[34] "The power of the image," they acknowledge, "or the work of art, to fold time, was neither discovered nor invented in the Renaissance. What *was* distinctive about the European Renaissance, so called, was its apprehensiveness about the temporal instability of the artwork, and its recreation of the artwork as a reflection on that instability."[35] Based on this rich account, we might rethink artworks and artifacts of various sorts from this period not as defined solely in terms of the time of their creation but as objects that foreground and interrogate the simultaneous or potential presence of multiple temporal frames, and, if they cannot anticipate the *specific* temporal stages through which they move, they do at least anticipate that they *will*, most likely, move through various temporal stages (their futurity, as opposed to a predetermined future). Historical interpretation "tends not to want to take up the possibility of the work's symbolic reach *beyond* this historical life-world that created it—its ability to symbolize realities unknown to its own makers."[36] To the list of these unknowable realities we must add the possibility that such works can become children's playthings; it is not a fate that can be anticipated, but it is one that can be imagined, and it is in this spirit that I am suggesting we approach a whole range of works from the past in terms of what I have called their *toy potential*. It is helpful to shift here from the *intentions* underpinning an object's creation to what James Gibson calls its subsequent *affordances*: "what it *offers* the animal, what it *provides* or *furnishes*, either for good or ill" (and Gibson does include "the affordance of a toy" for kinds of play among his examples).[37] *Do we know that this object survived as an object of iconoclastic child's play?* This is the wrong question. *Once we know that iconoclastic child's play took place, how might it change our sense of the sorts of play that we understand an object to afford, the ludic actions that it might make possible or available?* This, I think, is a question worth asking, one that has the potential to expand what we consider possible, or imaginable, when confronted by the remnants of the past.

———————

Nagel and Wood's analysis is predicated on the distinctive ability of the visual arts to foreground these clashes or interplays between the temporal dimensions of an object: "Visual artifacts collapsed past and present with a force not possessed by texts. They proposed an immediate, present-tense, somatic encounter with the people and things of the past."[38] I am not so sure: the notion of a single object as polychronic, interweaving various forms and experiences of time that in turn inflect its futurity, the temporal experience that we might have of the object, strikes me as having potentially useful and still underexploited potential for addressing the linguistic texture of literary works, including those from the early modern period, whose overlaid strategies of allusion, historical and mythical reference, and experiential immediacy frequently lend them the sense of belonging to more than one time at once. I would like to end this book by pointing toward these possibilities via an example from the English poetry of the period, which is both the closest analogy to iconoclastic child's play that I have encountered and, I hope, illuminates the benefits of approaching texts and the entities that they describe and contain via the temporalities and interpretative instabilities of play as I have presented them in the preceding chapters, including my closing suggestion of the *toy potential* of a wide array of objects.

The episode that I have in mind occurs near the end of book 1 of Edmund Spenser's allegorical epic romance *The Faerie Queene*. This first book, "The Legend of Holiness," culminates with a titanic battle between the book's hero, the

Red Crosse Knight, and the malevolent dragon whose defeat has been the ultimate aim of his quest. The dragon seems to be crammed almost with more significance than it can bear: religious and historical allegory sit conspicuously alongside fairy tale and myth amid its many resonances.[39] Once the dragon is defeated, however, the proliferation of potential meanings with which it seems to thrum fall suddenly away. It is reduced to a hulking carcass, "so huge and horrible a masse" of flesh.[40] Shorn of its allegorical significance, this creature becomes a mere slab of meat.

In reducing this horribly lively figure of satanic malevolence to lifeless inertia, the Red Crosse Knight behaves like a good iconoclast, in keeping with his belatedly revealed identity as "Saint George of merry England"; indeed, many critics have seen an iconoclastic impulse at work in both the subject matter and the technique of Spenser's first book.[41] "In the 'Legend of Holiness,'" writes James Kearney, "Spenser not only depicts a range of idolatrous texts and books but also elaborates an iconoclastic hermeneutics that distinguishes between a properly transcendent reading and an idolatrous tarrying with letters and things."[42] In making this claim, Kearney joins a number of critics who have recognized the centrality of iconoclasm to *The Faerie Queene*.[43] As with the case of Francis Bacon, this iconoclastic impulse is part and parcel of the view of Spenser as constitutionally opposed to play. Milton's famous characterization of "our sage and serious poet Spenser" has largely remained the horizon within which the tone of his work has been interpreted.[44] Again like Bacon, even when Spenser's playfulness has been acknowledged, it is interpreted *in terms of* an underlying seriousness that is taken for granted rather than unsettling what this seriousness is and what it might mean.[45]

If the fate of the dragon at the end of book 1 seems to exemplify this serious, iconoclastic impulse, it is notable that the creature is not reduced to ashes and powder: like the holy thing allowed to remain in situ in broken form, it lingers as a material mass subjected to new practices and interpretations. When the "raskall many . . . Heaped together in rude rabblement" pour from the city to behold the fallen beast, "The sight with ydle feare did them dismay, / Ne durst approach him nigh, to touch, or once assay" (1.12.9.1–2, 8–9). It is not the anxieties of the adult townspeople, however, that most richly embody the propensity of Spenser's allegorical villains to continue accruing meanings even after they have been broken and laid low. The "rude rabblement" who approach the giant carcass are accompanied by "the fry of children yong," who "their wanton

sports and childish mirth did play" (1.12.9.2, 7.1–2). If the adults approach the
dragon with extreme trepidation, theirs is an anxiety from which these children
are blithely liberated, though the adults remain anxious on the children's behalf,
alarmed at their gaming:

> One mother, whenas her foolehardy chyld
> Did come too neare, and with his talants play
> Halfe dead through feare, her litle babe reuyld,
> And to her gossibs gan in counsel say;
> How can I tell, but that his talants may
> Yet scratch my sonne, or rend his tender hand. (1.12.11.1–6)

The horrifying dragon is reduced not only to a lifeless carcass but to a child's plaything. On one level the emergence of the children makes sense: the titanic clash
has had the feel of a fairy tale, a rattling yarn emerging from popular culture;
indeed, both St. George and the Dragon often lived on in sixteenth-century England even after they were proscribed as popish idols.[46] Even this context, however,
cannot account for the delicate modulations of this moment in Spenser's poem.
The effect of the children who surround and play with the dragon is not to continue the grand spectacle that has gone before: given the *sturm und drang* of the
preceding battle, it is a startling tonal shift. Despite the dragon's vast size, the fact
that its threat is now so humdrum draws it, like the object of iconoclastic child's
play, into the realm of the domestic and the ordinary. The mother is not afraid
because her son is toying with an allegory of satanic malevolence; the dragon's
claws are just another sharp surface that might endanger the boy's "tender hand,"
no different in kind from a pair of mishandled scissors. The children are happy
to play with the fearsome talons of the fallen monster, cheerfully unaware of the
hermeneutic problems posed by its continued presence in the poem and, indeed,
in Reformation culture, after it has outworn its allegorical usefulness.

The narrator's adjectives in describing the children's activity—"wanton sports
and childish mirth"—seem to protest too much, and the force of this narrative
dismissal and the mother's anxiety serves to heighten the focus on this fleetingly
mentioned play. There is the sense that a radical change has silently occurred,
a profound shift in the assumptions about the kinds of beings who populate
Spenser's poem and our potential ways of relating to them, that we only now
realize we had been adopting until this point. We would never have thought that
an apocalyptic, heavily allegorical dragon might serve as a plaything, and now

we cannot help but wonder what it might look and feel like to the children, what sort of games might be spun around its vast, ungainly bulk. We are suddenly put in the remarkable and unexpected position of viewing this vast allegorical demon in terms of its *toy potential*. The sense that the status of the fallen dragon changes and shifts at this moment, and will continue to change through the rhythms of the play converging on it (the children's and the reader's), is heightened by the very brevity and opacity of the description, the powerful sense that these games—the motives of the children and the changed nature of the dragon as it becomes a plaything—are allowed to remain opaque and mysterious to the reader as well as to the diegetic parents and the narrator. Finally, the terrified sense among the townspeople that the dragon might not be truly dead—"for yet perhaps remaynd / Some lingering life within his hollow brest" (1.12.10.3–4)— is both nullified and realized by the playing children: they calm such anxiety in their blithe inadvertence, even as they confirm its basis by showing that the dragon will continue to verge on the animate, stubbornly refusing to vanish or to die, precisely by virtue of its becoming a plaything.

Its lingering as a giant toy ensures that this creature will not vanish entirely from the landscape of the poem. Just as Bruegel's playing children staged the parallel questions of what it meant to interpret both their play and the painting in which they were depicted, the playing children in Faerieland are integral to, and a figure for, Spenser's compulsive interrogation of the cognitive and representational commitments of his own poem and his equally compulsive need to acknowledge forms of action and life that stand outside the totalized meaningfulness of his allegory.[47] Spenser's dragon, like the images played with by the children whom Edgeworth describes, is not reduced to mere triviality when it becomes a toy. Instead, it becomes a new sort of being. It is impossible to specify just what it becomes because to do so, to assign it a new determinate meaning, would be to fold it back into the logic of the allegory; Spenser allows both the children and the dragon to retain the uncomfortable, electrifying, exclusionary blankness that Bruegel allows his children and their games. The dragon here becomes an "Idoll," to repeat Edgeworth's potentially punning orthography: not an object definitively shorn of meaning but one for which play opens up the possibility of newly emerging and oscillating temporalities and forms of attachment, potentially both caring and violent, that cannot be delimited or anticipated. The reader must ask at this point what it means for the techniques and commitments of Spenser's poem (and his wider culture) if even the most threatening allegorical being can become a toy—and if this change can occasion an opaque delight, for the children and for the reader of the poem, that seems entirely separate from the violently iconoclastic energies responsible for the dragon's destruction.

If the dragon's transformation into an everyday plaything gives a thrill of playful pleasure through the unanticipated possibility that an allegorical hulk might have *toy potential*, it is also, in Gordon Teskey's terms "a destabilizing element in a totality," prompting the reader both to respond differently to the entire poem and to respond wonderingly to her or his own response.[48] This shifting rhythm of response to *The Faerie Queene* might itself be understood or experienced as a form of play, radically discontinuous, its terms and logic shifting as we progress, like the unfolding rhythms of a child with a toy. Prominent among the thrilling and terrifying challenges with which Spenser's poem confronts its readers is the challenge of retrospection created by such moments. It is not enough to forge onward with the single-mindedness of a questing knight in order to interpret *The Faerie Queene*; instead, it can sometimes feel, impossibly, as if the reader needs constantly to start again and reread the entire poem up to that point in light of a new revelation about the ways in which it proves able to operate.

Although it arrives in the poem bearing an overabundance of symbolic malevolence, a terrifying panoply of fangs, fire, and flaggy wings, once reread in terms of its eventually realized *toy potential*, the dragon's behavior on its first appearance can be seen retrospectively as hardly in keeping with its demonic status. When Redcrosse and Una first spot the dragon, it is engaged in noticeably unthreatening behavior: "stretcht he lay vpon the sunny side, / Of a great hill, himselfe like a great hill" (1.11.4.5–6). The dragon is lazily lolling beneath the sun's warm rays, not aggressively poised to strike. Several stanzas are devoted to the beast's terrifying visage and bulk, but, as it approaches the knight, the effect is once again rather different:

> So dreadfully he towardes him did pas,
> Forelifting vp aloft his speckled brest,
> And often bounding on the brused gras,
> As for great ioyaunce of his newcome guest. (1.11.15.1–4)

The reader has been led since the third stanza of the poem to anticipate the knight's eventual conflict with "a Dragon horrible and stearne" (1.1.3.9), but this is hardly what is initially encountered when the long-anticipated, titanic struggle finally arrives. The dragon's behavior when it first appears is itself remarkably

playful and makes comparisons to domestic pets feel irresistible. It is first apprehended stretched out like a cat in the sun, but, once it catches sight of the Red
Cross Knight, it behaves less like a malevolent foe and more like a dog bouncing
with excitement and anticipation at the sight of its returning owner. The adverb
dreadfully is seemingly undercut by the ensuing lines, in which the dragon appears engaging and exuberant. It does not approach with implacable malice but
with joyous hospitality.

Even this joy could bring its own horrors: it might be nothing but the grisly
relish of a predator, who plans to play with the knight like a cat with a mouse (or
perhaps in the way that Montaigne's cat played with him).[49] After all, the description of bouncing delight quickly evaporates, and the reader is subjected to a series
of stanzas in which the dragon's threatening characteristics are exhaustively and
exhaustingly enumerated. But the ebullient mood that returns when the children
emerge and play with the dragon's corpse retrospectively clarifies and amplifies
the dragon's initial happiness. Spenser frames this threatening allegorical figure
within a surplus of playful energy, and when his dragon enters, it is glimpsed as
a playful individual in its own right, almost a character, as prophesying its destiny as a toy. The dragon *delights* in its allegorical function. While the reader had
been waiting for it to arrive since the poem's third stanza, the dragon, it suddenly
and startlingly seems, has also been waiting excitedly, not only for the knight but
for the reader to turn up. Here, at the apparent pinnacle of allegorical and typo-
logical explicitness—the peak of iconoclastic fervor—we find an abundance of
childish play, not only in the way that the dragon's body is finally treated but also
in the mood of its arrival. This is an urge to play that the overt aims of the poem
scarcely require and for which it can hardly account. Spenser accords the dragon
pronounced pleasure in its ability to fulfill its allegorical function. "You're here at
last, after quite a wait for both of us!" its actions seem to suggest.

In making this claim, I am seeking to go beyond the well-worn argument
that the literal surface of the poem can be enjoyed for its own sake, which has
informed many readings since Hazlitt's famous claim regarding readers of *The
Faerie Queene* that "if they do not meddle with the allegory, it will not meddle
with them"—a claim that he notably develops by comparing those terrified of
the allegory with "a child [who] looks at a painted dragon, and thinks it will
strangle them in its shining folds."[50] What the reader experiences is neither blithe
indifference to the allegory nor fear before it; and, after all, Spenser's children
play with the dragon in the conspicuous absence of the adults' fear. The reader

does not rest contented and unthinking at the literal level but both delights in it and wonders questioningly at the terms of this very delight. Once the dragon is revealed to have been waiting for the knight and to delight doggishly at his arrival, the reader cannot resist speculating about what kind of creature it is. What are its joys and its pleasures? How does it feel about being a vast, malevolent allegory? How was it passing the time as it waited for Redcrosse on the sunny hillside, before leaping up and practically wagging its vast, terrifying tail? Did it get bored? Did it play its own dragon games? And, following from questions of this sort—which are, I am suggesting, at once fanciful, extravagant, and inescapable—a second set of questions: what does it say about me as a reader that I find myself asking such bizarre questions? What does it say about *The Faerie Queene*, and about the iconoclastic Reformation culture of which it is often taken as the quintessential expression, that it creates pockets of space within which such play and such questions seem to emerge? Am I reading too much into the dragon's behavior? Or, conversely, might it be that I have missed opportunities to ask such questions of other moments in the poem (and in other poems, as well as other texts and objects from Spenser's wider culture, to which seriousness is so often imputed)—passed unwittingly on other invitations to play?

Spenser's toy dragon provokes his readers both to bizarre speculations of this sort and to reflections on them. It is impossible to know what the dragon is truly thinking, but it is remarkable to be put in a position of even wondering about the inner life of this allegorical beast. William Oram has recently written that *The Faerie Queene* as a whole tends toward the comic, since "evil figures die by the score while, if one excepts Una's lion, no character we care about loses his life."[51] But there are evil figures in the poem about whom we *do* care and who, precisely because they are *not* fully fleshed-out characters, possess the thrilling ability to exceed their assigned role in the moral universe of the poem. We both postulate inner lives for such figures, who at first seemed constructed from the most flimsy and tired of conventions, and enjoy the extravagance of our own investments, as well as the possibility that they might be wonderfully misplaced.[52] We cannot access the dragon's inner life, but it is the sense that such a life both exists and remains opaque that ensures our playful, shifting relationship with the poem as a vast, playful, polychronic entity with a *toy potential* of its own. Likewise, it cannot be known what sorts of games the children will play with the fallen dragon's claws. Spenser seems determined to allow their play to remain a blank, unscrutinized interval beyond adult interpretation and co-option; he is resolved *not* to imagine their imagination. It is the reader's very exclusion from the details of their games that opens new possibilities—that the joyous, bouncing dragon that is first encountered will live on in a curious fashion in the responsive and opaque cavorting of the playing children, much as a holy thing taken from a church and placed in a child's hands might thereby be imbued with unsettling and lingering traces of life.

ACKNOWLEDGMENTS

The closing pages of this book are about the strange forms of delight and affection toward a particularly malevolent dragon that I found myself feeling when reading Spenser's *Faerie Queene*. In the course of working on it, I have been introduced to many other delightful dragons: an audience member at a seminar recommended to me a children's book about a clockwork dragon; one scholar friend showed me a picture-book about a dragon that her daughter had written; one of my former teachers, renowned for his fearsomely detailed knowledge of seventeenth-century politics, spoke up in the Q&A following a conference paper to tell me about a toy crocodile that terrified and captivated him as a child.

I mention this parade of reptiles because one of the pleasures of working on *Iconoclasm as Child's Play* has been that, while it has led me to have many serious scholarly discussions, it has also reminded me that intellectual interests are always complexly located amid memories, families, and stories of all kinds. The "debt to childhood," writes Jean-François Lyotard, "is one which we never pay off. But it is enough not to forget it in order to resist it and perhaps, not to be unjust. It is the task of writing, thinking, literature, arts, to venture to bear witness to it."* I hope that this book bears witness of this sort, and if I cannot repay my own debt to childhood, I am no less indebted to those who have left a mark on its pages. Above all, conversations with them have been perpetually surprising and a huge amount of fun, and, since their names are too many to list, I would like to collectively thank all of these friends and colleagues, and seminar and conference participants, for their searching and generous questions and suggestions

* Jean-François Lyotard, *The Inhuman: Reflections on Time*, trans. Geoffrey Bennington and Rachel Bowlby (Stanford: Stanford University Press, 1991), 7.

(numerous specific recommendations for reading are acknowledged in my endnotes). For their particular hospitality during visits on which parts of the book were presented, I would like to thank Ayesha Ramachandran, Rob Watson, and Leah Whittington. I must make special mention of Mike Schoenfeldt, who read the whole thing with characteristic generosity. So, too, did David Hillman: our friendship is sustaining, and our countless conversations are so woven into these pages that I have doubtless laid claim to many thoughts that were really his (all criticisms therefore to be directed to him, please).

Much of the work was undertaken while I was a fellow of Trinity College, Cambridge, and I would like to thank the entire college community, especially my colleagues and students in English and the members of the "Early Modern Club," on whom I tested my ideas. The book was completed after I had moved to Oxford, and I would like to thank my colleagues there in the English faculty and at University College for providing the warm and welcoming environment in which I finished it.

At Stanford University Press I would like to thank my editor Emily-Jane Cohen for her immediate and continued enthusiasm for the project, her patience, and her cajoling; Faith Wilson Stein for her clear and good-humored guidance; Anne Fuzellier for help during the production process; and Joe Abbott for meticulous copyediting. Parts of the preface and conclusion appeared, in significantly different form, in my article "Spenser at Play," *PMLA* 133, no. 1 (2018): 19–35; I am grateful for permission to reprint some of that material here.

Having written a book that's partly about the nervousness and horror that children often provoke and the weird stakes that adults have in them, it's probably safest to swerve altogether any cod-psychological reflection on how I got interested in these questions and simply say thank you to my parents, Chana and Raf, and my siblings, Gabe and Ruby, for pretty much everything. The help that my wife, Rosa Andújar, once again gave me with ancient Greek is just the tip of a towering iceberg of reasons to be grateful for her presence in my life.

When I began thinking hard about children at play, my thoughts were based largely on dim recollections and imaginings of my childhood; by the time I finished, my own children, Alejandro and Beatriz, had arrived and made every day thrum. This book is dedicated to them, with boundless love.

NOTES

PREFACE

1. The history of the area gave Latimer hope: the surroundings of Bristol had a rich tradition of Lollardy and vernacular religious practice and was therefore seen as fertile ground for reform. See Martha C. Skeeters, *Community and Clergy: Bristol and the Reformation, c. 1530–1570* (Oxford: Clarendon, 1993), chaps. 3–4, for an excellent account of this context. The best overview of his life and theology is the introduction to Roger Edgeworth, *Sermons Very Fruitfull, Godly and Learned*, ed. Janet Wilson (Cambridge: D. S. Brewer, 1993).

2. For the context of this dispute see Susan Wabuda, "'Fruitful Preaching' in the Diocese of Worcester: Bishop Hugh Latimer and His Influence, 1535–39," in *Religion and the English People, 1500–1640: New Voices, New Perspectives*, ed. Eric Josef Carlson (Kirksville, MO: Thomas Jefferson University Press, 1998), 49–74, esp. 64.

3. Edgeworth, *Sermons*, 143.

4. This general view is summed up in the title of Lee Palmer Wandel's excellent study, *Voracious Idols and Violent Hands: Iconoclasm in Reformation Zurich, Strasbourg, and Basel* (Cambridge: Cambridge University Press, 1994).

5. Thomas M. Greene, "Rescue from the Abyss: Scève's Dizain 378," in *The Vulnerable Text: Essays on Renaissance Literature* (New York: Columbia University Press, 1986), 99–115, 101.

6. For a thought-provoking exploration of these attachments see Carolyn Dinshaw, *How Soon Is Now? Medieval Texts, Amateur Readers, and the Queerness of Time* (Durham, NC: Duke University Press, 2012).

7. Donald F. Tuzin, *The Voice of the Tambaran: Truth and Illusion in Ilahita Arapesh Religion* (Berkeley: University of California Press, 1980), 216. See 35–46 for a detailed account of how children are initiated into the spirit cult, as well as the observation that "the novices are reduced to being pawns in the serious games grown-ups play" (101).

8. Michael Taussig, *Defacement: Public Secrecy and the Labor of the Negative* (Stanford: Stanford University Press, 1999), 204 (my emphasis).

9. Adam Phillips and Barbara Taylor, *On Kindness* (New York: Picador, 2009), 10.

10. Much of this work has responded to Philippe Ariès, *Centuries of Childhood: A Social History of Family Life*, trans. Robert Baldock (New York: Random House, 1965).

For a useful overview see Peter N. Stearns, *Childhood in World History* (London: Routledge, 2017). On early modern children in (and as) literature see Michael Witmore, *Pretty Creatures: Children and Fiction in the English Renaissance* (Ithaca, NY: Cornell University Press, 2007).

11. Ernst Kris and Otto Kurz, *Legend, Myth and Magic in the Image of the Artist* (New Haven, CT: Yale University Press, 1979), 76–77. See the excellent discussion of this passage and the issues that it raises in David Freedberg, *The Power of Images: Studies in the History and Theory of Response* (Chicago: University of Chicago Press, 1989), 201–4.

12. Anthony Pagden, *The Fall of Natural Man: The American Indian and the Origins of Comparative Ethnology* (Cambridge: Cambridge University Press, 1982), 106; see esp. 44, 104–5, and the quotations on 222n275, which straightforwardly state of the "Indians": "ellos son como niños."

13. Jacqueline Rose, *The Case of Peter Pan, or, The Impossibility of Children's Fiction*, rev. ed. (London: Macmillan, 1994), 3–4.

14. Michael Fried, *Absorption and Theatricality: Painting and Beholder in the Age of Diderot* (Chicago: University of Chicago Press, 1980), 10.

15. Fried, *Absorption and Theatricality*, 46, 47, 49, 51.

16. Ian Hacking, *Historical Ontology* (Cambridge, MA: Harvard University Press, 2002), 17.

17. See Dinshaw, *How Soon Is Now?* and the summaries of scholars including Chakrabarty, Bhabha, Kristeva, and Grosz in Jeffrey J. Cohen, *Medieval Identity Machines* (Minneapolis: University of Minnesota Press, 2003); and Jonathan Gil Harris, *Untimely Matter in the Age of Shakespeare* (Philadelphia: University of Pennsylvania Press, 2009).

18. Elizabeth Freeman, *Time Binds: Queer Temporalities, Queer Histories* (Durham, NC: Duke University Press, 2010), 3.

19. Wai Chi Dimock, "A Theory of Resonance," *PMLA* 112, no. 5 (1997): 1060–71; Rita Felski, *The Limits of Critique* (Chicago: University of Chicago Press, 2015), esp. chap. 5: "Context Stinks!"

20. Dimock, "A Theory of Resonance." Dimock's use of *resonance* both builds on and departs from the wide currency given to it by Stephen Greenblatt: see "Resonance and Wonder," in *Learning to Curse* (London: Routledge, 1990), 216–46.

21. Felski, *The Limits of Critique*, 15, 110.

22. Stephen K. White, *Sustaining Affirmation: The Strengths of Weak Ontology in Political Theory* (Princeton, NJ: Princeton University Press, 2000), ix.

23. See Angela Vanhaelen, *The Wake of Iconoclasm: Painting the Church in the Dutch Republic* (University Park, PA: Pennsylvania State University Press, 2012), 159, 178, discussing images by Herman Saftleven.

24. Gregory Bateson, *Mind and Nature: A Necessary Unity* (New York: E. P. Dutton, 1979), 139.

25. Stephen Greenblatt, *Renaissance Self-Fashioning from More to Shakespeare* (Chicago: University of Chicago Press, 1980), 220, 209.

26. Jacques Derrida, "Structure, Sign and Play in the Discourse of the Human Sciences," in *Writing and Difference*, trans. Alan Bass (London: Routledge, 1978), 351–70, 369–70 (emphases in the original). For useful discussion of Derrida's account see James Hans, "Derrida and Freeplay," *MLN* 94, no. 4 (1979): 809–26; and Robert R. Wilson,

"Play, Transgression and Carnival: Bakhtin and Derrida on *Scriptor Ludens*," *Mosaic* 19, no. 1 (1986): 73–89.

27. Friedrich Nietzsche, *Beyond Good and Evil*, trans. Marion Faber (Oxford: Oxford University Press, 1998), 62. On Nietzsche and play see Lawrence M. Hinman, "Nietzsche's Philosophy of Play," *Philosophy Today* 18, no. 2 (1974): 106–24.

28. Teresa L. Ebert, *Ludic Feminism: Postmodernism, Desire, and Labor in Late Capitalism* (Ann Arbor: University of Michigan Press, 1996), 148 and passim.

29. D. W. Winnicott, *Playing and Reality* (London: Routledge, 1971), 41 (emphasis in the original).

INTRODUCTION

1. Charles Baudelaire, "The Philosophy of Toys," trans. Paul Keegan, in *On Dolls*, ed. Kenneth Gross (London: Notting Hill, 2012), 11–21, 19.

2. Max Weber, *The Protestant Ethic and the Spirit of Capitalism*, trans. Talcott Parsons (New York: Routledge, 2002), 104, 113.

3. Weber, *The Protestant Ethic*, 124.

4. Johan Huizinga, *Homo Ludens: A Study of the Play Element in Culture* [trans. R. F. C. Hull] (London: Routledge, 1949), 179, 181. For useful commentary on Huizinga's account of the playfulness of the medieval period see Laura Kendrick, "Games Medievalists Play: How to Make Earnest of Game and Still Enjoy It," *New Literary History* 40, no. 1 (2009): 43–61.

5. Victor Turner, "Liminal to Liminoid, in Play, Flow, and Ritual: An Essay in Comparative Symbology," *Rice University Studies* 60, no. 3 (1974): 53–92, 69–71.

6. See Jane Bennett, *The Enchantment of Modern Life: Attachments, Crossings, Ethics* (Princeton, NJ: Princeton University Press, 2001), esp. 57–65 on Weber. For a judicious overview of these narratives in relation to early modern religion see Alexandra Walsham, "The Reformation and 'The Disenchantment of the World' Reassessed," *Historical Journal* 51, no. 2 (2008): 497–528; for a compelling account of the unevenness of secularization from a literary-theoretical perspective see Regina Schwartz, *Sacramental Poetics at the Dawn of Secularism: When God Left the World* (Stanford: Stanford University Press, 2008), esp. chaps.1–2.

7. Joseph Leo Koerner, *The Reformation of the Image* (Chicago: University of Chicago Press, 2004), 104. Koerner makes clear that this was an ideal impossible to realize in practice.

8. Huizinga, *Homo Ludens*, 206; Fredric Jameson, *Postmodernism, or, The Cultural Logic of Late Capitalism* (Durham, NC: Duke University Press, 1991), 147.

9. From Diderot's critique of the *Salon* of 1765, in *Magazin encyclopédique* III (I795): 52–53. Cited and translated by Stanley Idzerda, "Iconoclasm in the French Revolution," *American Historical Review* 60, no. 1 (1954): 13–26, 13.

10. Bruno Latour, "A Few Steps Toward an Anthropology of the Iconoclastic Gesture," *Science in Context* 10, no. 1 (1998): 63–83, 66.

11. Matthew Arnold, *Culture and Anarchy and Other Writings*, ed. Stefan Collini (Cambridge: Cambridge University Press, 1993), 193.

12. Michael Camille, *The Gothic Idol: Ideology and Image-Making in Medieval Art* (Cambridge: Cambridge University Press, 1989).

13. Tom Wilkinson, "Empty Niche Syndrome: On ISIS' Iconoclasm," *Architectural Review*, March 10, 2015, www.architectural-review.com/opinion/empty-niche-syndrome -on-isis-iconoclasm/8679747.article; Jesse Hirsch, "ISIS and Iconoclasm: The History of the Museum Smash," www.atlasobscura.com/articles/isis-and-iconoclasm-the-history-of -the-museum-smash. See also the excellent discussion of similar issues raised by earlier Islamic iconoclasm by Finbarr Barry Flood, "Between Cult and Culture: Bamiyan, Islamic Iconoclasm, and the Museum," *Art Bulletin* 84, no. 4 (2002): 641–59.

14. James Simpson, *Under the Hammer: Iconoclasm in the Anglo-American Tradition* (Oxford: Oxford University Press, 2010), 11.

15. This paradoxical dynamic has been pointed out by many writers, most influentially David Freedberg, *The Power of Images: Studies in the History and Theory of Response* (Chicago: University of Chicago Press, 1989), 415–16 (on the recurrent focus on eyes); and Bruno Latour, *On the Modern Cult of the Factish Gods*, trans. Catherine Porter and Heather MacLean (Durham, NC: Duke University Press, 2010).

16. Michael Taussig, *Defacement: Public Secrecy and the Labor of the Negative* (Stanford: Stanford University Press, 1999), 1 (emphasis in the original).

17. Taussig, *Defacement*, 27.

18. See Michael Kelly, *Iconoclasm in Aesthetics* (Cambridge: Cambridge University Press, 2003); and Dario Gamboni, *The Destruction of Art: Iconoclasm and Vandalism Since the French Revolution* (London: Reaktion, 1997).

19. Hans Belting, *Likeness and Presence: A History of the Image Before the Era of Art*, trans. Edmund Jephcott (Chicago: University of Chicago Press, 1994), 458–59 (emphasis in the original).

20. Hans-Georg Gadamer, "The Relevance of the Beautiful: Art as Play, Symbol, and Festival," in *The Relevance of the Beautiful and Other Essays*, trans. Nicholas Walker, ed. Robert Bernasconi (Cambridge: Cambridge University Press, 1986), 3–53, 3–4.

21. He is presumably referring to the Second Council of Nicaea in 787 CE, which made explicit and official the church's support for images and brought to an end the first cycle of Byzantine iconoclasm. For a useful overview of Byzantine iconoclasm see Alain Besançon, *The Forbidden Image: An Intellectual History of Iconoclasm*, trans. Jane Marie Todd (Chicago: University of Chicago Press, 2000), 123–42. For a brief and cogent account of the Second Council and its defense of images see Charles Barber, *Figure and Likeness: On the Limits of Representation in Byzantine Iconoclasm* (Princeton, NJ: Princeton University Press, 2002), 112–15.

22. Gadamer, "The Relevance of the Beautiful," 47. Gadamer develops a related and important aesthetics of play at points throughout his major philosophical work: see *Truth and Method*, trans. Joel Weinsheimer and Donald G. Marshall (London: Continuum, 1975), 102–10, 115–17, 483–84, 498–99; and Paul Guyer, *A History of Modern Aesthetics*, 3 vols. (Cambridge: Cambridge University Press, 2014), 3:50–56.

23. Gadamer, "The Relevance of the Beautiful," 29 (emphasis in the original).

24. Maurizio Bettini, *The Portrait of the Lover*, trans. Laura Gibbs (Berkeley: University of California Press, 1999), 216. For other, contrasting discussions of the indefinability of play see Taussig, *Defacement*, 188; Jeffrey Irving Israel, "The Capability of Play," University of Chicago Divinity School Religion and Culture Web Forum, Jan. 2009, 21–22, http://divinity.uchicago.edu/sites/default/files/imce/pdfs/webforum/012009/WF%20

J%20Israel%20January%202009.pdf; and Brian Upton, *The Aesthetic of Play* (Cambridge, MA: MIT Press, 2015), 9–21.

25. Huizinga, *Homo Ludens*, 7–8. A recent account of playfulness from a zoological and behavioral perspective similarly claims at the outset that true play must be "spontaneous and rewarding to the individual" and "intrinsically motivated": Patrick Bateson and Paul Martin, *Play, Playfulness, Creativity and Innovation* (Cambridge: Cambridge University Press, 2013), 2.

26. Martha C. Nussbaum, *Frontiers of Justice: Disability, Nationality, Species Membership* (Cambridge, MA: Harvard University Press, 2006), 77; see the discussion in Israel, "The Capability of Play."

27. Friedrich Schiller, *On the Aesthetic Education of Man, in a Series of Letters*, ed. and trans. Elizabeth M. Wilkinson and L. A. Willoughby (Oxford: Clarendon, 1967), 107.

28. Eugen Fink, "The Oasis of Happiness: Toward an Ontology of Play," trans. Ute Saine and Thomas Saine, *Yale French Studies* 41 (1968): 19–30, 24. Fink did acknowledge, however, that "we do occasionally find in play the opposite pole of freedom, namely a withdrawal from the real world, which can go so far as enslavement and trance" (25). For Fink's account of play and his broader ontology, still relatively little known in the English-speaking world, see D. F. Krell, "Towards an Ontology of Play: Eugen Fink's Notion of Spiel," *Research in Phenomenology* 2 (1972): 62–93.

29. Schiller, *On the Aesthetic Education of Man*, 107.

30. Immanuel Kant, *Critique of Judgment*, trans. Werner S. Pluhar (Indianapolis, IN: Hackett, 1987), 62.

31. Guyer, *A History of Modern Aesthetics*, 1:32; see also the discussions of free aesthetic play scattered throughout this work, esp. 1:67–78, 340, 431–36, 449–52, 2:4–8, 11–17. For play as a crucial category in Kant's *Anthropology*, see Rosalind C. Morris and Daniel H. Leonard, *The Returns of Fetishism: Charles de Brosses and the Afterlives of an Idea* (Chicago: University of Chicago Press, 2017), 170–74.

32. Schiller, *On the Aesthetic Education of Man*, 104–5.

33. Sianne Ngai, *Our Aesthetic Categories: Zany, Cute, Interesting* (Cambridge, MA: Harvard University Press, 2012), 241, 7. See especially 239–40 for Ngai's explicit discussion of traditions of aesthetic play, including Schiller.

34. Karl Marx, *Grundrisse*, trans. Martin Nicolaus (London: Penguin, 1993), 712. The target of this remark is not Schiller but Fourier. See Moishe Postone, *Time, Labour and Social Domination: A Reinterpretation of Marx's Critical Theory* (Cambridge: Cambridge University Press, 1993), esp. 33n48, 382.

35. Herbert Marcuse, *Eros and Civilization: A Philosophical Enquiry into Freud* (Boston: Beacon, 1966), 189. See the discussion in Francis Hearn, "Toward a Critical Theory of Play," *Telos* 30 (Dec. 1976): 145–60, 148–49; and Theodor W. Adorno, *Aesthetic Theory*, trans. Robert Hullot-Kentor (London: Continuum, 1997), 417. Play nonetheless occupies a crucial place in Adorno's aesthetic and social theory, which will be integral to my later discussion.

36. Paul de Man, "Kant and Schiller," in *Aesthetic Ideology*, ed. Andrzej Warminski (Minneapolis: University of Minnesota Press, 1996), 129–62, 150–51.

37. See, e.g., the wonderful account by Stephen Miller, "Ends, Means, and Galumphing: Some Leitmotifs of Play," *American Anthropologist* 75, no. 1 (1973): 87–98; and the

convenient overview with bibliography in Bateson and Martin, *Play, Playfulness*, esp. chaps. 2 and 6.

38. Michel de Montaigne, *The Essayes or Morall, Politike and Millitarie Discourses of Lo: Michaell de Montaigne*, trans. John Florio (London, 1603), 260. For discussion see Jacques Derrida, "The Animal That Therefore I Am (More to Follow)," trans. David Wills, *Critical Inquiry* 28, no. 2 (2002): 369–418, 375.

39. See Bennett, *Enchantment of Modern Life*, 137–48; Doris Sommer, *The Work of Art in the World* (Durham, NC: Duke University Press, 2014), chap.5: "Play Drive in the Hard Drive: Schiller's Poetics of Politics" (quotation at 135); and Gayatri Chakravorty Spivak, *An Aesthetic Education in the Era of Globalization* (Cambridge, MA: Harvard University Press, 2012), 2, 10.

40. Adorno, *Aesthetic Theory*, 7.

41. Bill Brown, "Reification, Reanimation, and the American Uncanny," *Critical Inquiry* 32, no. 2 (2006): 175–207, 175.

42. Bill Brown, *A Sense of Things: The Object Matter of American Literature* (Chicago: University of Chicago Press, 2003), 12; *The Material Unconscious: American Amusement, Stephen Crane, and the Economies of Play* (Cambridge, MA: Harvard University Press, 1996). See also Bill Brown, "How to Do Things with Things (A Toy Story)," *Critical Inquiry* 24, no. 4 (1998): 935–64.

43. Barbara Johnson, *Persons and Things* (Cambridge, MA: Harvard University Press, 2008), chaps. 1, 11.

44. Jane Bennett, *Vibrant Matter: A Political Ecology of Things* (Durham, NC: Duke University Press, 2010), vii (emphasis in the original).

45. C. S. Lewis, *An Experiment in Criticism* (Cambridge: Cambridge University Press, 1961), 17–18. I am grateful to Sean Geddes for this reference.

46. Alfred Gell, *Art and Agency: An Anthropological Theory* (Oxford: Clarendon, 1998), 7.

47. Gell, *Art and Agency*, 17–18. A similar comparison was the implicit basis of E. H. Gombrich's famous essay "Meditations on a Hobby Horse or the Roots of Artistic Form," in *Meditations on a Hobby Horse and Other Essays on the Theory of Art* (London: Phaidon, 1965), 1–11.

48. Antony Gormley, remarks made at the seminar on the inauguration of *Free Object*, Feb. 8, 2018, Trinity College, University of Cambridge. I am grateful to Sir Antony Gormley for permission to print his remarks.

CHAPTER 1

1. Henry Gee, *The Elizabethan Prayer-Book and Ornaments* (London: Macmillan, 1902), 147.

2. See Eamon Duffy, *The Stripping of the Altars: Traditional Religion in England, c. 1400–c. 1580* (New Haven, CT: Yale University Press, 1992), 572–73. The definitive account of these visitations is now Margaret Aston, *Broken Idols of the English Reformation* (Cambridge: Cambridge University Press, 2016), 164–83.

3. The surviving lists were published as *English Church Furniture, Ornaments and Decorations, at the Period of the Reformation: As Exhibited in a List of the Goods Destroyed in Certain Lincolnshire Churches, A.D. 1566*, ed. Edward Peacock (London: John

Camden Hotten, 1866), 30 (for breaking and burning), 33, 35, 36, 151, and elsewhere for profane usage.

4. Peacock, *English Church Furniture*, 57. Pyxes were targeted by fifteenth-century Lollards in a spate of robberies in London churches, so were established iconoclastic targets: see Duffy, *Stripping of the Altars*, 101.

5. Tinkers mentioned as recipients: Peacock, *English Church Furniture*, 33, 71; donations to the poor: 30, 104, 120.

6. Peacock, *English Church Furniture*, 95.

7. Peacock, *English Church Furniture*, 39 (for altar stones as paving slabs), 40, 147 (for rood-lofts as seats), 119 (for a rood loft converted into a bed).

8. Peacock, *English Church Furniture*, 55, 108.

9. See, e.g., J. W. Blench, *Preaching in England in the Late Fifteenth and Sixteenth Centuries* (Oxford: Basil Blackwell, 1964), 122; Keith Thomas, *Religion and the Decline of Magic* (London: Penguin, 1971), 86 (citing Blench as his authority); and Nicholas Orme, *Medieval Children* (New Haven, CT: Yale University Press, 2001), 172.

10. *The Catechism of Thomas Becon*, ed. John Ayre (Cambridge: Cambridge University Press, 1845), 62.

11. Edmund Spenser, "Maye," lines 236, 238–40, and commentary, in *The Shorter Poems*, ed. Richard A. McCabe (London: Penguin, 1999), 85. See the discussion in Jeffrey Knapp, *An Empire Nowhere: England, America and Literature from "Utopia" to "The Tempest"* (Berkeley: University of California Press, 1992), 118–19.

12. Johannes Bugenhagen, *Der ehrbaren Stadt Hamburg christliche Ordnung 1529: De Ordeninge Pomerani*, ed. Hans Wenn (Hamburg: Friedrich Wittig, 1976), 5–7. See the brief discussion by Amy Knight Powell, *Depositions: Scenes from the Late Medieval Church and the Modern Museum* (New York: Zone, 2012), 195.

13. See Alexandra Walsham, "The Pope's Merchandise and the Jesuit's Trumpery: Catholic Relics and Protestant Polemic in Post-Reformation England," in *Religion, the Supernatural and Visual Culture in Early Modern England*, ed. Jennifer Spinks and Dagmar Eichberger (Leiden: Brill, 2015), 370–409.

14. Peacock, *English Church Furniture*, 170.

15. Powell, *Depositions*, 106 (my emphasis).

16. E. H. Gombrich, "Huizinga's *Homo Ludens*," in *Johan Huizinga, 1872–1972*, ed. W. R. H. Koops et al. (The Hague: Martinus Nijhoff, 1973), 133–54, 145 (my emphasis).

17. Webb Keane, "From Fetishism to Sincerity: On Agency, the Speaking Subject, and Their Historicity in the Context of Religious Conversion," *Comparative Studies in Society and History* 39, no. 4 (1997): 674–93, 678n7 (my emphasis).

18. Aston, *Broken Idols*, 183.

19. Jean Calvin, *A very profitable treatise made by M. Ihon Caluyne, declarynge what great profit might come to al christendome, yf there were a regester made of all sainctes bodies and other reliques*, trans. Steven Wythers (London, 1561), sig.A.ii, sig.H.v.

20. "Hugh Rhodes's Book of Nurture," in *The Babees Book*, ed. Frederick J. Furnivall (London: N. Trübner, 1868), line 151; Ben Jonson, *Discoveries*, ed. Lorna Hutson, in *The Cambridge Edition of the Works of Ben Jonson*, ed. David Bevington, Martin Butler, and Ian Donaldson (Cambridge: Cambridge University Press, 2012), 7:481–596, 548.

21. Patricia Fumerton, *Cultural Aesthetics: Renaissance Literature and the Practice of*

Social Ornament (Chicago: University of Chicago Press, 1991), 37, 43, 44. See also Michael Witmore, *Pretty Creatures: Children and Fiction in the English Renaissance* (Ithaca, NY: Cornell University Press, 2007), esp. 13, on "the trifling interests and actions of children" and the "aesthetics of the trifling" in which they played a part.

22. Bill Brown, "The Tyranny of Things (Trivia in Karl Marx and Mark Twain)," *Critical Inquiry* 28, no. 2 (2002): 442–69, 460. For a relevant attempt to rethink the status of the trivial in the context of microhistorical analysis, see Edward Muir, "Introduction: Observing Trifles," in *Microhistory and the Lost People of Europe*, ed. Edward Muir and Guido Ruggiero (Baltimore: Johns Hopkins University Press, 1991), vii–xxviii.

23. Eusebius, *Life of Constantine*, bk. 3, sec. 54, trans. Averil Cameron and Stuart G. Hall (Oxford: Clarendon, 1999), 143. For the Greek text see *Über das Leben des Kaisers Konstantin*, ed. Friedhelm Winkelmann (Berlin: De Gruyter, 1991), 107–8. For discussion of this passage in the context of ancient attitudes to broken and salvaged works see Jaś Elsner, "From the Culture of Spolia to the Cult of Relics: The Arch of Constantine and the Genesis of Late Antique Forms," *Papers of the British School at Rome* 68 (2000): 149–84, 155.

24. See, e.g., *Iliad*, 15.363; and *Odyssey*, 18.323.

25. *Homeric Hymn to Hermes*, 30, 40; Apollonius of Rhodes, *Jason and the Golden Fleece*, trans. Richard Hunter (Oxford: Oxford University Press, 1993), 69.

26. For the history of responses to these and other tensions in Christian tradition see Diana Wood, ed., *The Church and Childhood* (Oxford: Blackwell, 1994); and Marcia J. Bunge, ed., *The Child in Christian Thought* (Cambridge: William B. Eerdmans, 2001).

27. A notable example, which I cannot discuss at length here, occurs in Clement of Alexandria's *Exhortation to the Greeks*, in which the "perfectly savage" mysteries of Dionysus are denounced by describing the ripping apart of the infant god by the Titans after they have "beguiled him with childish toys [*paidariōdesin athurmasin*]," which are enumerated in a quotation from the Orphic poems—"Top, wheel, and jointed dolls" [*paignia kampesiguia*] (*Clement of Alexandria*, trans. G. W. Butterworth [Cambridge, MA: Harvard University Press, 1919], 37, 39). For rich accounts of the background to this myth see M. L. West, *The Orphic Poems* (Oxford: Clarendon, 1983), 155–59; and Olga Levaniouk, "The Toys of Dionysos," *Harvard Studies in Classical Philology* 103 (2007): 165–202, esp. 174–75, on the various resonances of *athurmata*.

28. *The Homilies of S. John Chrysostom, Archbishop of Constantinople, on the First Epistle of St. Paul the Apostle to the Corinthians: Part I, Hom. I–XXIV*, trans. Hubert Kestell Cornish and John Medley (Oxford: John Henry Parker, 1839), 48–49.

29. *The Homilies of S. John Chrysostom, Archbishop of Constantinople, on the Gospel of St. Matthew: Part I, Hom. I–XXV*, trans. Hubert Kestell Cornish and John Medley (Oxford: John Henry Parker, 1852), 360–61.

30. For an excellent analysis of this strand in Chrysostom's work see Blake Leyerle, "Appealing to Children," *Journal of Early Christian Studies* 5, no. 2 (1997): 243–70.

31. Roberte Hamayon, *Why We Play: An Anthropological Study*, trans. Damien Simon (Chicago: Hau, 2016), 37. I am grateful to Anthony Pickles for this reference and for a stimulating discussion of his work.

32. *Homilies of S. John Chrysostom . . . on the Gospel of St. Matthew*, 89.

33. Jean Delumeau, *Sin and Fear: The Emergence of a Western Guilt Culture, 13th–18th Centuries*, trans. Eric Nicholson (New York: St. Martin's, 1990), 455–62.

34. *Luther's Works*, vol. 20, *Lectures on the Minor Prophets III: Zechariah*, ed. Hilton C. Oswald (Saint Louis, MO: Concordia, 1973), 271–72. For discussions of this Lutheran strain that somewhat underplay the equivocality of this moment, see Sergiusz Michalski, *The Reformation and the Visual Arts: The Protestant Image Question in Western and Eastern Europe* (London: Routledge, 1993), 188–89; and Powell, *Depositions*, 195–97.

35. I follow the citation and translation by Mary Carruthers, *The Experience of Beauty in the Middle Ages* (Oxford: Oxford University Press, 2013), 21. I cite the Vulgate because the emphasis on play is obscured in the King James Version.

36. In both of these instances Jerome chose the Latin verb *ludere* as the translation for the Hebrew verb קחש [*sachak*], which can mean to laugh, to play, to delight in but also to deride: see the entry on the verb in the *Thesauri Hebraicae Linguae* appended to the Antwerp Polyglot Bible, which suggests as possible meanings: "Ridere, ludere, laetari, deridere, irridere, subsannare" (*Biblia Sacra Hebraice, Chaldaice, Græce, & Latine* [Antwerp, 1569–72], 7.129).

37. Plato, *Laws*, trans. A. E. Taylor, in *Collected Dialogues*, ed. Edith Hamilton and Huntington Cairns (Princeton, NJ: Princeton University Press, 1961), 1375; Greek text from Plato, *Laws*, trans. R. G. Bury (Cambridge, MA: Harvard University Press, 1926), 2:52.

38. John Forde, *Sermo* 14:6; see the citation, translation, and discussion in Carruthers, *The Experience of Beauty*, 21–22.

39. St. Thomas Aquinas, *An Exposition of the "On the Hebdomads" of Boethius*, trans. Janice L. Schultz and Edward A. Synan (Washington, DC: Catholic University of America Press, 2001), 2–3, 5. Elsewhere in his writings, Aquinas develops a rich account of play and pleasure, even "a moral virtue about playing" [*circa ludos potest esse aliqua virtus*], endorsing a moderate Aristotelian conception of *eutrapelia*: see *Summa Theologiæ*, vol. 44, *Well-Tempered Passion*, trans. Thomas Gilby (Cambridge: Cambridge University Press, 2006), 215–17 (quotations at 218–19); and Alain Besançon, *The Forbidden Image: An Intellectual History of Iconoclasm*, trans. Jane Marie Todd (Chicago: University of Chicago Press, 2000), 158–62.

40. Franz Pfeiffer, *Meister Eckhart*, trans. C. de B. Evans (London: J. M. Watkins, 1924), 1:148.

41. Cited in H. H. Brinton, *The Mystic Will: Based upon a Study of the Philosophy of Jakob Boehme* (London: G. Allen and Unwin, 1931), 217–18.

42. Paula Findlen, "Between Carnival and Lent: The Scientific Revolution at the Margins of Culture," *Configurations* 6, no. 2 (1998): 256–61, 259.

43. Kepler, *Gesammelte Werke* 2:19, cited in Fernand Hallyn, *The Poetic Structure of the World: Copernicus and Kepler*, trans. Donald M. Leslie (New York: Zone, 1993), 163.

44. Johannes Kepler, *Tertius Interveniens*, cited in Findlen, "Between Carnival and Lent," 259.

45. "Difficulty 71," in *Maximus the Confessor*, trans. Andrew Louth (London: Routledge, 1996), 162–63. For important discussions of these strands in Maximus's thought see Carlos Steel, "Le Jeu du verbe: À Propos de Maxime, *Amb. Ad Ioh.* LXVII," in *Philohistor: Miscellanea in Honorem Caroli Laga Septuagenarii*, ed. A. Schoors and P. Van Deun (Leuven: Peeters, 1994), 281–93; Paul M. Blowers, "On the 'Play' of Divine Providence in Gregory Nazianzen and Maximus the Confessor," in *Re-reading Gregory of Nazianzus:*

Essays on History, Theology and Culture, ed. Christopher A. Beeley (Washington, DC: Catholic University of America Press, 2012), 199–217; and Joshua Lollar, *To See into the Life of Things: The Contemplation of Nature in Maximus the Confessor and His Predecessors* (Turnhout: Brepols, 2013), 35–40, 331–32.

46. Maximus, "Difficulty 71," 163.

47. Hans-Georg Gadamer, *Truth and Method*, trans. Joel Weinsheimer and Donald G. Marshall (London: Continuum, 1975), 103–4.

48. Roland Barthes, *The Grain of the Voice: Interviews, 1962–1980*, trans. Linda Coverdale (New York: Hill and Wang, 1985), 103–4.

49. Romano Guardini, *The Spirit of the Liturgy*, trans. Ada Lane (London: Sheed and Ward, 1935), 182–83, chap. 5, "The Playfulness of the Liturgy," passim.

50. Walter Ong SJ, preface to Hugo Rahner SJ, *Man at Play, or, Did You Ever Practice Eutrapelia?* trans. Brian Battershaw and Edward Quinn (New York: Herder and Herder, 1965), 6–7; Rahner, *Man at Play*, 104–5.

51. Gerardus van der Leeuw, *Sacred and Profane Beauty: The Holy in Art*, trans. David E. Green (London: Weidenfeld and Nicolson, 1963), 77–85, 110–12 (quotations at 111, 80).

52. Jürgen Moltmann, *Theology of Play*, trans. Reinhard Ulrich (New York: Harper and Row, 1972), 48. For other notable accounts of theology and/as play see David L. Miller, *Gods and Games: Toward a Theology of Play* (New York: Harper and Row, 1970); and Bernhard Lang, *Sacred Games: A History of Christian Worship* (New Haven, CT: Yale University Press, 1997).

53. T. M. Luhrmann, *When God Talks Back: Understanding the American Evangelical Relationship with God* (New York: Alfred A. Knopf, 2012), esp. 92–100, 321–23, 374–75.

54. *St. Thomas More: Selected Letters*, ed. Elizabeth Frances Rogers (New Haven, CT: Yale University Press, 1961), 82; Latin from *The Correspondence of Sir Thomas More*, ed. Elizabeth Frances Rogers (Princeton, NJ: Princeton University Press, 1947), 85.

55. Knapp, *An Empire Nowhere*, 52–53. I am indebted throughout to Knapp's perceptive account of early modern trifling.

56. Thomas More, *Utopia*, trans. Ralph Robinson, in *Three Early Modern Utopias*, ed. Susan Bruce (Oxford: Oxford University Press, 1999), 71–72. For the Latin text see Thomas More, *Utopia: Latin Text and English Translation*, ed. George M. Logan, Robert M. Adams, and Clarence H. Miller (Cambridge: Cambridge University Press, 1995), 150.

57. On *serio ludere* see Walter M. Gordon, *Humanist Play and Belief: The Seriocomic Art of Desiderius Erasmus* (Toronto: University of Toronto Press, 1990). On "spatial play" see Louis Marin, *Utopics: Spatial Play*, trans. Richard A. Vollrath (Atlantic Highlands, NJ: Humanities Press, 1984), esp. the "Second Preface: The Neutral: Playtime in Utopia," and 8–10, 26–28, 96–97, 220.

58. Louis Marin, "Utopic Rabelaisian Bodies," in *Food for Thought*, trans. Mette Hjort (Baltimore: Johns Hopkins University Press, 1989), 85–113, 86, 92–93, 100, 104–5.

59. Gordon, *Humanist Play and Belief*, 129; Michael Holquist, "How to Play Utopia," *Yale French Studies* 41 (1968): 106–23, 119.

60. Stephen Greenblatt, *Renaissance Self-Fashioning from More to Shakespeare* (Chicago: University of Chicago Press, 1980), 33; see especially 24 on Humanist playfulness, and 57 on the text as "a playground in which a shifting series of apparently incompatible

impulses can find expression without flying apart or turning violently on one another"; and 27–31 on More's theatricality.

61. *The Complete Works of St. Thomas More*, vol. 9, ed. J. B. Trapp (New Haven, CT: Yale University Press, 1979), 117–18.

62. Thomas More, *A Dialogue of Comfort Against Tribulation*, in *The Complete Works of St. Thomas More*, vol. 12, ed. Louis L. Martz and Frank Manley (New Haven, CT: Yale University Press, 1976), 192. See the valuable discussion by Walter M. Gordon, "The Ominous Play of Children: Thomas More's Adaptation of an Image from Antiquity," *Journal of the Warburg and Courtauld Institutes* 47 (1984): 204–5. I owe this reference to the distracted assiduousness of Micha Lazarus.

63. Kendall L. Walton, *Mimesis as Make-Believe: On the Foundations of the Representational Arts* (Cambridge, MA: Harvard University Press, 1990).

64. Dio Chrysostom, *Discourses* 32.13, trans. J. W. Cohoon and H. Lamar Crosby (London: William Heinemann, 1940), 3:184–85; Aelian, *On the Characteristics of Animals* 11.10, trans. A. F. Scholfield (London: William Heinemann, 1958–59), 2:370–71 (translation slightly altered).

65. Plutarch, "Isis and Osiris," 5.1.356E, in *Plutarch's Moralia*, trans. Frank Cole Babbitt (London: William Heinemann, 1936), 5:36–39.

66. Susan Willis, "Earthquake Kits: The Politics of the Trivial," *South Atlantic Quarterly* 89, no. 4 (1990): 761–85, 761. A related conviction underpins Alexander Kluge's description of "an economy of combined trivials"; see Devin Fore's introduction to Alexander Kluge and Oskar Negt, *History and Obstinacy*, trans. Richard Langston et al. (New York: Zone, 2014), 15–67, 54; and Jeff Dolven, "Obstinate Spenser," *Spenser Review* 47.1.2 (Winter 2017): www.english.cam.ac.uk/spenseronline/review/item/47.1.2.

CHAPTER 2

1. Robert W. Scribner, "Ritual and Reformation," in *Popular Culture and Popular Movements in Reformation Germany* (London: Hambledon Press, 1987), 103–22, 114.

2. Nicholas Orme, *Medieval Children* (New Haven, CT: Yale University Press, 2001), 172.

3. I have found only one direct attempt to derive *doll* from *idol*: see Ruth Freeman and Larry Freeman, *A Cavalcade of Toys* (New York: Century House, 1942), 19. The Freemans' suggestion is given short shrift by Lois Kuznets, *When Toys Come Alive: Narratives of Animation, Metamorphosis, and Development* (New Haven, CT: Yale University Press, 1994), 11. A link is teasingly made, though without suggesting an explicitly etymological link, by Alfred Gell, in his comparison of a girl at play to a connoisseur beholding the statue of David: "From dolls to idols is but a small step," he writes, "and from idols to sculptures by Michelangelo another, hardly longer." Alfred Gell, *Art and Agency: An Anthropological Theory* (Oxford: Clarendon, 1998), 18.

4. Keith Thomas, "Children in Early Modern England," in *Children and Their Books*, ed. Gillian Avery and Julia Briggs (Oxford: Clarendon, 1989), 45–77, 60.

5. Maurizio Bettini, *The Portrait of the Lover*, trans. Laura Gibbs (Berkeley: University of California Press, 1999), 219, 221: "it is as if the doll is able to appropriate a kind of 'life' from her referent in order to acquire for herself (as much as is possible) the living nature of the object that she reproduces by similarity."

6. Lactantius, *Divine Institutes* 2.4.12–15, trans. Anthony Bowen and Peter Garnsey

(Liverpool: Liverpool University Press, 2003), 127; *L. Caeli Firmiani Lactanti Opera Omnia*, ed. Samuel Brandt and Georg von Laubmann (Berghof: F. Tempsky, 1890–93), 1:110. On the smallness of divine figures causing them to resemble dolls see also the discussion of ancient Egyptian worship in Gell, *Art and Agency*, 129, 133.

7. Heinrich Bullinger, *De origine erroris libri duo* (Zurich, 1529), 156–57. Cited and translated in Keith P. F. Moxey, *Peter Aertsen, Joachim Beuckelaer, and the Rise of Secular Painting in the Context of the Reformation* (New York: Garland, 1977), 136–37; see also Amy Knight Powell, *Depositions: Scenes from the Late Medieval Church and the Modern Museum* (New York: Zone, 2012), 195.

8. For this description—and the confirmation that this was a derogatory phrase, not an actual account of Nunziata's vocation—see Louis A. Waldman, "'Se Bene era Dipintore di Fantocci': Nunziata d'Antonio, Painter, Pyrotechnician and Bombardier of Florence," *Paragone* 59 (2008): 72–86, esp. 74. See also Alexander Nagel, *The Controversy of Renaissance Art* (Chicago: University of Chicago Press, 2011), 37–38.

9. This was a common strain in Byzantine writings and images, where laments written in the voice of Mary as she held Christ's body frequently drew a direct connection with her holding him in her arms as an infant; see Henry Maguire, *Art and Eloquence in Byzantium* (Princeton, NJ: Princeton University Press, 1981), 99–100.

10. Lilian M. C. Randall, "Games and the Passion in Pucelle's Hours of Jeanne d'Évreux," *Speculum* 47, no. 2 (1972): 248; Jeffrey Hamburger, *The Visual and the Visionary: Art and Female Spirituality in Late Medieval Germany* (New York: Zone, 1998), 23.

11. See Leah Sinanoglou Marcus, *Childhood and Cultural Despair: A Theme and Variations in Seventeenth-Century Literature* (Pittsburgh, PA: University of Pittsburgh Press, 1978), 16–23.

12. Richard Leighton Greene, ed., *The Early English Carols* (Oxford: Clarendon, 1935), 37, 57. The former example is discussed in Marcus, *Childhood and Cultural Despair*, 19.

13. See Victor Lasareff, "Studies in the Iconography of the Virgin," *Art Bulletin* 20, no. 1 (1938): 41–46.

14. For useful discussions of some of these objects see Alexa Sand, "*Materia Meditandi*: Haptic Perception and some Parisian Ivories of the Virgin and Child, ca. 1300," *Different Visions* 4 (2014): http://differentvisions.org/materia-meditandi-haptic-perception-parisian-ivories-virgin-child-ca-1300; and especially Jacqueline Jung, "The Tactile and the Visionary: Notes on the Place of Sculpture in the Medieval Religious Imagination," in *Looking Beyond: Visions, Dreams, and Insights in Medieval Art and History*, ed. Colum Hourihane (University Park: Pennsylvania State University Press, 2010), 203–40, to which I am indebted throughout this section.

15. For examples of such figures see *Krone und Schleier: Kunst aus Mittelalterlichen Frauenklöstern*, ed. Jutta Frings and Jan Gerchow (Essen: Ruhrlandmuseum, 2005), 113; *Spiegel der Seligkeit: Privates Bild und Frömmigkeit im Spätmittelalter*, ed. Frank Matthias Kammel (Nürnberg: Germanischen Nationalmuseums, 2000), 176. For discussion see Christiane Klapisch-Zuber, "Holy Dolls: Play and Piety in Florence in the Quattrocento," in *Women, Family and Ritual in Renaissance Italy*, trans. Lydia Cochrane (Chicago: University of Chicago Press, 1985), 310–29; and Giovanni Previtali, "Il Bambin Gesù come immagine devozionale nella scultura italiana del Trecento," *Paragone* 21 (1970): 31–40.

16. Klapisch-Zuber writes that in Florentine nunneries the effigy of the Christ child "was not only interpreted and adored, but handled, coddled and taken for walks through the convent" ("Holy Dolls," 311). Ulinka Rublack writes that in their visions and prayers some nuns "typically saw the infant Jesus as a child with whom they played, joked, and kissed" ("Female Spirituality and the Infant Jesus in Late Medieval Dominican Convents," in *Popular Religion in Germany and Central Europe, 1400–1800*, ed. Bob Scribner and Trevor Johnson [Basingstoke: Macmillan, 1996], 16–37, 20). See also the discussions of holy dolls in Henk van Os, *The Art of Devotion in the Late Middle Ages in Europe*, trans. Michael Hoyle (London: Merrell Holberton, 1994), 98–104; Hamburger, *The Visual and the Visionary*, 22–26, 386; and Caroline Walker Bynum, *Christian Materiality: An Essay on Religion in Late Medieval Europe* (New York: Zone, 2010), 38–40, 56–57, 61–65.

17. Isa Ragusa and Rosalie B. Green, eds., *Meditations on the Life of Christ: An Illustrated Manuscript of the Fourteenth Century*, trans. Isa Ragusa (Princeton, NJ: Princeton University Press, 1961), 38; Margaretha Ebner cited in Rosemary Drage Hale, "Rocking the Cradle: Margaretha Ebner (Be)Holds the Divine," in *Performance and Transformation: New Approaches to Late Medieval Spirituality*, ed. Mary A. Suydam and Joanna E. Ziegler (London: Macmillan, 1999), 211–39, 214.

18. Jung, "The Tactile and the Visionary," 235–36.

19. Hamburger, *The Visual and the Visionary*, 22.

20. Klapisch-Zuber, "Holy Dolls," 324; Hamburger, *The Visual and the Visionary*, 23.

21. *The Book of Margery Kempe*, ed. Barry Windeatt (Cambridge: D. S. Brewer, 2004), 177. See the brief discussions in Margaret Aston, *England's Iconoclasts*, vol. 1, *Laws Against Images* (Oxford: Clarendon, 1988), 403; and Orme, *Medieval Children*, 171.

22. Henry Adams, *Mont Saint Michel and Chartres*, in *Novels, Mont Saint Michel, The Education* (Cambridge: Cambridge University Press, 1983), 323, 424.

23. See, e.g., Antonia Fraser, *Dolls* (London: Octopus, 1963); and Maria Argyriadi, *Dolls in Greek Life and Art from Antiquity to the Present Day*, trans. Alexandra Doumas (Athens: Lucy Braggiotti, 1991).

24. Philippe Ariès, *Centuries of Childhood: A Social History of Family Life*, trans. Robert Baldock (New York: Random House, 1965), 69.

25. See Kate McK Elderkin, "Jointed Dolls in Antiquity," *American Journal of Archaeology* 34, no. 4 (1930): 455–79, 456; L. Y. Rahmani, "Finds from a Sixth to Seventh Centuries Site Near Gaza I: The Toys," *Israel Exploration Journal* 31, no. 1/2 (1981): 72–80, 74, 78; Rosalind M. Janssen, "Soft Toys from Egypt," in *Archaeological Research in Roman Egypt*, ed. Donald M. Bailey (Ann Arbor, MI: Journal of Roman Archaeology, 1996), 231–39, 231; and Brigitte Pitarakis, "The Material Culture of Childhood in Byzantium," in *Becoming Byzantine: Children and Childhood in Byzantium*, ed. Arietta Papaconstantinou and Alice-Mary Talbot (Cambridge, MA: Harvard University Press, 2009), 167–251, 243. For more general discussions of the interpretative challenges raised in the archaeology of childhood, see especially Laurie Wilkie, "Not Merely Child's Play: Creating a Historical Archaeology of Children and Childhood," in *Children and Material Culture*, ed. Joanna Sofaer Derevenski (London: Routledge, 2000), 100–113. For a powerful account of the ways in which modern concerns are used to interpret ancient figurines with an undue degree of specificity, see Lynn Meskell, "Goddesses, Gimbutas and 'New Age' Archaeology," *Antiquity* 69 (1995): 74–86.

26. Fraser, *Dolls*, 5.

27. For the importing of dolls see T. S. Willan, ed., *A Tudor Book of Rates* (Manchester: Manchester University Press, 1962), 48; and Thomas, "Children in Early Modern England," 46. For the materials from which dolls were fashioned, with illustrations, see Orme, *Medieval Children*, 169–70.

28. Thomas, "Children in Early Modern England," 60.

29. David Freedberg, *The Power of Images: Studies in the History and Theory of Response* (Chicago: University of Chicago Press, 1989), esp. 202–6.

30. Edgar Allan Poe, "The Angel of the Odd: An Extravaganza," in *Poetry and Tales*, ed. Patrick F. Quinn (New York: Library of America, 1984), 756–65; see the brief discussion in Giorgio Agamben, *Stanzas: Word and Phantasm in Western Culture*, trans. Ronald L. Martinez (Minneapolis: University of Minnesota Press, 1993), 51; Franz Kafka, "The Cares of a Family Man," trans. Willa Muir and Edwin Muir, in *On Dolls*, ed. Kenneth Gross (London: Notting Hill, 2012), 63–64. For a brief discussion of Kafka's figure as exemplifying the vivacity of objects, see Jane Bennett, *Vibrant Matter: A Political Ecology of Things* (Durham, NC: Duke University Press, 2010), 7–8.

31. Stanley Cavell, *The Claim of Reason: Wittgenstein, Skepticism, Morality and Tragedy* (Oxford: Oxford University Press, 1979), 401 (emphasis in the original).

32. See Kenneth Gross, *The Dream of the Moving Statue* (Ithaca, NY: Cornell University Press, 1992); see also Freedberg, *The Power of Images*, esp. 36–37, 74–76.

33. I return to a broader account of what I call the "toy potential" of objects in my conclusion.

34. For an excellent overview of his reign see Warren Treadgold, *The Byzantine Revival, 780–842* (Stanford: Stanford University Press, 1988), 263–329.

35. John Skylitzes, *A Synopsis of Byzantine History, 811–1057*, trans. John Wortley (Cambridge: Cambridge University Press, 2010), 54–55. Skylitzes misidentifies the woman responsible as Theodora's mother, Theoktiste. For the Greek text see *Ioannis Scylitzae Synopsis Historiarum*, ed. Hans Thurn (Berlin: De Gruyter, 1973), 52–53. The term used for dolls here—*ninia*—is not present in classical Greek but was a standard Byzantine term: see the relevant entry in Eric Trapp et al., *Lexikon zur byzantinischen Gräzität* (Vienna: Österreichischen Akademie der Wissenschaften, 1994–).

36. Skylitzes, *Synopsis*, 55.

37. See Treadgold, *The Byzantine Revival*, 310–11, 446–47n427, who considers the latter anecdote simply a derivation and repetition of the former. See also the brief discussion in Arne Effenberger, "Images of Personal Devotion: Miniature Mosaic and Steatite Icons," in *Byzantium: Faith and Power (1261–1557)*, ed. Helen C. Evans (New Haven, CT: Yale University Press, 2004), 209–14, 209–10, who assumes that "all such stories were later inventions, of course" (210).

38. See the discussions of Byzantine dolls, and this object in particular, in Argyriadi, *Dolls in Greek Life and Art*, 25–27; Demetra Papanikola-Bakirtzi, ed., *Everyday Life in Byzantium* (Athens: Hellenic Ministry of Culture, 2002), 493–95; Peter Hatlie, "The Religious Life of Children and Adolescents," in *A People's History of Christianity*, vol. 3, *Byzantine Christianity*, ed. Derek Krueger (Minneapolis: Fortress Press, 2006), 182–200, 191; and Pitarakis, "The Material Culture of Childhood in Byzantium."

39. Lactantius, *Divine Institutes* 1.22.13, 115; *L. Caeli Firmiani Lactanti Opera Omnia*, 1:90.

40. Freedberg, *The Power of Images*, 283.

41. Sigmund Freud, "The Uncanny," in *The Standard Edition of the Complete Psychological Works of Sigmund Freud*, ed. James Strachey (London: Hogarth Press, 1953–74), 17:217–56, 233.

42. Barbara Johnson, *Persons and Things* (Cambridge, MA: Harvard University Press, 2008), 163.

43. John Hall of Richmond, *Of Government and Obedience* (London, 1654), 440; cited in Thomas, "Children in Early Modern England," 60.

44. For an excellent account see Fanny Dolansky, "Playing with Gender: Girls, Dolls, and Adult Ideals in the Roman World," *Classical Antiquity* 31, no. 2 (2012): 256–92. For a useful discussion of "the gendering of childhood pastimes in the early modern period" see Katherine R. Larson, "'Certein Childeplayes Remembred by the Fayre Ladies': Girls and Their Games," in *Gender and Early Modern Constructions of Childhood*, ed. Naomi J. Miller and Naomi Yavneh (Farnham: Ashgate, 2011), 67–86, 68.

45. Gross, introduction to *On Dolls*, xi–xii. Doug Bailey has (somewhat controversially) made comparisons with Barbie dolls in his analysis of prehistoric figurines, while emphasizing that they are neither simply "goddesses or votives . . . or that they were toys for children . . . or that they were teaching tools"; he argues, instead, that "any individual Neolithic figurine would have had several different functions and meanings each of which would have changed during the artefact's lifetime." Doug Bailey, "Touch and the Cheirotic Apprehension of Prehistoric Figurines," in *Sculpture and Touch*, ed. Peter Dent (Farnham: Ashgate, 2012), 27–44, 28.

46. Susan Stewart, *On Longing: Narratives of the Miniature, the Gigantic, the Souvenir, the Collection* (Durham, NC: Duke University Press, 1993), 57.

47. Sigmund Freud, "Beyond the Pleasure Principle," in *The Penguin Freud Reader*, ed. Adam Phillips (London: Penguin, 2006), 132–95. I derive the language of "rhythm" and "coping" in this scene from the account by Alexander Freer, "Rhythm as Coping," *New Literary History* 46, no. 3 (2015): 549–68, esp. 551–52.

48. Jonathan Lear, *Happiness, Death and the Remainder of Life* (Cambridge, MA: Harvard University Press, 2000), 96 (see 90–98 on this scene more generally). See also the important discussions of the orderly meanings of the Fort-Da game as a reflection of Freud's drive toward psychoanalytic systematicity in Jacques Derrida, "Freud's Legacy," in *The Post Card: From Socrates to Freud and Beyond*, trans. Alan Bass (Chicago: University of Chicago Press, 1987), 292–337.

49. Christopher Bollas, *The Mystery of Things* (London: Routledge, 1999), 69.

50. Charles Baudelaire, "The Philosophy of Toys," trans. Paul Keegan, in *On Dolls*, ed. Kenneth Gross (London: Notting Hill, 2012), 11–21, 20 (emphasis in the original).

51. Quoted in Eva Maria Simms, "Uncanny Dolls: Images of Death in Rilke and Freud," *New Literary History* 27, no. 4 (1996): 663–77, 670.

52. Walter Benjamin, "Toys and Play: Marginal Notes on a Monumental Work," in *Selected Writings: Volume 2, Part 1: 1927–1930*, ed. Michael W. Jennings, Howard Eiland, and Gary Smith (Cambridge, MA: Harvard University Press, 1999), 117–21, 118. For discussions of the role of children in Benjamin's thought see Susan Buck-Morss, *The*

Dialectics of Seeing: Walter Benjamin and the Arcades Project (Cambridge, MA: MIT Press, 1991), 262–68, 274–79; and Astrid Deuber-Mankowsky, "Spiel und zweite Technik: Walter Benjamins Entwurf einer Medienanthropologie des Spiels," in *Mediale Anthropologie*, ed. Christiane Voss and Lorenz Engell (Munich: Fink, 2015), 35–62.

53. Benjamin, "Toys and Play," 118.

54. See the exhibition catalogue *Madonnas and Miracles: The Holy Home in Renaissance Italy*, ed. Maya Corry, Deborah Howard, and Mary Laven (Cambridge: Fitzwilliam Museum, 2017), 92.

55. *Madonnas and Miracles*, 92. I am very grateful to Mary Laven for discussion of this object and logistical assistance.

56. Gell, *Art and Agency*, 97.

57. Michael Camille, review of *Bild und Kult*, by Hans Belting, *Art Bulletin* 74, no. 3 (1992): 514.

58. See the catalogue of the exhibition *Art Under Attack: Histories of British Iconoclasm*, ed. Tabitha Barber and Stacey Boldrick (London: Tate, 2013), 62–63, which first drew my attention to this object.

59. Bruno Latour, "'Thou Shalt Not Freeze-Frame,' or, How Not to Misunderstand the Science and Religion Debate," in *Science, Religion and the Human Experience*, ed. James D. Proctor (Oxford: Oxford University Press, 2005), 27–48, 44.

60. I rely here on the discussion in Glyn Redworth, *The She-Apostle: The Extraordinary Life and Death of Luisa de Carvajal* (Oxford: Oxford University Press, 2008), 83–84.

61. I first encountered extracts from this project reproduced in *Cabinet Magazine*, Winter 2002–3, 86–89.

62. Shelley Jackson and Pamela Jackson, The Doll Games, www.ineradicablestain.com /dollgames/intros.html. All citations are from this site. This page comprises two columns of paragraphs, the left headed "Shelley" and the right "Pamela"; hence, I assume that these particular words are Pamela's, although it should be observed that part of the polyvocal challenge of the project is its destabilizing of just which voice belongs to which sister.

63. For excellent analyses of the way in which modern dolls project and shape gender roles see Judy Attfield, "Barbie and Action Man: Adult Toys for Girls and Boys, 1959–93"; and Heather Hendershot, "Dolls: Odour, Disgust, Femininity and Toy Design," both in *The Gendered Object*, ed. Pat Kirkham (Manchester: Manchester University Press, 1996), 81–89, and 90–102, respectively.

CHAPTER 3

1. Albert Angele, *Altbiberach um die Jahre der Reformation* (Biberach-Birkendorf: Stadtpfarramt St. Josef, 1962), 163–64; cited by Sergiusz Michalski, "Das Phänomen Bildersturm: Versuch einer Übersich," in *Bilder und Bildersturm im Spätmittelalter und in der frühen Neuzeit*, ed. Bob Scribner (Wiesbaden: Otto Harrassowitz, 1990), 69–124, 88n76; Amy Knight Powell, *Depositions: Scenes from the Late Medieval Church and the Modern Museum* (New York: Zone, 2012), 341–42n24.

2. See Robert W. Scribner, "Ritual and Popular Religion in Catholic Germany at the Time of the Reformation," in *Popular Culture and Popular Movements in Reformation Germany* (London: Hambledon Press, 1987), 17–47, 28.

3. Scribner, "Ritual and Popular Religion," 22, 30–31.

4. This is especially true of the well-known festival of the Boy Bishop, which Scribner discusses. For a rich discussion of the ways in which a ritual traditionally understood by anthropologists as profoundly "serious"—the ceremony of *potlatch*—could incorporate and overlap with play-forms of the same practice, see Helen Codere, "The Amiable Side of Kwakiutl Life: The Potlatch and the Play Potlatch," *American Anthropologist* 58, no. 2 (1956): 334–51.

5. Scribner, "Ritual and Popular Religion," 30, 26–28.

6. William Lambarde, *Alphabetical Description of the Chief Places in England and Wales* (London, 1730), 459 (written c. 1570).

7. On religious puppetry in the late medieval and early modern periods see Margaret Rogerson, "English Puppets and the Survival of Religious Theatre," *Theatre Notebook* 52, no. 2 (1998): 91–111.

8. Powell, *Depositions*, 195.

9. The line between doll and puppet was often blurry: the word *puppet* derives from the Latin *pupa*, which, as I discussed in the previous chapter, was a standard term both for a little girl and for her doll. See the discussions in Scott Cutler Shershow, *Puppets and "Popular" Culture* (Ithaca, NY: Cornell University Press, 1995), 69–71; and Kenneth Gross, *Puppet: An Essay on Uncanny Life* (Chicago: University of Chicago Press, 2011), 3–4. Powell obscures this ambiguity in her otherwise valuable analysis.

10. See, e.g., Thomas Becon, *The Catechism of Thomas Becon*, ed. John Ayre (Cambridge: Cambridge University Press, 1845). See also Powell, *Depositions*, 195; and Philip Butterworth, *Magic on the Early English Stage* (Cambridge: Cambridge University Press, 2005), 127–28. The term used as synonymous with puppet—*mawmet* or *mammet*—is a bowdlerized form of the name *Mahomet* or *Muhammad*, used from the Middle Ages onward to mean either an idol or false religious image or a toy or puppet. See Dorothy Metlitzki, *The Matter of Araby in Medieval England* (New Haven, CT: Yale University Press, 1977), 208; Shershow, *Puppets and "Popular" Culture*, 27–29; and Butterworth, *Magic on the Early English Stage*, 134.

11. The richest general accounts are Shershow, *Puppets and "Popular" Culture*; Gross, *Puppet*; and Victoria Nelson, *The Secret Life of Puppets* (Cambridge, MA: Harvard University Press, 2001).

12. Marjorie Garber, "Out of Joint," in *The Body in Parts: Fantasies of Corporeality in Early Modern Europe*, ed. David Hillman and Carla Mazzio (New York: Routledge, 1997), 23–51.

13. See Susan Brigden, "Youth and the English Reformation," *Past and Present* 95 (May 1982): 37–67; Alexandra Walsham, "The Reformation of the Generations: Youth, Age and Religious Change in England, c. 1500–1700," *Transactions of the Royal Historical Society* 21 (Dec. 2011): 93–121, esp. 101–3.

14. Charles Wriothesley, *A Chronicle of England During the Reign of the Tudors*, ed. William Douglas Hamilton (London: Camden Society, 1877), 2:1.

15. Carlos Eire, *War Against the Idols: The Reformation of Worship from Erasmus to Calvin* (Cambridge: Cambridge University Press, 1986), 145.

16. Youth and childhood were relatively discrete early modern categories and should not be conflated; see Paul Griffiths, *Youth and Authority: Formative Experiences in England, 1560–1640* (Oxford: Clarendon, 1996), 132–40, 178–86.

17. Robert W. Scribner, "Ritual and Reformation," in *Popular Culture and Popular Movements in Reformation Germany* (London: Hambledon Press, 1987), 103–22, 105. Scribner builds on the interesting account (though ultimately one that makes overly certain distinctions) by Don Handelman, "Play and Ritual: Complementary Frames of Meta-communication," in *It's a Funny Thing, Humour*, ed. Antony J. Chapman and Hugh C. Foot (Oxford: Pergamon, 1977), 185–92.

18. Scribner, "Ritual and Reformation," 116.

19. *Letters and Papers, Foreign and Domestic, of the Reign of Henry VIII: Preserved in the Public Record Office, the British Museum, and Elsewhere in England, Arranged and Catalogued by J. S. Brewer, J. Gairdner and R. H. Brodie*, vol. 13, pt. 1 (London: Longman, 1862–1910), 120; Stephen Reed Cattley, ed., *The Acts and Monuments of John Foxe* (London: R. B. Seeley and W. Burnside, 1838), 5:407. See the excellent account by Peter Marshall, "The Rood of Boxley, the Blood of Hailes and the Defence of the Henrician Church," *Journal of Ecclesiastical History* 46, no. 4 (1995): 689–96.

20. *Letters and Papers, Foreign and Domestic*, 13:1.120.

21. Cattley, *The Acts and Monuments of John Foxe*, 5:409. For the case against see Butterworth, *Magic on the Early English Stage*, 126. The case in favor is made by Leanne Groeneveld, "A Theatrical Miracle: The Boxley Rood of Grace as Puppet," *Early Theatre* 10, no. 2 (2007): 11–50. See also Aura Satz, "Attacks on Automata and Eviscerated Sculpture," in *Iconoclasm: Contested Objects, Contested Terms*, ed. Stacy Boldrick and Richard Clay (Farnham: Ashgate, 2007), 35–49.

22. See, e.g., the "puppets with jointed limbs" (*paignia kampesiguia*) involved in the rites of Dionysus that were derided by Clement of Alexandria, of which M. L. West writes, "Most surviving Greek dolls are of terracotta, and many of them have 'jointed limbs' . . . and could be operated by strings marionette fashion. They are normally just toys but magical use is readily imaginable. One could also envisage the use of frightening, animated puppets in an initiation ritual." M. L. West, *The Orphic Poems* (Oxford: Clarendon, 1983), 158.

23. See Scribner, "Ritual and Reformation," 110; Powell, *Depositions*, 81–90.

24. See Garber, "Out of Joint," 37: "What has the jointedness of puppets to do with the jointedness of language?"

25. Gesine Taubert and Johannes Taubert, "Mittelalterliche Kruzifixe mit schwenkbaren Armen: Ein Beitrag zur Verwendung von Bildwerken in der Liturgie," *Zeitschrift der deutschen Vereins für Kunstwissenschaft* 23 (1969): 79–121, 79; Johannes Taubert, *Polychrome Sculpture: Meaning, Form, Conservation*, trans. Carola Schulman (Los Angeles: Getty Conservation Institute, 2015), 38–53.

26. Matthew Isaac Cohen, "Puppetry and the Destruction of the Object," *Performance Research* 12, no. 4 (2007): 123–31, 127.

27. See Powell, *Depositions*, plate 3.

28. Bruno Latour, "How to Be Iconophilic in Art, Science, and Religion?" in *Picturing Science, Producing Art*, ed. Caroline A. Jones and Peter Galison (New York: Routledge, 1998), 418–40, 432.

29. Gross, *Puppet*, 95, chap. 7 *passim*.

30. Samuel Sharp, *Letters from Italy, Describing the Customs and Manners of That Country, in the Years 1765, and 1766* (London, 1767), 183–84.

31. Caroline Walker Bynum, *Christian Materiality: An Essay on Religion in Late Medieval Europe* (New York: Zone, 2010), 150, 145.

32. Bynum, *Christian Materiality*, 221, 267.

33. Tertullian, Q. *Septimii Florentis Tertulliani de carne Christi liber / Tertullian's Treatise on the Incarnation*, trans. Ernest Evans (London: SPCK, 1956), 14–17.

34. M. A. Screech, *Erasmus: Ecstasy and the Praise of Folly* (London: Penguin, 1980), 19.

35. Tertullian, *Tertullian's Treatise on the Incarnation*, 18–19.

36. See the entry in C.T. Lewis and C. Short, *Latin Dictionary: Based on Andrews's Edition of Freund's Latin Dictionary* (Oxford: Oxford University Press, 1963). An explicit discussion and definition is provided in Cicero, *De Oratore*, 2.4.17. For a useful discussion of Tertullian's "*certum est, quia imposibile*" in the context of conceptions of belief, see Rodney Needham, *Belief, Language and Experience* (Oxford: Basil Blackwell, 1972), 64–66.

37. Desiderius Erasmus, *The Praise of Folly*, trans. Clarence H. Miller (New Haven, CT: Yale University Press, 1973), 128.

38. Martin Dorp to Erasmus, Sept. 1514, in *The Correspondence of Erasmus: Letters 298 to 445, 1514 to 1516*, trans. R. A. B. Mynors and D. F. S. Thomson, *Collected Works of Erasmus*, general editor Manfred Hoffman, 78 vols. (Toronto: University of Toronto Press, 1978–), 3:18. Subsequent references to this edition abbreviated *CWE*.

39. See Myron P. Gilmore, "*Apologiae*: Erasmus's Defenses of Folly," in *Essays on the Works of Erasmus*, ed. Richard L. DeMolen (New Haven, CT: Yale University Press, 1978), 111–23, 111.

40. Erasmus, *Enchiridion*, trans. John W. O'Malley, *CWE* 66:90.

41. Screech, *Erasmus*, 22; see also Screech, *Laughter at the Foot of the Cross* (London: Penguin, 1997), 124–26.

42. Origen, *Homilies on Jeremiah*, trans. John Clark Smith (Washington, DC: Catholic University of America Press, 1998), 83 (emphasis in the original).

43. I use here the translation in Screech, *Erasmus*, 24.

44. Citations from Screech, *Erasmus*, 24–25.

45. Margaret Mann Phillips, *The "Adages" of Erasmus: A Study with Translations* (Cambridge: Cambridge University Press, 1964), 269. For discussion see Screech, *Laughter*, 90–92; and Walter M. Gordon, *Humanist Play and Belief: The Seriocomic Art of Desiderius Erasmus* (Toronto: University of Toronto Press, 1990), 73–76.

46. Erasmus does not explicitly describe the Silenus figurine as a plaything, though some modern scholars have done so: Simon Goldhill writes that Alcibiades compares Socrates to "a doll of Silenus (a satyr): the Silenus is ugly, of course, with a pot-belly and snub nose . . . but when you open up the doll inside are lovely statues of the gods." Simon Goldhill, *The Invention of Prose* (Oxford: Oxford University Press, 2002), 85.

47. Phillips, *The "Adages" of Erasmus*, 271–72; Latin cited from *Desiderii Erasmi Roterodami Opera omnia emendatiora et avctiora, ad optimas editiones praecipve qvas ipse Erasmvs postremo curavit svmma fide exacta, doctorvmqve virorvm notis illvstrata* (Lyon, 1703–6), 2:771.

48. See Joe Moshenska, *Feeling Pleasures: The Sense of Touch in Renaissance England* (Oxford: Oxford University Press, 2014), 17–30.

49. Erasmus, "A Pilgrimage for Religion's Sake," trans. Craig R. Thompson, *CWE* 40:647; Latin cited from *Desiderii Erasmi Roterodami Opera Omnia*, 1:785.

50. See the discussion of the word and its background by Guillermo Galán Vioque, *Martial, Book VII: A Commentary*, trans. J. J. Zoltowski (Leiden: Brill, 2002), 150–51.

51. Erasmus, "Ye Pylgremage of Pure Deuotyon," in *The Earliest English Translations of Erasmus's Colloquia, 1536–1566*, ed. Henry de Vocht (Louvain: Librairie Universitaire, Uystpruyst, 1928), 183 (my emphasis).

52. Peter Brown, *The Cult of the Saints: Its Rise and Function in Latin Christianity* (Chicago: University of Chicago Press, 1981), 78.

53. Quoted in Jonathan Sumption, *Pilgrimage: An Image of Mediaeval Religion* (London: Faber and Faber, 1975), 28.

54. On the portability of relics see Julia M. H. Smith, "Portable Christianity: Relics in the Medieval West (c. 700–1200)," *Proceedings of the British Academy* 181 (2012): 143–67.

55. Paulinus of Nola, "Carmen 19," lines 363–65, in *The Poems of St. Paulinus of Nola*, trans. P. G. Walsh (New York: Newman Press, 1975), 143; *Sancti Pontii Meropii Paulini Nolani Carmina*, ed. Guilelmus de Hartel (Vienna: Österreichischen Akademie der Wissenschaften, 1999), 130–31. For Paulinus's place in wider Late Antique discourses of fragmentation see the excellent analysis in Patricia Cox Miller, "'Differential Networks': Relics and Other Fragments in Late Antiquity," *Journal of Early Christian Studies* 6, no. 1 (1998): 113–38.

56. Paulinus of Nola, "Carmen 27," lines 404–5, in *Poems of St. Paulinus*, 285; *Sancti Pontii Meropii Paulini Nolani Carmina*, 280.

57. Brown, *The Cult of the Saints*, 166n62, 79.

58. Julia Reinhard Lupton, *Afterlives of the Saints: Hagiography, Typology, and Renaissance Literature* (Stanford: Stanford University Press, 1996), 66. This is most famously implied in the scatological jokes of Chaucer's Pardoner. For an important treatment of fragmentation and scatology in this tale see Carolyn Dinshaw, *Chaucer's Sexual Poetics* (Madison: University of Wisconsin Press, 1989), chap. 6, esp. 163–65.

59. On the "consecrated residues" left behind by saints, see David Frankfurter, "On Sacrifices and Residues: Processing the Potent Body," in *Religion im Kulturellen Diskurs*, ed. Brigitte Luchesi and Kocku von Stuckrad (Berlin: De Gruyter, 2004), 511–33. On the excremental holy see also Georges Bataille, "The Use Value of D. A. F. de Sade (An Open Letter to My Current Comrades)," in *Visions of Excess: Selected Writings, 1927–1939*, trans. Allan Stoekl et al. (Minneapolis: University of Minnesota Press, 1985), 91–102, esp. 94.

60. For discussion see Daniel Knapp, "The Relyk of a Seint: A Gloss on Chaucer's Pilgrimage," *ELH* 39, no. 1 (1972): 1–26, esp. 6.

61. Brown, *The Cult of the Saints*, 87.

62. I draw here on the analysis of Cynthia Hahn, "Metaphor and Meaning in Early Medieval Reliquaries," in *Seeing the Invisible in Late Antiquity and the Early Middle Ages*, ed. Giselle de Nie, Karl F. Morrison, and Marco Mostert (Turnhout: Brepols, 2005), 239–63, esp. 255.

63. Cynthia Hahn, *Strange Beauty: Issues in the Making and Meaning of Reliquaries, 400–circa 1204* (University Park: Pennsylvania State University Press, 2012), 230. *Myron* is perfume or fragranced oil.

64. See my discussion in Moshenska, *Feeling Pleasures*, 15–16, of Hugh of Lincoln,

who snapped and bit the finger from an arm of Mary Magdalen at Fécamp not because he reviled it but precisely to disseminate its holiness.

65. See Patrick Geary, "Humiliation of Saints," in *Saints and Their Cults: Studies in Religious Sociology, Folklore and History*, ed. Stephen Wilson (Cambridge: Cambridge University Press, 1983), 123–40; and Powell, *Depositions*, 91–95.

66. See Dennis Flynn, *John Donne and the Ancient Catholic Nobility* (Bloomington: Indiana University Press, 1995), 21; citing Anthony à Wood, *Athenae Oxoniensis* (London, 1691).

67. Alfred Gell, *Art and Agency: An Anthropological Theory* (Oxford: Clarendon, 1998), 129. Also germane here is Michel Foucault's discussion of the "grotesque" forms in which political power is capable "of conveying its effects, and, even more, of finding their source, in a place that is manifestly, explicitly, and readily discredited as odious, despicable, or ridiculous." Michel Foucault, *Abnormal: Lectures at the Collège de France, 1974–1975*, trans. Graham Burchell (London: Verso, 2003), 12.

68. Philippe Buc, "Conversion of Objects," *Viator* 28 (1997): 99–144, 101–2.

69. On the possibility of the Eucharist as abject or disgusting see Moshenska, *Feeling Pleasures*, 34–35; and Powell, *Depositions*, 242–43. On miracle tales see the rich account by Steven Justice, "Eucharistic Miracle and Eucharistic Doubt," *Journal of Medieval and Early Modern Studies* 42, no. 2 (2012): 307–32.

70. John Foxe, *Actes and Monuments* (London: John Face, 1563), 1360 (incorrectly numbered 1361).

71. *OED*, s.v. "Jack-in-the-Box." I am grateful to Anne Stillman for alerting me to this first recorded use of the phrase. See also Shershow, *Puppets and "Popular" Culture*, 79–81. I cannot discuss here the complex ways in which structures of thought and feeling informed by the Eucharist continued to permeate the early modern period; see the excellent accounts by Regina Schwartz, *Sacramental Poetics at the Dawn of Secularism: When God Left the World* (Stanford: Stanford University Press, 2008); and Louis Marin, "The Discourse of the Example: An 'Example,' Chapter IV of the First Part of 'The Logic of Port Royal,'" in *Unruly Examples: On the Rhetoric of Exemplarity*, ed. Alexander Gelley (Stanford: Stanford University Press, 1995), 104–17; as well as the excellent summary and analysis of Marin's complex account in Milad Doueihi, "Traps of Representation," *Diacritics* 14, no .1 (1984): 66–77.

72. Philippe Mornay du Plessis, *A Woorke Concerning the Trewnesse of the Christian Religion*, trans. Sir Philip Sidney and Arthur Golding (London, 1587), 191.

73. Heinrich von Kleist, "On the Marionette Theatre," trans. Idris Parry, in *On Dolls*, ed. Kenneth Gross (London: Notting Hill, 2012), 10. Kleist's story has been given particularly wide currency owing to the influential reading in Paul de Man, "Aesthetic Formalization: Kleist's *Über das Marionettentheater*," in *The Rhetoric of Romanticism* (New York: Columbia University Press, 1984), 263–90. For accounts indebted to de Man see Daniel Tiffany, *Toy Medium: Materialism and Modern Lyric* (Berkeley: University of California Press, 2000), 64–68; Garber, "Out of Joint"; and Powell, *Depositions*, 198–203.

74. Plato, *Laws*, trans. A. E. Taylor, in *Collected Dialogues*, ed. Edith Hamilton and Huntington Cairns (Princeton, NJ: Princeton University Press, 1961), 1244.

75. William Shakespeare, *King Lear*, ed. Jay L. Halio (Cambridge: Cambridge University Press, 1992), 4.1.37–38; Mihai Spariosu, *God of Many Names: Play, Poetry, and Power in Hellenic Thought from Homer to Aristotle* (Durham, NC: Duke University Press, 1991), 190.

76. See the excellent readings of Plato's puppets in Timothy Power, "Cyberchorus: Pindar's *Keledones* and the Aura of the Artificial," in *Archaic and Classical Choral Song: Performance, Politics and Dissemination*, ed. Lucia Athanassaki and Ewen Bowie (Berlin: De Gruyter, 2011), 67–113; and Leslie Kurke, "Imagining Chorality: Wonder, Plato's Puppets, and Moving Statues," in *Performance and Culture in Plato's Laws*, ed. Anastasia-Erasmia Peponi (Cambridge: Cambridge University Press, 2013), 123–70.

77. Bruno Latour, *On the Modern Cult of the Factish Gods*, trans. Catherine Porter and Heather MacLean (Durham, NC: Duke University Press, 2010), 62.

78. Alexander Nagel, *Medieval Modern: Art out of Time* (London: Thames and Hudson, 2012), chap. 17: "Relics and Reproducibles."

79. Richard Wollheim, "Minimal Art," in *On Art and the Mind: Essays and Lectures* (London: Allen Lane, 1973), 101–11, 109. See also Howard Caygill's rich and challenging account of the destruction of artworks as an expression of their existence as objects in time—and as the norm rather than the exception: "The Destruction of Art," in *The Life and Death of Images: Ethics and Aesthetics*, ed. Diarmuid Costello and Dominic Willsdon (London: Tate, 2008), 163–73; and Michel Serres's account of the hammer-wielding sculptor who blurs creation and destruction into an inextricable web of gestures: "With a hammer in his hand, Phidias, Michelangelo, Houdon, Rodin sculpted; Polyeuctes along with Nearchus and every other iconoclast broke the statues of the idols into tiny pieces, hammer in hand. Nietzsche wanted to philosophize by hammer blows.... Rodin decapitated bodies: he started the fragmentation. A headless statue remains a statue: Venus is more beautiful without arms.... Any fragment can substitute for a statue." Michel Serres, *Statues: The Second Book of Foundations*, trans. Randolph Burks (London: Bloomsbury, 2015), 111–12. Serres's mention of Nietzsche echoes Alexander Nehamas's claim that the famous desire to philosophize with a hammer was in fact a mixture of the destructive and the constructive: Nietzsche's hammer is "part tuning fork to sound out hollow idols, part instrument of their destruction, and part sculptor's mallet to fashion new statues out of the forms as well as the materials of the old" Alexander Nehamas, *Nietzsche: Life as Literature* (Cambridge, MA: Harvard University Press, 1985), 97.

80. Matthew Bown, "Traces of the Holy," *Times Literary Supplement*, Oct. 28, 2016, 155–56, 155. On the perpetuation of Eucharistic categories as a way of understanding the modern artwork, see Donald Preziosi, *Rethinking Art History: Meditations on a Coy Science* (New Haven, CT: Yale University Press, 1989), 102–6.

81. Patrick Collinson, "Fundamental Objections," *Times Literary Supplement*, Feb. 17, 1989, 14–15.

82. I am grateful to Amy Morris for this observation.

83. *A Fifteenth-Century School Book from a Manuscript in the British Museum* (MS. Arundel 249), ed. William Nelson (Oxford: Clarendon, 1956), 13; see the discussion in Rebecca Bushnell, *A Culture of Teaching: Early Modern Humanism in Theory and Practice* (Ithaca, NY: Cornell University Press, 1996), 40.

CHAPTER 4

1. "About an Inventory: A Conversation Between Natalie Zemon Davis and Peter N. Miller," in *Dutch New York Between East and West: The World of Margrieta van Varick*, ed. Deborah L. Krohn and Peter N. Miller (New Haven, CT: Yale University Press, 2009), 117–29, 123–24. I am grateful to Jason Scott-Warren for first alerting me to this discussion.

2. The fact that these objects existed as part of a carefully curated collection also calls to mind the interesting if not always particularly convincing or sophisticated claim, advanced by Werner Muensterberger, that collected objects are always akin to toys and act as forms of compensation for unhappy childhoods: "What else are collectibles but toys grown-ups take seriously? . . . The toys achieve what nothing else can. . . . They transform the child's feelings of loss and anxiety into well-springs of activity and imagination." He interprets the medieval passion for relics in the same way. Werner Muensterberger, *Collecting: An Unruly Passion—Psychological Perspectives* (Princeton, NJ: Princeton University Press, 1994), 31, 28.

3. Tara Alberts, *Conflict and Conversion: Catholicism in South East Asia, 1500–1700* (Oxford: Oxford University Press, 2013), 148.

4. Alberts, *Conflict and Conversion,* 139.

5. My account here is informed by Webb Keane's analysis of twentieth-century missionary contexts as sites of particularly complex "encounter" characterized not by a simple binary of peoples who have and have not been shaped by disenchanted modernity but rather by "*multiple* modalities of object creation." Webb Keane, *Christian Moderns: Freedom and Fetish in the Mission Encounter* (Berkeley: University of California Press, 2007), 12 (emphasis in the original).

6. The most thorough and useful recent account of the vicissitudes of the fetish and fetishism as concepts is now Rosalind C. Morris, "After de Brosses," in Rosalind C. Morris and Daniel H. Leonard, *The Returns of Fetishism: Charles de Brosses and the Afterlives of an Idea* (Chicago: University of Chicago Press, 2017), 133–320.

7. William Pietz, "The Problem of the Fetish, I," *RES* 9 (1985): 5–17; William Pietz, "The Problem of the Fetish, II: The Origin of the Fetish," *RES* 13 (1987): 23–45; William Pietz, "The Problem of the Fetish, IIIa: Bosman's Guinea and the Enlightenment Theory of Fetishism," *RES* 16 (1988): 105–24. See Rosalind Morris's valuable engagement with Pietz's argument in Morris, "After de Brosses," 153–66.

8. Webb Keane, "From Fetishism to Sincerity: On Agency, the Speaking Subject, and Their Historicity in the Context of Religious Conversion," *Comparative Studies in Society and History* 39, no. 4 (1997): 674–93, 677; see also Keane's more extended analysis of the fetish in his *Christian Moderns.*

9. Keane, "From Fetishism to Sincerity," 677.

10. For a valuable overview of psychoanalytic theories see E. L. McCallum, *Object Lessons: How to Do Things with Fetishism* (Albany: State University of New York Press, 1999).

11. Keane, "From Fetishism to Sincerity," 677–78. See also McCallum, *Object Lessons,* xi–xii: "fetishism is a form of subject-object relation that informs us about basic strategies of defining, desiring and knowing subjects and objects in Western culture."

12. See, in particular, Anne McClintock, *Imperial Leather: Race, Gender and Sexuality in the Colonial Context* (New York: Routledge, 1995), chap. 4: "Psychoanalysis, Race and Female Fetishism."

13. Claude Lévi-Strauss, *The Savage Mind* (London: Weidenfeld and Nicolson, 1966), 30–32, 23.

14. Claude Lévi-Strauss, "Father Christmas Executed," in *Unwrapping Christmas,* ed. Daniel Miller (Oxford: Oxford University Press, 1995), 38–51, 46, 49, 51.

15. Boris Wiseman, *Lévi-Strauss, Anthropology and Aesthetics* (Cambridge: Cambridge University Press, 2007), 1–2.

16. Morris, "After de Brosses," 149.

17. For an extended analysis of Lévi-Strauss's interest in this body-painting see Wiseman, *Lévi-Strauss*, 135–46. For the killing and adoption of children see Morris, "After de Brosses," 235.

18. Claude Lévi-Strauss, *Tristes Tropiques*, trans. John Weightman and Doreen Weightman (London: Jonathan Cape, 1973), 224–25. I have altered this quite unreliable translation to restore Lévi-Strauss's rhetorical questions. For the original text see Claude Lévi-Strauss, *Tristes Tropiques*, in *Œuvres*, ed. Vincent Debaene et al. (Paris: Gallimard, 2008), 164.

19. On these objects see the exhibition catalogue *Brésil Indien: Les Arts des Amérindiens du Brésil*, ed. Luís Donisete Benzi Grupioni (Paris: Réunion des Musées Nationaux, 2005), 348. For the Kachina dolls sold to Lacan see Wiseman, *Lévi-Strauss*, 2.

20. I return to this notion of blank, masked effigies in my final chapter.

21. Guido Boggiani, *Os Caduveo*, trans. Amadeu Amaral Júnior (Sãao Paolo: Livraria Martins Editõra, 1945), 200; A. V. Frič, "Onoenrgodi-Gott und Idole der Kaďuveo in Matto Grosso," in *International Congress of Americanists, Proceedings of the XVIII. Session, London, 1912* (London: Harrison and Sons, 1913), 397–407, figs. 2, 3.

22. Kalervo Oberg, *The Terena and the Caduveo of Southern Mato Grosso, Brazil* (Washington, DC: United States Government Printing Office, 1949), 64; Darcy Ribeiro, *Religião e Mitologia Kadiuéu* (Rio de Janeiro: Conselho Nacional de Proteção aos Indios, 1950), 80–81. I am grateful to Maria Cecília de Miranda Nogueira Coelho and Rodrigo Tadeu Gonçalves for kindly providing scans from this latter work. For Lévi-Strauss's likely reference to these sources see *Œuvres*, ed. Debaene et al., 1751n6.

23. Lévi-Strauss, *Tristes Tropiques*, 225–26.

24. A similar account of Kachina dolls—probably indebted to *Tristes Tropiques*—was mentioned in passing by Roger Caillois in his seminal account of play: *Man, Play and Games*, trans. Meyer Barash (London: Thames and Hudson, 1962), 61. Brian Sutton-Smith, a modern authority on play and toys, quotes Lévi-Strauss and Caillois but simply states that such activity "does not seem to have been widespread" and moves on. See Brian Sutton-Smith, *Toys as Culture* (New York: Gardner Press, 1986), 27.

25. Jacques Derrida, "Structure, Sign and Play in the Discourse of the Human Sciences," in *Writing and Difference*, trans. Alan Bass (London: Routledge, 1978), 351–70, 365, 369 (emphases in the original).

26. Though I cannot do justice to this aspect of Lévi-Strauss's thought here, my thinking about his work has been inspired indirectly by the dense and electrifying reconsideration offered by Eduardo Viveiros de Castro, *Cannibal Metaphysics*, trans. Peter Skafish (Minneapolis, MN: Univocal, 2014), especially his discussion of the interplay between stabilizing and destabilizing elements in Lévi-Strauss's writing (200–209).

27. Sigmund Freud, "Creative Writers and Day-Dreaming," in *The Standard Edition of the Complete Psychological Works of Sigmund Freud*, ed. James Strachey (London: Hogarth, 1953–74), 9:143–53, 143–44.

28. For the role of play in and after Klein see Mary Jacobus, *The Poetics of Psychoanalysis in the Wake of Klein* (Oxford: Oxford University Press, 2005), chap. 4: "Magical Arts: The Poetics of Play."

29. My thinking on these competing urges in Freud and psychoanalysis as a whole

have been principally informed by the work of Adam Phillips; see, especially, his *Terrors and Experts* (London: Faber, 1995).

30. Melanie Klein, "The Psycho-analytic Play Technique: Its History and Significance," in *The Selected Melanie Klein*, ed. Juliet Mitchell (New York: Free Press, 1986), 35–54, 42, 46; Melanie Klein, "The Psychological Principles of Infant Analysis," in *The Selected Melanie Klein*, 58–68, 66.

31. Klein, "Psychological Principles," 67.

32. D. W. Winnicott, *Playing and Reality* (London: Routledge, 1971), 96. I am grateful to Elizabeth Harvey for pushing me to clarify my thinking on Winnicott.

33. Barbara Johnson, *Persons and Things* (Cambridge, MA: Harvard University Press, 2008), 98. See also the illuminating discussion of Winnicott's account, specifically in relation to the aliveness of the toy, in Anne Stillman, "Distraction Fits," *Thinking Verse* 2 (2012): 27–67, 51.

34. Winnicott, *Playing and Reality*, 51.

35. Winnicott, *Playing and Reality*, 62.

36. Brian Upton, *The Aesthetic of Play* (Cambridge, MA: MIT Press, 2015), 9.

37. See, e.g., Margaret Mead, "An Investigation of the Thought of Primitive Children, with Special Reference to Animism," *Journal of the Royal Anthropological Society of Great Britain and Ireland* 62 (Jan.–June 1932): 173–90.

38. Gregory Bateson, *Naven: A Survey of the Problems Suggested by a Composite Picture of the Culture of a New Guinea Tribe Drawn from Three Points of View* (Cambridge: Cambridge University Press, 1936), 125.

39. Bateson, *Naven*, 137.

40. Gregory Bateson, "A Theory of Play and Fantasy," in *Steps to an Ecology of Mind: Collected Essays in Anthropology, Psychiatry, Evolution and Epistemology* (London: Intertext, 1972), 177–93, 182. For an important extrapolation of Bateson's consideration of play-frames as a way of understanding the structuring of social action generally, see Erving Goffman, *Frame Analysis: An Essay on the Organization of Experience* (Boston: Northeastern University Press, 1986), esp. 40–43, 49–52, 87–92, on the necessarily unstable ways in which playful behavior is undertaken and recognized.

41. For an account that connects *Naven* to Bateson's later work on play, see Don Handelman, "Is Naven Ludic? Paradox and the Communication of Identity," *Social Analysis*, no. 1 (Feb. 1979): 177–91.

42. Steven Lee Rubenstein, "Circulation, Accumulation, and the Power of Shuar Shrunken Heads," *Cultural Anthropology* 22, no. 3 (2007): 357–99, 364. I am grateful to Joel Robbins for alerting me to this article.

43. Philippe Descola, *The Spears of Twilight: Life and Death in the Amazon Jungle*, trans. Janet Lloyd (New York: New Press, 1996), 275; cited in Rubenstein, "Circulation," 365.

44. F. W. Up de Graff, *Head Hunters of the Amazon: Seven Years of Exploration and Adventure* (Garden City, NJ: Garden City Publishing, 1923), 283; cited in Rubenstein, "Circulation," 388n16.

45. Jean-Jacques Rousseau, *Emile*, in *The Collected Writings of Rousseau*, vol. 13, trans. Christopher Kelly and Allan Bloom (Hanover, NH: Dartmouth College Press, 2010), 413; Sarah Kofman, "Baubô: Theological Perversion and Fetishism," trans. Tracy B. Strong,

in *Feminist Interpretations of Friedrich Nietzsche*, ed. Kelly Oliver and Marilyn Pearsall (University Park: Pennsylvania State University Press, 1999), 21–49, 22; Sigmund Freud, "Fetishism," in *On Sexuality: Three Essays on the Theory of Sexuality and Other Works*, vol. 7, ed. James Strachey (Harmondsworth: Penguin, 1977), 351–408; T. W. Adorno, "On the Fetish Character in Music and the Regression of Listening," in *The Culture Industry: Selected Essays on Mass Culture*, ed. J. M. Bernstein (London: Routledge, 2001), 29–60, 46–47. I return to Adorno's account of the fetish below.

46. Charles de Brosses, "On the Worship of Fetish Gods; or, A Parallel of the Ancient Religion of Egypt with the Present Religion of Nigritia," trans. Daniel H. Leonard, in Morris and Leonard, *The Returns of Fetishism*, 44–132, 101. The original is cited from de Brosses, *Du Culte des dieux fétiches* (Paris, 1760), 184, 185–86. See the discussion in the fascinating article by Keston Sutherland, "Marx in Jargon," *World Picture* 1 (2008): 1–25, which first drew it to my attention.

47. Bruno Latour, *On the Modern Cult of the Factish Gods*, trans. Catherine Porter and Heather MacLean (Durham, NC: Duke University Press, 2010), 28, 42.

48. Bruno Latour, "The Slight Surprise of Action: Facts, Fetishes, Factishes," in *Pandora's Hope: Essays on the Reality of Science Studies* (Cambridge, MA: Harvard University Press, 1999), 266–92, 271–72.

49. Pietz, "The Problem of the Fetish, II," 41.

50. Samuel Purchas, *Purchas His Pilgrimes in Five Books, the Second Part* (London, 1625), 960, 943.

51. Pietz, "The Problem of the Fetish, II," 41.

52. Purchas, *Purchas His Pilgrimes*, 935.

53. Cited in Pietz, "The Problem of the Fetish, II," 39.

54. Purchas, *Purchas His Pilgrimes*, 960, 943, 944.

55. "Sir George Peckham's True Reporte," in *The Voyages and Colonising Enterprises of Sir Humphrey Gilbert*, ed. David Beers Quinn (London: Hakluyt Society, 1940), 2:450.

56. "Sir George Peckham's True Reporte," 2:450, 452. See the discussion of these linguistic strains by James J. Kearney, "Trinket, Idol, Fetish: Some Notes on Iconoclasm and the Language of Materiality in Reformation England," *Shakespeare Studies* 28 (2000): 257–61.

57. Jeffrey Knapp, *An Empire Nowhere: England, America, and Literature from "Utopia" to "The Tempest"* (Berkeley: University of California Press, 1992), 145.

58. *The Libelle of Englyshe Polycye: A Poem on the Use of Sea Power, 1436*, ed. George Warner (Oxford: Clarendon, 1926), lines 345, 348–49. For this widespread anxiety see Knapp, *An Empire Nowhere*; Smith cited by G. V. Scammell, "Hakluyt and the Economic Thought of His Time," in *The Hakluyt Handbook*, ed. D. B. Quinn (London: Hakluyt Society, 1974), 1:15–22.

59. Purchas, *Purchas His Pilgrimes*, 931.

60. On the way in which fetishes promulgate new forms of connectivity and interrelation see David Graeber, "Fetishism as Social Creativity, or, Fetishes Are Gods in the Process of Construction," *Anthropological Theory* 5, no. 4 (2005): 407–38.

61. Purchas, *Purchas His Pilgrimes*, 930–31.

62. Thomas Hariot, *A Briefe and True Report of the New Found Land of Virginia* (New York: Dover, 1972), 25, 45.

63. Andrew Cole, *The Birth of Theory* (Chicago: University of Chicago Press, 2014), 86.

64. G. W. F. Hegel, *The Philosophy of History*, trans. J. Sibree (New York: Dover, 1956), 94, 390–91.

65. Hegel, *The Philosophy of History*, 94. Similar behavior is noted in recent anthropological accounts; see, e.g., Roy Ellen, "Fetishism," *Man* 23, no. 2 (1988): 213–35, 228.

66. Morris, "After de Brosses," 170.

67. In his *Theories of Surplus Value* Marx aligned the fetish and the consecrated Host: "It is in *interest-bearing capital* . . . that capital finds its most objectified form, its pure fetish form. . . . The transubstantiation, the fetishism, is complete." Karl Marx, *Theories of Surplus Value, Part 3*, trans. Jack Cohen and S. W. Ryazanskaya (Moscow: Progress, 1971), 494, 498. On this passage, and the date of Marx's reading of de Brosses, see William Pietz, "Fetishism and Materialism: The Limits of Theory in Marx," in *Fetishism as Cultural Discourse*, ed. Emily Apter and William Pietz (Ithaca, NY: Cornell University Press, 1993), 119–51, 149, 134.

68. Karl Marx, *Capital*, vol. 1, trans. Ben Fowkes (London: Penguin, 1990), 163–64.

69. On Marx's satirical strategies see Pietz, "Fetishism and Materialism," 130; and Sutherland, "Marx in Jargon."

70. Giorgio Agamben, *Stanzas: Word and Phantasm in Western Culture*, trans. Ronald L. Martinez (Minneapolis: University of Minnesota Press, 1993), 56–57; on the toy and the Marxist fetish see also Daniel Tiffany, *Toy Medium: Materialism and Modern Lyric* (Berkeley: University of California Press, 2000), 25–26, 174.

71. Agamben, *Stanzas*, 57.

72. Walter Benjamin, "The Cultural History of Toys," in *Selected Writings: Volume 2, Part 1: 1927–1930*, ed. Michael W. Jennings, Howard Eiland, and Gary Smith (Cambridge, MA: Harvard University Press, 1999), 113–16, 115.

73. W. J. T. Mitchell, "Totemism, Fetishism, Idolatry," in *What Do Pictures Want? The Lives and Loves of Images* (Chicago: University of Chicago Press, 2005), 188–96, 193, 194, 196 (emphases in the original). See also Mitchell's rich and influential account, "The Rhetoric of Iconoclasm: Marxism, Ideology, and Fetishism," in *Iconology: Image, Text, Ideology* (Chicago: University of Chicago Press, 1986), 160–208.

74. Jean-Luc Nancy, "The Two Secrets of the Fetish," trans. Thomas C. Platt, *Diacritics* 31, no. 2 (2001): 2–8, 5; see also 7–8.

75. Jane Bennett, *Vibrant Matter: A Political Ecology of Things* (Durham, NC: Duke University Press, 2010), 15–16; see also Theodor W. Adorno, *Negative Dialectics*, trans. E. B. Ashton (London: Routledge, 1973), 14.

76. Theodor W. Adorno, *Aesthetic Theory*, trans. Robert Hullot-Kentor (London: Continuum, 1997), 49; Theodor W. Adorno, "Free Time," in *The Culture Industry: Selected Essays on Mass Culture*, ed. J. M. Bernstein (London: Routledge, 2001), 187–97, 194.

77. Adorno, *Aesthetic Theory*, 400.

78. Adorno, *Aesthetic Theory*, 401–2.

79. Adorno, "Fetish Character," 39.

80. Adorno, *Aesthetic Theory*, 22.

81. Adorno, *Aesthetic Theory*, 149.

82. Adorno, *Aesthetic Theory*, 298.

83. Theodor W. Adorno, *Minima Moralia: Reflections on a Damaged Life*, trans. Edmund Jephcott (London: Verso, 1974), 109.

84. Adorno, *Minima Moralia*, 228. This account of the child "rescuing" things echoes Benjamin's claim: "In waste products [children] recognize the face that the world of things turns directly and solely to them. In using these things, they do not so much imitate the works of adults as bring together, in the artefact produced in play, materials of widely differing kinds in a new, intuitive relationship. Children thus produce their own small world of things within the greater one." Walter Benjamin, "One Way Street," in *Selected Writings: Volume 1: 1913–1926*, ed. Marcus Bullock and Michael W. Jennings (Cambridge, MA: Harvard University Press, 1999), 449–50. On the unstable processes by which objects become detritus see Michael Thompson, *Rubbish Theory: The Creation and Destruction of Value* (Oxford: Oxford University Press, 1979).

85. Adorno, *Minima Moralia*, 228.

86. Adorno, *Minima Moralia*, 178.

CHAPTER 5

1. Richard Lord Braybrooke, *The History of Audley End, to Which Are Appended Notices of the Town and Parish of Saffron Walden in the County of Essex* (London: Samuel Bentley, 1836), 203. See the brief discussion in Margaret Aston, *Broken Idols of the English Reformation* (Cambridge: Cambridge University Press, 2016), 997.

2. Anthony Ossa-Richardson, "Cry Me a Relic: The Holy Tear of Vendôme and Early Modern Lipsanomachy," unpublished manuscript; I am grateful to Anthony Ossa-Richardson for sharing this work with me.

3. Charles H. Kahn, *The Art and Thought of Heraclitus: An Edition of the Fragments with Translation and Commentary* (Cambridge: Cambridge University Press, 1979), 227–28. See also the brief discussion of Heraclitus's claim by Mihai Spariosu, *God of Many Names: Play, Poetry, and Power in Hellenic Thought from Homer to Aristotle* (Durham, NC: Duke University Press, 1991), 65–66; and the extensive account, building on Kahn and discussing *pessoi* and their place in Greek life, in Leslie Kurke, *Coins, Bodies, Games, and Gold: The Politics of Meaning in Archaic Greece* (Princeton, NJ: Princeton University Press, 1999), chap. 7: "Games People Play," esp. 263–64.

4. Bruno Bettelheim, "The Importance of Play," *Atlantic Monthly*, March 1987, 35–46, 40.

5. Elizabeth Freeman, *Time Binds: Queer Temporalities, Queer Histories* (Durham, NC: Duke University Press, 2010), 3. Also relevant here is Lee Edelman's account of the ways in which ideologically constructed images of childhood are used to naturalize specific, heteronormative political agendas, with "the image of the Child, not to be confused with the lived experience of any historical children," used to create an idealized image of "an innocence seen as continuously under siege" and a future that must be protected. Lee Edelman, *No Future: Queer Theory and the Death Drive* (Durham, NC: Duke University Press, 2004), 11, 21.

6. John Milton, *Paradise Regained*, 1.201–4, in *Shorter Poems*, ed. John Carey (London: Longman, 1968).

7. *Magna Vita Sancti Hugonis: The Life of St. Hugh of Lincoln*, ed. and trans. Decima L. Douie and David Hugh Farmer (Oxford: Clarendon, 1985), 6: "iocos numquam didici, numquam sciui."

8. J. A. Burrow, *The Ages of Man: A Study in Medieval Writing and Thought* (Oxford: Clarendon, 1988), 90.

9. John Lydgate, *The Pilgrimage of the Life of Man*, ed. F. J. Furnivall (London: Kegan Paul, 1899), lines 11204–6; Jean Froissart, "L'Espinette Amoureuse," lines 23–248, in *Jean Froissart: An Anthology of Narrative and Lyric Poetry*, ed. and trans. Kristen M. Figg with R. Barton Palmer (New York: Routledge, 2001).

10. Ptolemy, *Tetrabiblos*, bk. 4, chap. 10, cited from the appendix to Burrow, *The Ages of Man*, 198.

11. Rebecca Bushnell, *A Culture of Teaching: Early Modern Humanism in Theory and Practice* (Ithaca, NY: Cornell University Press, 1996), 30, 18; see also the discussion of the normative formation of male children in Diane Purkiss, *Literature, Gender and Politics During the English Civil War* (Cambridge: Cambridge University Press, 2005), 9–19.

12. Quintilian, *The Orator's Education: Books 1–2*, trans. Donald A. Russell (Cambridge, MA: Harvard University Press, 2001), 74 (I have chosen to translate this as "let it be play" rather than Russell's "let it be a game"—either is possible); *Selected Letters of Saint Jerome*, trans. F. A. Wright (London: Heinemann, 1933), 345–47; Erasmus, *De lusu*, trans. Craig R. Thompson, in *Collected Works of Erasmus*, general editor Manfred Hoffman, 78 vols. (Toronto: University of Toronto Press, 1978–), 39:75.

13. Bushnell, *A Culture of Teaching*, 109.

14. Plato, *Laws*, in *Collected Dialogues*, ed. Edith Hamilton and Huntington Cairns (Princeton, NJ: Princeton University Press, 1961), 1243. Greek gloss from Plato, *Laws*, trans. R. G. Bury (Cambridge, MA: Harvard University Press, 1926), 1:62.

15. Plato, *Laws*, 1243.

16. Kahn, *Heraclitus*, 228; see also the discussion of these etymological links in Mark Golden, *Children and Childhood in Classical Athens* (Baltimore: Johns Hopkins University Press, 1990), 53. The verbal parallel is noted in the classic study by Werner Jaeger, *Paideia: The Ideals of Greek Culture*, vol. 2, *In Search of the Divine Centre*, trans. Gilbert Highet (Oxford: Oxford University Press, 1971), 317. See also Steven H. Londsdale, *Ritual Play in Greek Religion* (Baltimore: Johns Hopkins University Press, 1993), 33–36.

17. Aristotle, *Politics* 1336a, in *Complete Works of Aristotle*, ed. Jonathan Barnes (Princeton, NJ: Princeton University Press, 1984), 2:2120; Greek cited from *Politics*, trans. H. Rackham (Cambridge, MA: Harvard University Press, 1932), 626. For useful discussion of Aristotle on play—including his points of agreement and disagreement with Plato's *Laws*—see Friedrich Solmsen, "Leisure and Play in Aristotle's Ideal State," *Rheinisches Museum für Philologie* 107 (1964): 193–220, esp. 209–15.

18. Mauss refers specifically at numerous points in his essay to the imitative capacity of children and mentions his recourse to "the Platonic position on technique" in relation to dance and music: Marcel Mauss, "Techniques of the Body," in *Beyond the Body Proper: Reading the Anthropology of Material Life*, ed. Margaret Lock and Judith Farquhar (Durham, NC: Duke University Press, 2007), 50–68, esp. 54–55. See also the discussion of this pioneering emphasis on child-rearing in Mauss's essay in Claude Lévi-Strauss, *Introduction to the Work of Marcel Mauss*, trans. Felicity Baker (London: Routledge, 1987), 4–5.

19. For important accounts see Amelie Rorty, "Plato and Aristotle on Belief, Habit and Akrasia," *American Philosophical Quarterly* 7, no. 1 (1970): 50–61; and Richard Sorabji, "Aristotle on the Role of Intellect in Virtue," in *Essays on Aristotle's Ethics*, ed. Amelie Oksenberg Rorty (Berkeley: University of California Press, 1980), 201–19, esp. 214–18. For Plato and Aristotle on the malleability of the child see Golden, *Children and Childhood*, 7.

20. Paul Ricoeur, *Freedom and Nature: The Voluntary and the Involuntary*, trans. Erazim V. Kohák (Evanston, IL: Northwestern University Press, 1966), 298.

21. Steven Ozment, *Ancestors: The Loving Family in Old Europe* (Cambridge, MA: Harvard University Press, 2001), 69.

22. For this side of habit as a fixed "second nature" see Paul Ricoeur, *Oneself as Another*, trans. Katherine Blamey (Chicago: University of Chicago Press, 1992), 121.

23. Michel de Montaigne, *The Essayes or morall, politike and millitarie discourses of Lo: Michaell de Montaigne*, trans. John Florio (London, 1603), 46.

24. Montaigne, *Essayes*, 47.

25. Montaigne, *Essayes*, 47. These words were echoed and generalized by Walter Pater, who observed that "play is often that about which people are most serious." Walter Pater, *Appreciations* (London: Macmillan, 1889), 170. I am grateful to David Hillman for this reference.

26. Ozment, *Ancestors*, 69.

27. John Duffy, "Playing at Ritual: Variations on a Theme in Byzantine Religious Tales," in *Greek Ritual Poetics*, ed. Dimitrios Yatromanolakis and Panagiotis Roilos (Washington, DC: Center for Hellenic Studies, 2004), 199–209, 200.

28. Duffy, "Playing at Ritual," 203.

29. Duffy, "Playing at Ritual," 206–7. For Rufinus's original account see Thomas Wiedemann, *Adults and Children in the Roman Empire* (London: Routledge, 1989), 153.

30. Duffy, "Playing at Ritual," 201–2.

31. Giovanni Dominici, "On the Education of Children," trans. Arthur Basil Cote (PhD thesis, Catholic University of America, 1927), 34, 42; cited in Richard Trexler, "Ritual in Florence: Adolescence and Salvation in the Renaissance," in *The Pursuit of Holiness in Late Medieval and Renaissance Religion*, ed. Charles Trinkaus with Heiko A. Oberman (Leiden: Brill, 1974), 200–264, 233–34.

32. Thomas Elyot, *The Boke Named the Gouernour*, ed. Henry Herbert Stephen Croft (London: Kegan Paul, 1880), 1:30–31.

33. Martin Luther, *Exhortation to All Clergy Assembled at Augsburg* (1530), trans. Lewis W. Spitz, in *Luther's Works*, ed. Helmut T. Lehmann (Philadelphia: Muhlenberg Press, 1960), 34:59; see the discussion in Scott Cutler Shershow, *Puppets and "Popular" Culture* (Ithaca, NY: Cornell University Press, 1995), 38.

34. *The Homilies of S. John Chrysostom, Archbishop of Constantinople, on the First Epistle of St. Paul the Apostle to the Corinthians*, trans. Hubert Kestell Cornish and John Medley (Oxford: John Henry Parker, 1839), 49.

35. *Batman upon Bartholome His Booke De Proprietatibus rerum* (London, 1582), f.73r.

36. *The Book of Curtesie, That Is Clepid, Stans Puer ad Mensam*, in *The Babees Book*, ed. Frederick J. Furnivall (London: N. Trübner, 1868), lines 85–87.

37. Spariosu, *God of Many Names*, 181.

38. Golden, *Children and Childhood*, 54, 56. For the range of toys and games that Plato would actually have encountered in Athens, see Jennifer Neils and John H. Oakley, *Coming of Age in Ancient Greece: Images of Childhood from the Classical Past* (New Haven, CT: Yale University Press, 2003), 263–82.

39. Ian Hacking, *The Taming of Chance* (Cambridge: Cambridge University Press, 1990), 161; see also Hacking, "The Making and Molding of Child Abuse," *Critical Inquiry* 17, no. 2 (1991): 253–88, 286.

40. Brian Sutton-Smith, *The Ambiguity of Play* (Cambridge, MA: Harvard University Press, 1997), 42, 49.

41. Adam Phillips, *Going Sane* (New York: Fourth Estate, 2005), 79.

42. Phillips, *Going Sane*, 118. Relevant again here are Hacking's observations on "a fundamental tension in the idea of the normal—the normal as existing average, and the normal as a figure of perfection to which we may progress" (*The Taming of Chance*, 168). This double sense operates strongly, I would argue, in accounts of child's play as progression. There is of course a vast bibliography on child development and play; for a helpful overview see Daniel Miller, *Material Culture and Mass Consumption* (Oxford: Basil Blackwell, 1987), 86–95.

43. Ian Hacking, *Historical Ontology* (Cambridge, MA: Harvard University Press, 2002), 21 (emphases in the original).

44. Hacking, *Historical Ontology*, 21.

45. Hacking, *Historical Ontology*, 22.

46. Walter Benjamin, "Doctrine of the Similar" and "Toys and Play," both in *Selected Writings: Volume 2, Part 1: 1927–1930*, ed. Michael W. Jennings, Howard Eiland, and Gary Smith (Cambridge, MA: Harvard University Press, 1999), 694–98, 694; 117–121, 120.

47. Benjamin, "Doctrine of the Similar," 694.

48. Benjamin, "Old Toys," in *Selected Writings: Volume 2, Part 1: 1927–1930*, ed. Michael W. Jennings, Howard Eiland, and Gary Smith (Cambridge, MA: Harvard University Press, 1999), 98–102, 101. On Benjamin's conception of *Spielraum* see Miriam Bratu Hansen, "Room-for-Play: Benjamin's Gamble with Cinema," *October* 109 (Summer 2004): 3–45.

49. Gilles Deleuze and Félix Guattari, *Kafka: Toward a Minor Literature*, trans. Dana Polan (Minneapolis: University of Minnesota Press, 1986), 21.

50. Benjamin, "Toys and Play," 120.

51. Eamon Duffy, *The Voices of Morebath: Reformation and Rebellion in an English Village* (New Haven, CT: Yale University Press, 2001), 177.

52. Stephen Greenblatt, "Resonance and Wonder," in *Learning to Curse* (London: Routledge, 1990), 216–46, 218. For a trenchant critique of Greenblatt's account of this process—including the factual inaccuracies of the first edition—see Anne Barton, "Perils of Historicism," *New York Review of Books*, March 28, 1991.

53. *Records of Early English Drama: Cambridge*, ed. Alan Nelson (Toronto: University of Toronto Press, 1986), 2:756; see also the discussion in Peter Stallybrass and Ann Rosalind Jones, *Renaissance Clothing and the Materials of Memory* (Cambridge: Cambridge University Press, 2001), 192.

54. Christopher Bollas, *The Shadow of the Object: Psychoanalysis of the Unthought Known* (New York: Columbia University Press, 1987), 158–59.

55. Bollas, *The Shadow of the Object*, 163.

56. Webb Keane, *Signs of Recognition: Powers and Hazards of Representation in an Indonesian Society* (Berkeley: University of California Press, 1997), 251n34. I am grateful to Webb Keane for discussing this practice with me.

CHAPTER 6

1. Elizabeth Sharrett, "Shakespeare in 100 Objects: Doll," Shakespeare Birthplace Trust, www.shakespeare.org.uk/explore-shakespeare/blogs/shakespeare-100-objects -doll/; William Shakespeare, *The Taming of the Shrew*, ed. Barbara Hodgdon (London: Bloomsbury, 2010), 1.2.78 (Sharrett explains that aglets are pieces of metal at the end of a lace that makes threading them easier); Ellen Mackay, "The Curious Absence of Soft Matter: A Response to Cute Shakespeare," *Journal for Early Modern Cultural Studies* 16, no. 3 (2016): 138–44, 139.

2. Michael Taussig, *Defacement: Public Secrecy and the Labor of the Negative* (Stanford: Stanford University Press, 1999), 136, 204, 235, passim.

3. Octave Mannoni, "I Know Well, but All the Same . . . ," trans. G. M. Goshgarian, in *Perversion and the Social Relation*, ed. Molly Anne Rothenberg, Dennis Foster, and Slavoj Žižek (Durham, NC: Duke University Press, 2003), 68–92, 70.

4. Mannoni, "I Know Well," 73.

5. Mannoni, "I Know Well," 75–76.

6. Christian Metz, *Psychoanalysis and Cinema: The Imaginary Signifier*, trans. Celia Britton et al. (London: Macmillan, 1982), 73.

7. Taussig, *Defacement*, 120; see 234–35 for his engagement with Metz.

8. Metz, *Psychoanalysis and Cinema*, 70.

9. Jacques Derrida, *Dissemination*, trans. Barbara Johnson (London: Bloomsbury, 2016), 150–51 (emphases in the original).

10. Derrida, *Dissemination*, 152.

11. See Shulamith Shahar, *Childhood in the Middle Ages* (London: Routledge, 1990), 197.

12. Jeff Dolven, *Scenes of Instruction in Renaissance Romance* (Chicago: University of Chicago Press, 2007), 55; citing John Brinsley, *Ludus Literarius* (London, 1612), Qq2r.

13. Erasmus, *Confabulatio pia*, trans. Craig R. Thompson, in *Collected Works of Erasmus* (hereafter *CWE*), general editor Manfred Hoffman, 78 vols. (Toronto: University of Toronto Press, 1978–), 39:93.

14. See Jason Scott-Warren's entry on Harington in the *Oxford Dictionary of National Biography*, https://doi.org/10.1093/ref:odnb/12326.

15. John Harington, "A Treatise on Playe," in *Nugae Antiquae*, ed. Thomas Park (London: J. Wright, 1804), 1:186–232, 188.

16. Erasmus, *De civilitate morum puerilium*, trans. Brian McGregor, *CWE* 25:289.

17. Harington, "A Treatise on Playe," 202.

18. Huizinga quoted by E. H. Gombrich, "Huizinga's *Homo Ludens*," in *Johan Huizinga, 1872–1972*, ed. W. R. H. Koops et al. (The Hague: Martinus Nijhoff, 1973), 133–54, 154.

19. Harington, "A Treatise on Playe," 188–89.

20. I am indebted throughout this paragraph to the discussion in Bernard J. Verkamp, *The Indifferent Mean: Adiaphorism in the English Reformation to 1554* (Athens, OH: Ohio University Press, 1977), chaps. 1–3; see the discussion of Gardiner at 63.

21. Verkamp, *The Indifferent Mean*, 29–30.

22. For Harington's religious views see Debora Shuger, "A Protesting Catholic Puritan in Elizabethan England," *Journal of British Studies* 48, no. 3 (2009): 587–630.

23. "A Letter to John Campanus by Sebastian Franck," in *Spiritual and Anabaptist Writers*, ed. George Hunston Williams (London: SCM Press, 1957), 149, 155.

24. Harington, "A Treatise on Playe," 202.

25. Harington, "A Treatise on Playe," 211.

26. Harington, "A Treatise on Playe," 216.

27. Adam Phillips, *Going Sane* (New York: Fourth Estate, 2005), 78.

28. George Herbert Mead, *Mind, Self, and Society: From the Standpoint of a Social Behaviorist*, ed. Charles W. Morris (Chicago: University of Chicago Press, 1934), 152, 159.

29. Theodor W. Adorno, *Minima Moralia: Reflections on a Damaged Life*, trans. Edmund Jephcott (London: Verso, 1974), 130.

30. Adorno, *Minima Moralia*, 175. See also E. P. Thompson, "Time, Work-Discipline, and Industrial Capitalism," *Past and Present* 38 (Dec. 1967): 56–97.

31. Adorno, *Minima Moralia*, 130–31.

32. Adorno, *Minima Moralia*, 130.

33. Adorno, *Minima Moralia*, 130.

34. Tzachi Zamir, "Puppets," *Critical Inquiry* 36, no. 3 (2010): 386–409, 396–97.

35. Joseph Leo Koerner, *Bosch and Bruegel: From Enemy Painting to Everyday Life* (Princeton, NJ: Princeton University Press, 2016), 2.

36. Koerner, *Bosch and Bruegel*, 7.

37. Harry Berger Jr., *Fictions of the Pose: Rembrandt Against the Italian Renaissance* (Stanford: Stanford University Press, 1999), 57.

38. For a rich and playful meditation, in light of Wittgenstein's famous account, of the problem of defining games, see Bernard Suits, *The Grasshopper: Games, Life and Utopia* (Toronto: University of Toronto Press, 1978).

39. I cite from the best-known seventeenth-century translation: see François Rabelais, *The Lives, Heroic Deeds and Sayings of Gargantua and His Son Pantagruel*, trans. Thomas Urquhart (London: Chatto and Windus, 1921), 62–66; for these games in the context of the carnivalesque see Mikhail Bakhtin, *Rabelais and His World*, trans. Hélène Iswolsky (Bloomington: Indiana University Press, 1984), 231–39, esp. 235.

40. See the useful overview of this debate in Walter S. Gibson, *Pieter Bruegel and the Art of Laughter* (Berkeley: University of California Press, 2006), "Prologue: Deciphering Bruegel."

41. Sandra Hindman, "Pieter Bruegel's *Children's Games*, Folly, and Chance," *Art Bulletin* 63, no. 3 (1981): 447–75, 449. For a useful identification of the actual games depicted in Bruegel's painting, see Jeanette Hills, *Das Kinderspielbild von Pieter Bruegel d.Ä. (1560)* (Vienna: Österreichischen Museums für Volkskunde, 1957).

42. Edward Snow, "'Meaning' in *Children's Games*: On the Limitations of the Iconographic Approach to Bruegel," *Representations* 2 (Spring 1983): 26–60, 30. Snow makes passing reference to the practice of giving idols to children as dolls (41).

43. Snow, "'Meaning' in *Children's Games*," 46.

44. Joseph Leo Koerner, "Albrecht Dürer's *Pleasures of the World* and the Limits of Festival," in *Das Fest*, ed. Walter Haug and Rainer Warning (Munich: Fink, 1989), 181–216, 207.

45. For sensitive accounts of how to read Sedlmayr's essay in this context, see Koerner, "Albrecht Dürer's *Pleasures of the World*," 195–97; and Christopher Wood, introduction

to *The Vienna School Reader*, ed. Christopher Wood (New York: Zone, 2000), esp. 21, 33–34, 36–38, 46–48, 52–53.

46. Hans Sedlmayr, "Bruegel's *Macchia*," in *The Vienna School Reader*, ed. Christopher Wood (New York: Zone, 2000), 323–76, 325.

47. Sedlmayr, "Bruegel's *Macchia*," 326.

48. Sedlmayr, "Bruegel's *Macchia*," 330–31.

49. Koerner, "Albrecht Dürer's *Pleasures of the World*," 196, 197.

50. Sedlmayr, "Bruegel's *Macchia*," 336.

51. Mark Golden, *Children and Childhood in Classical Athens* (Baltimore: Johns Hopkins University Press, 1990), 7.

52. Sedlmayr, "Bruegel's *Macchia*," 341. It is not clear from whom these final words are quoted.

53. Jean-François Lyotard, *The Inhuman: Reflections on Time*, trans. Geoffrey Bennington and Rachel Bowlby (Stanford: Stanford University Press, 1991), 4; Avital Ronell, "On the Unrelenting Creepiness of Childhood: Lyotard, Kid Tested," in *The ÜberReader: Selected Works of Avital Ronell*, ed. Diane Davis (Urbana: University of Illinois Press, 2008), 101–27, 103. Thanks to David Hillman for the latter reference.

54. Koerner, *Bosch and Bruegel*, 325.

55. Sedlmayr, "Bruegel's *Macchia*," 342–43. Sedlmayr's thinly veiled racism also emerges in this discussion: "The faces of foreign races whose expressions one does not understand have the uncanny effect of masks" (342).

56. Koerner, *Bosch and Bruegel*, 325. See 318–27 generally for his excellent account of masking and unmasking, drawing on Taussig's *Defacement*.

57. Hindman, "Pieter Bruegel's *Children's Games*," 452.

58. Edward Snow, *Inside Bruegel: The Play of Images in "Children's Games"* (New York: FSG, 1997), 27.

59. From Lucas de Heere, *Den hof en boomgaerd der poësien* (Ghent, 1565); see also Koerner, *Bosch and Bruegel*, 328.

60. On holy cradles for dolls of the Christ child that are "shaped to echo a cathedral" see Caroline Walker Bynum, *Christian Materiality: An Essay on Religion in Late Medieval Europe* (New York: Zone, 2010), 62–63, 65.

61. Snow, "'Meaning' in *Children's Games*," 43.

62. Sedlmayr, "Bruegel's *Macchia*," 340. These words refer to *The Battle Between Carnival and Lent*, but they describe the estranging vision that he immediately says is also produced in *Children's Games*.

63. Eugen Fink, "The Oasis of Happiness: Towards an Ontology of Play," trans. Ute Saine and Thomas Saine, *Yale French Studies* 41 (1968): 19–30, 25.

64. For a good overview of the responses to children as victims and perpetrators of violence, see James Sharpe, *A Fiery and Furious People: A History of Violence in England* (London: Random House, 2016), 463–74.

65. Golden, *Children and Childhood*, 44.

66. Mariane C. Ferme, *The Underneath of Things: Violence, History, and the Everyday in Sierra Leone* (Berkeley: University of California Press, 2001), 199. See also the fascinating analysis of the analogy drawn from the other side of the human/spirit divide—spirits behaving like children—by Michael Lambek, *Human Spirits: A Cultural Account*

of *Trance in Mayotte* (Cambridge: Cambridge University Press, 1981), chap. 12: "The Spirits as Children."

67. John Duffy, "Playing at Ritual: Variations on a Theme in Byzantine Religious Tales," in *Greek Ritual Poetics*, ed. Dimitrios Yatromanolakis and Panagiotis Roilos (Washington, DC: Center for Hellenic Studies, 2004), 199–209, 200–201.

68. *A true and just Recorde of the Information, Examination and Confession of all the Witches, taken at S. Oses in the countie of Essex* (London, 1582); partly quoted in Scott Cutler Shershow, *Puppets and "Popular" Culture* (Ithaca, NY: Cornell University Press, 1995), 34; Anna French, "Possession, Puritanism and Prophecy: Child Demoniacs and English Reformed Culture," *Reformation* 13 (2008): 133–61, 144.

69. Particularly useful studies are French, "Possession, Puritanism and Prophecy"; and J. A. Sharpe, "Disruption in the Well-Ordered Household: Age, Authority, and Possessed Young People," in *The Experience of Authority in Early Modern England*, ed. Paul Griffiths, Adam Fox, and Steve Hindle (Houndmills: Macmillan, 1996), 187–212.

70. Diane Purkiss, *The Witch in History: Early Modern and Twentieth-Century Representations* (London: Routledge, 1996), 109.

71. Cited in Barbara Rosen, ed., *Witchcraft in England, 1558–1618* (Amherst: University of Massachusetts Press, 1969), 249–50, 251.

72. Lyndal Roper, "'Evil Imaginings and Fantasies': Child Witches and the End of the Witch Craze," *Past and Present* 167 (May 2000): 107–39, 110.

73. Roper, "'Evil Imaginings,'" 115–16.

74. Ian Hacking, "The Making and Molding of Child Abuse," *Critical Inquiry* 17, no. 2 (1991): 253–88, 277.

75. Jacqueline Rose, *The Case of Peter Pan, or the Impossibility of Children's Fiction*, rev. ed. (London: Macmillan, 1994), xv.

76. Roper, "'Evil Imaginings,'" 127.

77. See the account of the parallels between child's play and magic, in terms of the shared tendency to comment incessantly on the action as it unfolds, in Alfred Gell, "Technology and Magic," *Anthropology Today* 4, no. 2 (1988): 6–9, 8.

CONCLUSION

1. Francis Bacon, *Early Writings, 1584–96*, ed. Alan Stewart with Harriet Knight (Oxford: Clarendon, 2012), 568. I am grateful to David Hillman for first drawing these notes to my attention.

2. Francis Bacon, *The Works of Francis Bacon*, ed. James Spedding et al. (London: Longman, 1858–59), 7:210–11; Francis Bacon, *The Essays*, ed. John Pitcher (London: Penguin, 1985), 257; Bacon, *Early Writings*, 528.

3. Bacon, *Early Writings*, 527 (quoting *Works*, ed. Spedding et al., 7:210).

4. Theodor W. Adorno and Max Horkheimer, *Dialectic of Enlightenment*, trans. John Cumming (London: Verso, 1997), 4–5.

5. Paula Findlen, "Between Carnival and Lent: The Scientific Revolution at the Margins of Culture," *Configurations* 6, no. 2 (1998): 243–67, 267. I am grateful to Paula Findlen for sharing and discussing her work in progress with me.

6. Catherine Wilson, *The Invisible World: Early Modern Philosophy and the Invention of the Microscope* (Princeton, NJ: Princeton University Press, 1995), 23–24.

7. Alfred Gell, "Technology and Magic," *Anthropology Today* 4, no. 2 (1988): 6–9, 8.

8. Andrew Cole and D. Vance Smith, "Introduction: Outside Modernity," in *The Legitimacy of the Middle Ages*, ed. Andrew Cole and D. Vance Smith (Durham, NC: Duke University Press, 2010), 1–36, 3.

9. Hans Blumenberg, *The Legitimacy of the Modern Age*, trans. Robert M. Wallace (Cambridge, MA: MIT Press, 1985), 473.

10. Blumenberg, *The Legitimacy of the Modern Age*, 474–75.

11. John Palsgrave, *Lesclarcissement de la langue francoyse* (London, 1530), 281–82; *The dictionary of syr Thomas Eliot* (London, 1538); both cited in *OED*, s.v. "toy," sense 2.5.

12. Philip Sidney, *The Countesse of Pembrokes Arcadia* (London, 1590), sig. Nn3v; cited in *OED*, s.v. "toy," sense 6.

13. Katherine Duncan-Jones, "Philip Sidney's Toys," in *Sir Philip Sidney: An Anthology of Modern Criticism*, ed. Dennis Kay (Oxford: Clarendon, 1987), 61–80, 61, 78.

14. See Joseph Campana, *The Pain of Reformation: Spenser, Vulnerability, and the Ethics of Masculinity* (New York: Fordham University Press, 2012), 259n12, and the works listed there. Campana cites Ascham and Campion at 133–35. See also Michael Witmore, *Pretty Creatures: Children and Fiction in the English Renaissance* (Ithaca, NY: Cornell University Press, 2007), chap. 1.

15. Roland Barthes, *Mythologies*, trans. Annette Lavers (London: Jonathan Cape, 1972), 53 (emphases in the original). For a rich account of what it means to read toys from the past as part of developmental narratives and divergences from them, see J. Allan Mitchell, *Becoming Human: The Matter of the Medieval Child* (Minneapolis: University of Minnesota Press, 2014), esp. 59–115; I am grateful to Jackie Tasioulas for this reference.

16. Giorgio Agamben, "In Playland: Reflections on History and Play," in *Infancy and History: Essays on the Destruction of Experience*, trans. Liz Heron (London: Verso, 1993), 65–88, 79. For a useful commentary on the place of play in Agamben's thought see "Coda: Play," in Kevin Attell, *Giorgio Agamben: Beyond the Threshold of Deconstruction* (New York: Fordham University Press, 2015), 255–62.

17. Agamben, "In Playland," 79–80 (emphases in the original).

18. Agamben, "In Playland," 81.

19. Giorgio Agamben, "In Praise of Profanation," in *Profanations*, trans. Jeff Fort (New York: Zone, 2015), 73–92, 75.

20. Agamben, "In Praise of Profanation," 76.

21. Agamben, "In Praise of Profanation," 77; Giorgio Agamben, *State of Exception*, trans. Kevin Attell (Chicago: University of Chicago Press, 2005), 64. For commentary on this passage and its place within Agamben's thought see Catherine Mills, "Playing with Law: Agamben and Derrida on Postjuridical Justice," *South Atlantic Quarterly* 107, no. 1 (2008): 15–36.

22. Agamben, "Infancy and History," 53; see also Mills, "Playing with Law," 22.

23. Bruno Latour, *We Have Never Been Modern*, trans. Catherine Porter (New York: Harvester Wheatsheaf, 1993), 72.

24. Latour, *We Have Never Been Modern*, 72–73.

25. Michel Serres with Bruno Latour, *Conversations on Science, Culture, and Time*, trans. Roxanne Lapidus (Ann Arbor: University of Michigan Press, 1995), 57, 60. Serres's and Latour's accounts of temporality have had some impact on early modern studies; see

especially Julian Yates, *Error Misuse Failure: Object Lessons from the English Renaissance* (Minneapolis: University of Minnesota Press, 2003).

26. Siegfried Kracauer, *History: The Last Things Before the Last* (Oxford: Oxford University Press, 1969), 199. See Christopher Pinney, "Things Happen: Or, From Which Moment Does That Object Come?" in *Materiality*, ed. Daniel Miller (Durham, NC: Duke University Press, 2005), 256–72, for a rich discussion of Kracauer that stresses that for him, as for Serres, chronologically contemporaneous objects and events do not necessarily "belong" to the same epoch in the same way.

27. Igor Kopytoff, "The Cultural Biography of Things: Commoditization as Process," in *The Social Life of Things: Commodities in Cultural Perspective*, ed. Arjun Appadurai (Cambridge: Cambridge University Press, 1986), 64–91, 64, 73.

28. Arjun Appadurai, "Introduction: Commodities and the Politics of Value," in *The Social Life of Things*, ed. Arjun Appadurai, 3–63, 15 (first emphasis in the original, second emphasis mine).

29. Sally Crawford, "The Archaeology of Play Things: Theorising a Toy Stage in the 'Biography' of Objects," *Childhood in the Past* 2, no. 1 (2009): 55–70, 66. Only as I completed this chapter did I encounter this fascinating article, which anticipates my claims in various respects.

30. Robson Bonnichsen, "Millie's Camp: An Experiment in Archaeology," *World Archaeology* 4, no. 3 (1973): 277–91, 281, 285.

31. Webb Keane, "Signs Are Not the Garb of Meaning: On the Social Analysis of Material Things," in *Materiality*, ed. Daniel Miller (Durham, NC: Duke University Press, 2005), 182–205, 194.

32. Keane, "Signs Are Not the Garb of Meaning," 191.

33. Alexander Nagel and Christopher S. Wood, *Anachronic Renaissance* (New York: Zone, 2010), 9.

34. Alexander Nagel and Christopher S. Wood, "Toward a New Model of Renaissance Anachronism," *Art Bulletin* 87, no. 3 (2005): 403–15, 404; Nagel and Wood, *Anachronic Renaissance*, 117.

35. Nagel and Wood, *Anachronic Renaissance*, 13 (emphasis in the original).

36. Nagel and Wood, *Anachronic Renaissance*, 17 (emphasis in the original).

37. James J. Gibson, *The Ecological Approach to Visual Perception* (Hillsdale, NJ: Lawrence Erlbaum, 1986), 127, 141 (emphases in original).

38. Nagel and Wood, "Toward a New Model," 408.

39. On the dragon's various layers of meaning see, among others, Carol V. Kaske, "The Dragon's Spark and Sting and the Structure of Red Cross's Dragon-Fight: *The Faerie Queene*, I.xi–xii," *Studies in Philology* 66, no. 4 (1969): 609–38; and Mary Ellen Lamb, "The Red Crosse Knight, St. George, and the Appropriation of Popular Culture," *Spenser Studies* 18, no. 1 (2003): 185–208.

40. Edmund Spenser, *The Faerie Queene*, ed. A. C. Hamilton (London: Longman, 1977; rev. ed. 2006), book 1, canto 11, stanza 55, line 2. All further references are to this edition and appear parenthetically.

41. For St. George as both iconoclast and idol see Alexander Barclay, *The Life of St. George*, ed. William Nelson (London: Oxford University Press, 1955), 90; Margaret Aston, *Broken Idols of the English Reformation* (Cambridge: Cambridge University Press, 2016),

401–44; and Jerry Brotton, "Saints Alive: The Iconography of Saint George," in *Iconoclash*, ed. Bruno Latour and Peter Weibel (Cambridge, MA: MIT Press, 2002), 155–57.

42. James Kearney, *The Incarnate Text: Imagining the Book in Reformation England* (Philadelphia: University of Pennsylvania Press, 2009), 113.

43. See, e.g., Kenneth Gross, *Spenserian Poetics: Idolatry, Iconoclasm, and Magic* (Ithaca, NY: Cornell University Press, 1985); and Linda Gregerson, *The Reformation of the Subject: Spenser, Milton and the English Protestant Epic* (Cambridge: Cambridge University Press, 1995).

44. John Milton, *Areopagitica*, in *The Complete Prose Works of John Milton*, ed. Don M. Wolfe et al. (New Haven, CT: Yale University Press, 1959–82), 2:516.

45. I discuss this imputed seriousness further in "Spenser at Play," *PMLA* 133, no. 1 (2018): 19–35.

46. See Peter Burke, *Popular Culture in Early Modern Europe* (London: Temple Smith, 1978), 173, 216; and Lamb, "The Red Crosse Knight."

47. These children and their play have received surprisingly little attention in Spenser criticism: see James Nohrnberg, *The Analogy of "The Faerie Queene"* (Princeton, NJ: Princeton University Press, 1976), 197; William Nelson, "Spenser *ludens*," in *A Theatre for Spenserians*, ed. Judith M. Kennedy and James A. Reither (Toronto: University of Toronto Press, 1973), 83–100, 93–94, 99. An exception is the excellent recent account by Jane Grogan, "Style, Objects, and Heroic Values in Early Modern Epic," *Studies in English Literature* 57, no. 1 (2017): 23–44. For the allegorical drive toward totalized meaning see Gordon Teskey, *Allegory and Violence* (Ithaca, NY: Cornell University Press, 1996), 30.

48. Gordon Teskey, "Thinking Moments in *The Faerie Queene*," *Spenser Studies* 22 (2007): 103–25, 114.

49. I am grateful to Mike Schoenfeldt for this comparison. For Montaigne's reversible scene of play with his cat see the discussion in my introduction.

50. *The Complete Works of William Hazlitt*, ed. P. P. Howe (London: Dent, 1930–34), 5:38. I am grateful to Cathy Nicholson for pointing out this connection.

51. William Oram, "Human Limitation and Spenserian Laughter," *Spenser Studies* 30 (2015): 35–56, 50.

52. See my analysis of Archimago functioning in similar terms in "The Forgotten Youth of Allegory: Figures of Old Age in *The Faerie Queene*," *Modern Philology* 110, no. 3 (2013): 389–414, 407–8.

INDEX

Page numbers in italics refer to illustrations.

244   *Index*